Miriam C Merrel
111 College
Carrollton, Ga - 30117

DISCARD

Newton County

D1496239

The gracious old city of Covington has been called one of Georgia's best-kept secrets. While Madison, Greensboro, Washington and Athens are known far and wide for their ante-bellum houses, Covington has until recent years been off the beaten path for tourists and seekers after the old and beautiful.

In this book the reader will not only glimpse Covington's magnificent Greek Revival houses and a few less pretentious ones; he will be introduced to the persons who have lived in and loved them for a century and a half. From judges, preachers, Confederate generals and millionaires to simple and unassuming folk — they're all here waiting to welcome you.

The GLORY of COVINGTON

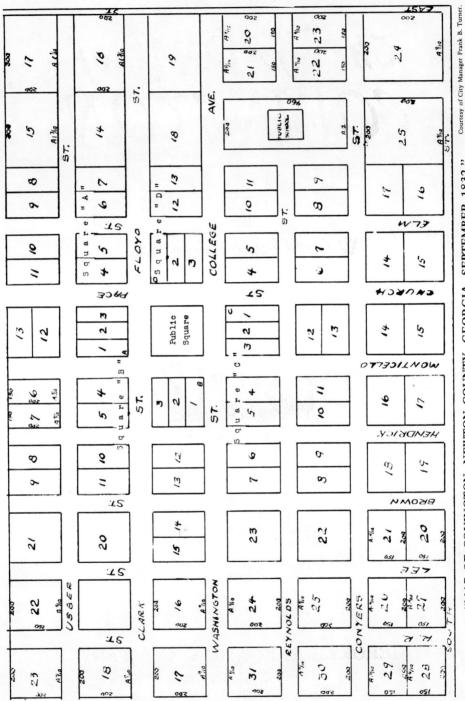

"MAP OF COVINGTON, NEWTON COUNTY, GEORGIA, SEPTEMBER 1832."

Courtesy of City Manager Frank B. Turner.

Probably ante-dated, as the men for whom some of the streets were named did not arrive in Covington until later.

The GLORY of
COVINGTON

By
William Bailey Williford

CHEROKEE PUBLISHING COMPANY
ATLANTA
1973

Library of Congress Catalog Card Number: 72-96820

ISBN: 0-87797-024-6

Copies of *The Glory of Covington* may be obtained from Cherokee
Publishing Company's sales office: P.O. Box 1081, Covington, Ga. 30209.
Send $10 plus 30¢ mailing charge. Georgia residents add 3% sales tax
and, where applicable, an additional 1% MARTA tax.

To My Wife

JULIA BENTON WILLIFORD

And

In Memory of Her Son

THOMAS CHALMERS SWANN, 3RD.

CONTENTS

	Acknowledgements	xi
	Foreword	xiii
I	The Setting	1
II	The Brown-Anderson House	11
III	"Swanscombe"	16
IV	The Neal-Sanders House	33
V	The Graham-Simms House	49
VI	"Edwards House"	68
VII	"Clark's Grove"	76
VIII	"The Floyd House"	89
IX	The Carr-Cody-Corley House	101
X	"The President's House"	109
XI	"Usher House"	122
XII	The Bates-Terrell House	136
XIII	"Dixie Manor"	145
XIV	"Whitehall"	157
XV	Home of "The Honest Man"	173
XVI	"Poverty Hill" and Others	183
XVII	"The Cottage"	201
XVIII	Dr. Archibald Camp's House	217
XIX	The Lee-Rogers House	230
XX	The Porter-Rogers-Tuck House	234
XXI	The Lee-Porter House	240
	Epilogue	245
	A Suggested Drive Past Covington's Old Houses	247
	Source Notes	251
	Bibliography	293
	Index	301

ACKNOWLEDGMENTS

The author is indebted to many persons for interest, assistance, and cooperation in the research which made possible this book. With the sole exception of one who retorted "Who cares!" when queried concerning one of the houses included in this book, everyone with whom I have talked has been most gracious.

I wish to acknowledge the assistance I have received from the following residents of Covington: Miss Julia Aiken, Mrs. William W. Aiken, Mrs. George S. Allen, Miss Annie Pauline Anderson, Franklin Anderson, Colonel William G. Borella, Mrs. Chris Bowen, Mr. and Mrs. David Butler, Miss Sarah White Callaway, Mr. and Mrs. Leon Cohen, Mrs. W. S. Cook Sr., Starr Corley, Mr. and Mrs. Wendell Crowe, Mrs. Harry Dietz, George Elliott, Dr. and Mrs. Robert L. Faulkner, Robert R. Fowler, Miss Lois Gray, former Clerk of Newton Superior Court Sam Hay and Mrs. Hay, Miss Dorothy Lee, Mrs. John F. Meacham, Miss Virginia Merck, Miss Sarah Mobley, Mrs. Leslie J. Moore, Mr. and Mrs. Dutton Morehouse, Mrs. Henry Odum Sr., Mrs. R. H. Patterson, Mrs. Everett Pratt, Mrs. P. W. Pratt Sr., Miss Martha Ramsey, the Misses Christine and Rose Rheburgh, the late Mrs. E. B. Rogers, Dr. J. R. Sams, Judge Donald Stephenson, Mr. and Mrs. Lee Stephenson, Charles D. Strickland, Mrs. W. H. Thompson, William D. Travis 3rd., Frank B. Turner, Mr. and Mrs. N. S. Turner, Mrs. William B. Williford, Miss Mary Willingham, and Edgar Wood.

Also, Mrs. Anita Stewart Armstrong, Bates Block, Mr. and Mrs. King Cleveland, Mrs. Asa G. DeLoach, Mrs. Fred Fletcher, Mrs. Hampton Flowers, Mrs. Cullen Gosnell, Miss Carroll Hart, Miss Leila Perry, Miss Geniveve Scully, Mrs. Charles S. Thompson, Mrs. Ralph L. Turner, Miss Marjorie Weldon, and Robert R. Wood, all of Atlanta.

Additionally, E. Marsh Adair, Trenton, Missouri; Tandy E. Bush, Tampa, Florida; Walton C. Clark, Chevy Chase,

Maryland; William Herbert Corley, Starrsville; Mrs. Fulton E. DeVane, Quitman; Mrs. Annie Laura Robinson Dodson, Oxford; O. Grant Gooden, Springfield, Pennsylvania; Mrs. David D. Harvey, Rome; Mrs. Lowry Hunt, Madison; Mrs. John B. Reeves, Brevard, North Carolina; Mrs. Ivy Smith, Jacksonville, Florida; Paul Swann, Dalton; Mrs. Hugh H. Trotti, Decatur; Miss Addie Augusta Wert, LaFayette; Mrs. Robert Wharton, St. Simons Island; and Mrs. D. Leon Wilson, Macon.

I acknowledge my indebtedness to David Butler for unknowingly providing the title for this book when he remarked in the course of a conversation that "the glory of Covington has always been its Greek Revival houses on Floyd Street."

Finally, I express to my wife my appreciation for providing the inspiration for this undertaking. Although her interest lies in what *is* rather than in what *was*, she has been an unfailing source of information. Through her I came to love one house and then to appreciate many others.

FOREWORD

This book is the outgrowth of an interest in the history of one of the beautiful ante-bellum houses for which Covington has long been known. Research opened so many avenues and revealed so much in the way of interesting historical data that soon the scope of my investigations was broadened to include *all* of the extant Greek Revival houses.

In writing this book I set out to confine it entirely to columned structures. The unfolding of the various chapters, however, provided opportunities for including a small number of houses *sans* columns which were worthy of mention because of interesting persons or events associated with them.

There are other old houses in Covington about which interesting stories could be related. By and large, however, they belong to that never-never style which might be termed *eclectic*. They have no architectural distinction; they are just houses.

The surrounding countryside has occasional examples of handsome ante-bellum architecture, and of course a book could be devoted to half a dozen houses in nearby Oxford and to several really noteworthy structures on the campus of Oxford College of Emory University.

This book is about Covington, some of its fine houses, and the persons who have lived in them. To a very great extent the histories of these houses forms the fabric upon which the history of Covington has been woven. This is not, however, in any sense a formal history of the city. It is, quite simply, a fragment of the whole — albeit the most fascinating and remarkable portion.

WILLIAM BAILEY WILLIFORD

Covington, Georgia
13 November 1972

I
THE SETTING

The area in which Covington is situated was once a part of the vast territory of the Creek Nation of Indians. Beginning with the landing of the first English settlers on Georgia's coast in 1733 and continuing until the last redskins were banished to Oklahoma via the " Trail of Tears " a hundred years later, the white man unrelentingly pushed the original Americans ever farther westward.

By a series of treaties signed in 1805, 1821 and 1825, the United States acquired ownership of the last remaining hunting grounds of the proud Creeks. The second of these treaties, signed at Indian Springs on 8 January 1821, permitted the opening up of a large virgin area which was soon overrun by white settlers. The newcomers were attracted by the opportunities afforded by the fertile and densely wooded terrain, and soon they were busy clearing land, building crude temporary living quarters, and putting slaves to work cultivating cotton for the textile mills which were beginning to spring up throughout middle Georgia.[1]

Newton County was created by Act of the General Assembly of Georgia on 24 December 1821. It was formed from parts of Jasper, Henry and Walton counties. Parts of it were given back to Jasper in 1822 and 1834, and a small portion was transferred to DeKalb County in 1826. The new county was named in honor of Sergeant John Newton, who had been a companion-at-arms of the man for whom nearby Jasper County was named. Both men had become heroes by recapturing American prisoners of war in Revolutionary War activity near Savannah.[2]

The first comers to Newton County were sturdy folk from Virginia, the Carolinas, and eastern Georgia. Many of them

1

seem to have been persons of means, and some of them were cultivated and well - educated. They settled originally in the eastern part of the new county, where they proposed to start a town which would be named Winton. It was on this site that Solomon Graves and his sons directed the construction of a store building for which bricks are said to have been brought from England. When completed it served as a combination general store, post office, and meeting place. At the rear was a frame building which was used as an inn and stage stop. This was the crossroads of the stage roads from Charleston to New Orleans and from Ruckersville to Milledgeville. After completion of the brick building the neighborhood around it became known as Brick Store, and thereafter the name of Winton was nothing more than a memory.[3]

The first session of Newton Superior Court was convened at Brick Store on 15 April 1822. The foreman of the jury was Solomon Graves and the presiding judge was the Honorable Augustin L. Clayton of the Western Judicial Circuit. On 23

BRICK STORE

Sadly neglected in recent years, the first brick structure in Newton County is being restored by the Newton County Historical Society, which was organized in 1971. The initial sum to be used in this undertaking was a gift from William A. Parker of Atlanta, whose antecedents were early residents of the county. Brick Store itself was deeded to the historical society by the late Charles M. Jordan on 1 May 1971.[4]

December of that year Newton was assigned to the Flint circuit, in which it remained until transferred to the Stone Mountain circuit on 1 January 1892. Newton is now one of two counties in the Alcovy Judicial Circuit, which was created on 9 March 1972.[5]

The lack of an adequate water supply caused the members of the first court to decide forthwith to meet next at Newtonsboro, a settlement a few miles to the west of Brick Store, and to designate it as the county seat.[6]

Newtonsboro was a crude hamlet located to the south of the Hightower Trail, an Indian path which had formed a boundary between Cherokee lands to the north and Creek lands to the south. Soon after Newtonsboro was unexpectedly selected as the seat of government for Newton County it became a beehive of activity. A plan for its orderly development as a town was drawn up which envisioned a central square from which streets radiated to the four points of the compass. One James Mize was directed to erect a temporary courthouse measuring 60' x 40' and 28' 8" in height, for which he was paid the sum of fifty dollars. This crude log structure, situated on a portion of the Square, was supplanted a few years later by a frame building in the center of the Square.[7]

Newtonsboro was incorporated on 6 December 1822 as the town of Covington, and in 1853 it was incorporated as a city. Covington's first commissioners, or governing body, were Dr. William D. Conyers, Richard S. Shackleford, Richard L. Simms and Cary Wood. Probably at the suggestion of Maryland-born Mr. Simms (see pages 53-55), the town was named for Leonard Covington of that state. He was born on 30 October 1768 and was killed in battle on 14 November 1813 while serving as a general officer in the War of 1812. General Covington had served in both the Maryland legislature and the Congress of the United States.[8]

The town soon began to attract residents who were ambitious, hard-working, and God-fearing. Provision was made early for Methodist and Baptists churches, both of which occupied several different structures in the first seventy-five years of their existence.[9]

The first church building was located on the east bank of Dried Indian Creek, a stream which received its name as the result of the first settlers' continuing efforts to rout the Indians who had long dwelt on its banks. Repeatedly foiled, the brave white men began to systematically exterminate their foe. Finally all of the red men except one old chieftain had been put to death. Alone and greatly outnumbered, he still breathed the defiant spirit of his race. One day while he was sleeping a band of settlers captured him and bound him to a tree. His body was pierced by many arrows and soon death ensued. His tormentors then took the Indian's body to the bank of the nearby creek and left it there to dry in the sun. Hence the name *Dried Indian Creek*. Subsequently the area immediately east of the creek was known for many years as Dried Indian Creek Common and was, in its early days, the scene of drills by local militia companies.[10]

The Founding Fathers of Covington were determined that their sons and daughters should have an opportunity to acquire an education. Accordingly, on 6 December 1822, Governor John Clark signed "An Act To Incorporate the Newton County Academy at Covington." First trustees were Solomon Graves, Martin Kolb, Harrison Jones, Samuel Brazil, Thomas Jones, Farr H. Townsend, and William H. Morrow. Subsequently separate schools were established for boys and for girls. In 1849 trustees of the Male Academy, which was located at the present southeast corner of Conyers Street and Legion Drive, included such prominent men as the Reverend Charles H. Sanders, Joseph H. Anderson, Dr. John B. Hendrick, Charles Strong, J. W. Murrell, John P. Carr and L. Q. C. Lamar.[11]

In its earliest days Covington was fortunate to be one of

the stops on a stage route from Milledgeville to Rock (now Stone) Mountain. The coming of the stage coach was an important event in the life of the village, and it served not only to provide a means of travel to important cities but also to keep the inhabitants in touch with the great world beyond their ken. The impending arrival of a stage was announced by a blast from a horn, and when the vehicle stopped to discharge passengers and take on others a quick change of horses was made. Soon the driver cracked his whip and the great coach lurched forward to resume its journey. [12]

Social life in ante-bellum Covington centered around the homes of the town's leading families, whose circle of friends was fairly rigidly defined by relationship and background. The most important social occasions were weddings and the subsequent receptions at the homes of the brides' parents, the second-day "infairs" at the homes of the bridegrooms' parents, and finally the housewarmings given at the homes of the newlyweds. On the last of these occasions, if the season were auspicious, fox hunting and other field sports with fine horses and dogs were enjoyed. [13]

The white-columned homes of that era were furnished with old mahogany, ebony, rosewood and walnut. Slaves being plentiful and well trained, the households were conducted on the most liberal and luxurious scale, and hospitality was a way of life. [14]

Until the end of the first quarter of the present century, Covington had no paved streets and few paved sidewalks. The hard ruts in dry weather and the ankle-deep mud in winter were an inconvenience which most residents accepted philosophically, but one visitor to the city was not so complacent. In a letter to the editor of *The Covington Star* he wrote,

> Your sidewalks are all in passable condition . . . , but the wagon tracks put me in mind of a city with a river running through it without a bridge or boat for crossing . . . Covington is a beautiful and lovely little city, with . . . broad thoroughfares, and wide, sandy

EARLY CHURCH

This structure at 1143 College Street was erected as a house of worship for Covington Baptists shortly after the site was purchased in 1877 from James T. Corley (*see page 106*). The church had been organized by the Reverend Joel Colley and Messrs. Luke Robertson and Richard Pace as Bethlehem Baptist Church on 21 June 1823. Prior to the Civil War it sponsored a Negro church which assumed the parent's name, and thereafter the latter was known as First Baptist Church.

The first structure occupied by the Baptists was on the east bank of Dried Indian Creek. After the congregation had moved to a new site, it was burned on 22 July 1864 when Union General Kenner Garrard's cavalry raiders found it filled with cotton. The second building was located on the west side of Pace Street, just south of the present Central of Georgia railroad tracks. It was occupied from 1856 until the edifice shown above was completed *circa* 1878.

For several years after the First Baptist Church moved into its present structure on Floyd Street (*see page 224*) in 1911, the College Street building was used by a Christian Science congregation of which Mrs. P. W. Godfrey (*see page 227*) was the motivating force. In recent years it has been an apartment house owned by Mr. and Mrs. J. C. Ward.

The Reverend Joel Colley (*11 December 1776–11 October 1851*), one of the organizers and the first pastor of the Baptist church, was a noted Primitive Baptist preacher. A native of Pittsylvania County, Virginia, he was ordained in Oglethorpe County, Georgia, in 1815. In 1824 he was elected first moderator of the Yellow River Baptist Association, a position which he held until death. After leaving the Covington church he served the nearby Holly Creek and Harris Springs churches. In a sermon at the latter when the Georgia Railroad was erecting a trestle over the Alcovy River in 1844 in preparation for the inauguration of service between Augusta and Atlanta via Covington, he prayed for God to derail the first train to reach it and to kill all the people who were fools enough to ride on the new-fangled contraption. [15]

sidewalks ... When your crossings are made with granite blocks, they will be all right.[16]

The same newspaper carried an editorial a year later which stated emphatically that "Covington must have a new first class hotel ... Everything is propitious for it ... [and] no improvement is needed as much at this time, to meet the growing demands of our city, as an elegant, first class, modern style brick hotel, with from 40 to 60 well furnished rooms. Let us build the hotel in advance of the needs of our city, and then build the town up to it ..." At that time there were several hostelries in the town: the old Cox Hotel at the

DELANEY HOTEL

northwest corner of the Square; the Flowers Hotel in the next block of Clark Street; and the Pitts Hotel at the northeast corner of the Square and College Street. Within a few years the editor's dream came true when the Delaney Hotel was erected upon the north portion of the residence lot of Mrs. W. D. Conyers (see pages 79-80). It became a popular hotel, noted for the excellence of its dining room, until the automobile age spawned interstate highways and motels. Today the last of Covington's hotel structures is occupied by a furniture store.[17]

Toward the end of the nineteenth century Covington was known as a wide-open and rather wild town. Saloons and bars were to be found on every side of the Square, and public drunkenness was rampant. Knifings, fights and even murders

Courtesy of the Atlanta Transit Co.

STREETCAR

circa 1900. Operated by the Covington & Oxford Street Railway Co., which was organized in the 1870's. Covington and New York are said to have had the last mule-drawn streetcars in the United States.

This picture was made in front of the present courthouse, which is the second on the site and the fourth since the naming of Newtonsboro as the county seat.[18]

were commonplace occurrences. Finally the more respectable
citizens of the town united in 1897 and in righteous indignation succeeded in outlawing legal whiskey. Drunkenness was
said to have decreased by forty percent once the nine local
saloons were closed.[19]

Long solely a trading center for planters and farmers from
the surrounding area, Covington became around the turn of
the century a community centered around textile mills. Thereafter it prospered to an extent unknown since the Civil War.

Now, three-quarters of a century later, textile operations in
Covington and environs have been drastically reduced. The
economy of the area has expanded, however, because of the
opening of branch plants by national corporations and, more
recently, the opening of an interstate highway from Augusta
to Atlanta and the concurrent phenomenal expansion of Met-
ropolitan Atlanta.

Merchants, bankers and real estate dealers smile happily over
Covington's recent growth and renewed prosperity. Some oldtimers who have no vested interest in the new state of affairs
comment gloomily about "the way Covington has *changed*."
As is true in any transitional community anywhere, they speak
longingly of old times and of the days when life was simpler.
They are pleased when newcomers acquire one of the city's
fine old houses and restore it lovingly to an approximation of
its former glory, much preferring that a "nice" new resident
live in it than that it be taken over by those who are
dismissed cooly with "I knew them *when*."

Whether they be long-time residents or newcomers, however,
all Covingtonians can enjoy and take pride in the dozen or so
beautiful columned houses which dot the city. Most of them
are Greek Revival in style and all but a few are a century and
a half in age. Their histories form, to a very large extent, the
history of the community which has loved and protected them
for so many years.

II
THE BROWN-ANDERSON HOUSE

One of the handsome columned houses in Covington is built around a log cabin which surely must have been among the first structures erected in the village, probably in the period 1822–1830.[1]

On 30 May 1822 pioneer resident Dr. William D. Conyers (*see pages 79-80*) paid $161 for Lot 8 in Square C "in the Town of Newtonsboro." This, together with Lot 9, formed the city block now bounded by Reynolds, Hendricks, Conyers and Lee streets. Subsequently a crude one-room log cabin was erected on Lot 9. Various frame additions were made as time passed, and eventually the property came into the possession of Purmedus Reynolds, a pioneer settler of Newton County who lived variously in Oxford and in several houses in Covington (*see page 43*). He "relinquished" it to one Coleman Brown, who lived there until he was killed in the Civil War in 1862.[2]

From an examination of deeds, marriage records, wills, and tombstones it has been determined that Coleman G. Brown was married on 11 October 1855 to Fannie E. Reynolds, daughter of Purmedus and Nancy Reynolds. Seven years later Mr. Brown was killed in battle (*see page 59*). On 21 November 1866 his widow became the wife of Dr. Gustavus A. Meritt.[3]

Less than two years later, on 21 March 1868, Dr. and Mrs. Meritt sold their home and the city block in which it was situated to James W. Anderson for $1000. Dr. Meritt died on 13 December 1883, at the age of fifty-two years, and was buried on the plot with three children born of his wife's first marriage. Although there are no extant markers to them, one assumes that Mrs. Meritt and Mr. Brown also are buried on the plot in what was originally the Methodist Cemetery.[4]

James Washington Anderson, purchaser of the Brown-Meritt residence, was one of Covington's most prominent and successful post-war residents. A native Georgian, he had served as a courier under General James Longstreet in the Civil War, being mustered out as a colonel. After spending a few months in Canada he settled in Covington. Shortly thereafter he and James Delaney started publication of *The Georgia Enterprise*, with the Reverend William L. Beebe as editor.[5]

The Reverend Mr. Beebe, a native of Middletown, New York, had come to Georgia in 1850 and to Covington two years later. He served as pastor of Holly Springs and Harris Springs Primitive Baptist churches, and immediately prior to the Civil War he was editor of the *Southern Baptist Messenger*. Captured at Conyers after volunteering for duty with the state militia, he was imprisoned at Camp Chase, Ohio. Upon returning to Covington he became editor of the new *Georgia Enterprise*. In 1858 he married as the second of his three wives Mrs. Eliza (Henderson) Hawkins, whose son Sion W. Hawkins subsequently became the newspaper's owner. In 1878 the Beebes left Covington for Canada and New York State. Mrs. Beebe died in 1880, her son in 1898, and her widower in 1901.[6]

After successfully launching *The Georgia Enterprise* and then disposing of his interest in it, Colonel James W. Anderson started *The Covington Star*. A few years later he erected an imposing two-story brick building at the northwest corner of the Square and Washington Street which was known for years thereafter as the Star Building. Upon his death in late January 1912 it was said that, "Col. James W. Anderson, known to every man in Newton County, . . . ran a clean, conservative publication, and himself was an honor to the fourth estate . . . He was very successful and at the time of his death owns [sic] some of the most valuable property in the city . . ." After a funeral at the Baptist church he was buried in Covington City Cemetery with Knights Templar rites.[7]

HOME OF COL. JAMES W. ANDERSON

During the period of Colonel Anderson's occupancy his home had been enlarged into a two-story structure with columns across the front. The will of the prominent newspaperman contained the following provisions:

> To my beloved wife, Mrs. Sarah Henrietta Anderson, I give all of my real estate consisting of the house and lot on the corner of Reynolds and Hendrix Streets ... together with all our household furnishings, as well as the tenement houses on the south-west corner of said lot: Also the two story brick building and lot ... known as the Star Building; also one story brick building [on the

East side of the Square] known as the Lula Building . . . Upon the
death of my wife all the . . . property . . . not consumed by her shall
descend to our two children, William Meredith Anderson and Mrs.
Nellie Virginia Wells . . . Sarah H. Anderson and George T. Wells . . .
executors. [Mrs. Wells was bequeathed outright twenty shares in
"Clark Banking Co., now Bank of Newton County."][8]

On 3 December 1923 the residuary legatees of the Anderson
estate sold the house and furnishings and the city block in
which it was situated to W. H. Pickett for $6500.[9]

William Henry Pickett was a native of Newton County who
had begun his adult years as a cotton planter. Farming formed
the basis of his fortune, which was augmented by the acquisition of much valuable property in Covington. On 16 March
1882 he had married Miss Sallie Hinton (*25 August 1861–19
July 1948*) of Newton County. Their children were Sallie Mae
and W. H. Pickett, Jr. Upon his death late in 1926 at the age
of eighty-one, Mr. Pickett was described as "one of the
wealthiest men in Newton County."[10]

W. H. Pickett did not move into the former Anderson house
after he acquired it in 1923. His own home, formerly the
residence of Dr. and Mrs. William D. Conyers (*see page 79*),
was located in the block immediately east of the property.
Twelve days after buying the former Anderson house Mr.
Pickett deeded it to his only daughter, Sallie Mae, for "$5
and love and affection." [11]

The new owner, who had become the wife of William S.
Cook on 24 December 1915, lived in the house with her
husband and their children, Sarah, Carter, and William S.
Cook, Jr., until it was sold on 26 September 1949 for
$15,000.[12]

The next owner of the property was George Scott Allen,
who was born in Powatan County, Virginia, on 21 February
1895. After attending a business college in Richmond he
moved to Georgia, where on 18 May 1935 he married Miss
Leonora Belcher of Starrsville, who had studied at the University of Georgia. In 1945 Mr. Allen opened a dry cleaning

establishment in Covington, to which city he and Mrs. Allen moved after purchasing the Brown-Anderson house. Mr. Allen, a Kiwanian and a one-time member of city council, died on 19 June 1969, and three years later his widow sold his business.[13]

The Allen children are Judy (now Mrs. Maurice A. Parker of Brunswick) and Nina (who is the wife of Harold M. Hendry of Lake Thonotosassa, Florida). The former was married on 20 June 1958 in a formal evening ceremony at the Methodist church, after which a reception was held at her parents' home. The bride wore a blush pink *peau de soie* gown with cathedral train, and the house was decorated for the occasion with pink flowers, pink table cloths, and a myriad of glowing pink candles.[14]

Since Mr. Allen's death his widow has continued to live in their handsome old home. Now almost totally surrounded by business and commercial property, the house provides a beautiful and surprising vista when a stranger sees it for the first time. It is a poignant reminder of what "Progress" has done to similar old houses in Covington, as well as an important link to the city's earliest days when its pioneers lived in simple log cabins such as the one incorporated into the present imposing structure.

III

"SWANSCOMBE"

The oldest house now standing in Covington was both the first clapboard house and one of the first frame houses to be erected in the village. This stately structure was built for Covington's first settler, Cary Wood. [1]

Mr. Wood was a native of Spotsylvania County, Virginia, where he was born on 10 February 1795. He moved to Georgia as a young man and lived briefly in Clarke County, where he served as private and ensign in a company of state militia. Soon he moved on and settled in that part of Walton County which in 1821 formed a portion of newly-created Newton County. The plantation upon which he first lived, and which remained in his family for many years, was located two or three miles east of Covington and was known later as the Echols Place. [2]

Cary Wood and Mary Richardson Billups, a native of South Carolina, were married in Walton County on 16 October 1823. Their first home in Covington was in rooms on the second floor of the split-log building which had been erected to house Mr. Wood's general store. This structure was located at the southeast corner of the present Washington and Brown streets, where in later years was built a beautiful house which was occupied successively by Mr. and Mrs. John R. Dyer and Dr. and Mrs. Luke Robinson. [3]

Cary Wood was, from the time of his arrival until the day of his death, a prominent and influential resident of Covington and Newton County; as one writer has stated, he was "the earliest settler on the site ... [and] in after years ... its most

16

conspicuous landmark." He was a successful merchant, a large-scale planter, one of the first three county commissioners of roads, an original commissioner of the town of Covington, and a justice of the inferior court (1825–'32). Mr. Wood owned vast tracts of land, much of which he sold to trustees of the Manual Labor School (*see pages 76-77*) for $10,000 on 8 October 1836. This acreage subsequently became the site of Emory College and the new town of Oxford.[4]

On 2 January 1827 Cary Wood foreclosed on a mortgage which he held from one Samuel Wynne. On that date Coroner William D. McCracken sold to him at public outcry for $610 the property involved. This was identified as Lot 18 in Square D, containing a 300-foot frontage and extending a depth of 200 feet.[5]

Later in the same year construction was begun upon a house into which Mr. Wood and his family moved in 1828. An account of this edifice written early in the twentieth century states that it originally consisted of two rooms downstairs and two upstairs; there also was a separate kitchen house behind the main structure. A careful examination of the structural underpinnings and of the floors and walls, however, indicates that the downstairs consisted of a central hallway and *three* rooms (living room, dining room and bedroom), that a hallway and two rooms were upstairs, and that a "lean-to" was at the rear of the dining room. This floor plan is remarkably similar to that of *The Cedars* at Milledgeville, which has been attributed to architect-industrialist Daniel Pratt during his ten-year residence in Georgia's capital city (1821–'31). It reflects the emerging transition from "plantation plain style" to the grandeur of the Greek Revival period.[6]

Several years after moving into his house Cary Wood had it enlarged, and at the same time added six beautiful Ionic columns across the front. An historian of an earlier period has written that "long before the [Civil] War the domicile achieved its present form." Records of litigation in which he became involved as a result of the refinements to his home present an interesting picture of the cost of labor and materials in that period. Among the items listed are four squares of 70-foot railing, $11.70; one door shutter, $1; one window shutter, $2; four window frames and sash, $24; putting on three locks, $1.25; four window panes, 50 cents; overhead ceiling, $46.50; weatherboarding, $39; shingling, $30; 300 brick, $2.40; 47 feet of sawed lumber, $1; and one writing desk, $2.50.[7]

The Wood family was the first to build a house in Covington on the road leading from the Square to Madison, Eatonton and Augusta. Within a few years, however, Dr. William P. Graham, Judge John J. Floyd and Robert O. Usher had built columned mansions close to the Wood residence. A similarity of detail in the Floyd, Usher and Wood houses, as well as in those built later for William P. Anderson and John Harris, suggests that the same architect may have been responsible for — or at least influenced the design of — all of them. The treatment of the front doorways is remarkably similar.

Cary Wood died on 6 May 1847 and was buried on the site of what later became the Georgia Railroad passenger station on Railroad (now Emory) Street. Years later his body and the tomb above it were removed to Covington City Cemetery. There his wife, Mary Billups Wood (*18 September 1803–10 May 1873*), and other members of their family later joined him.[8]

Mr. and Mrs. Wood were the parents of William, John and Stevens, who died in infancy; Laura and Paulina, who married the brothers Robert J. and John T. Henderson (*see page 158*) respectively; Mary Jane, who was married to (1) William Young Stokes and (2) Osborn Thorn Rogers (*see page 147*); Cecelia Billups, who became the wife of William Hulbert Gaither; and Robert Richardson Wood (*see pages 173-178*).[9]

The extent of Cary Wood's estate clearly set him apart as a rich man by the standards of the period. Four years after his death "arbitrators" apppointed by the superior court found that in 1861 the estate aggregated $208,617.33, "exclusive of the lot of land in litigation and the Inn safe and insolvent claims."[10]

Following Cary Wood's death his widow continued to maintain their home as the center of her family's life. When the South was engulfed by the Civil War, she watched her relatives and friends go off to battle while the women stayed behind to manage plantations and businesses, knit warm garments for their fighting menfolk, and pray for their early and safe return. Her only surviving son, Robert R. Wood, became a major in the Confederate States Army and ultimately was named quartermaster of Holtzclaw's Brigade. When General William T. Sherman's forces passed the handsome Wood residence en route from Atlanta to Savannah, a small group of men camped across the road and probably visited Mrs. Wood's property to forage for food. She had shrewdly buried the family silver, including a monogrammed punch bowl which is now owned by a great-grandson, before temporarily refugeeing to Forsyth.[11]

Mrs. Wood spent her last years in the home of her daughter Mrs. Gaither, during which time her own home was occupied by the family of another daughter, Mrs. Robert J. Henderson. In accordance with a specific request in the mother's will, her son and other daughters transferred their interest in the family home to Mrs. Henderson in 1875 and 1876.[12]

Robert Johnson Henderson was born in Newton County on 12 November 1822, a son of Maryland-born Isaac P. Henderson (see page 158). After receiving the Bachelor of Arts degree from Franklin College (now the University of Georgia) in 1843 he studied law under Judge John J. Floyd of Covington. Later he practiced law, served as judge of the county court, and represented Newton County in the General Assembly of 1859–'60. He was a prosperous lawyer, planter and miller and a major in the State Militia at the outbreak of the Civil War.[13]

Appointed colonel of the 42nd Regiment, Georgia Volunteer Infantry, on 20 March 1862, he was captured in the fighting at Vicksburg on 4 July 1863 and paroled two days later. Colonel Henderson was wounded in an engagement at Resaca, Georgia, in 1864, and in the following year he was made a brigadier general on the battlefield at Bentonville, North Carolina. He returned to Covington after the war to find that his farms and mill had been devastated by Sherman's army, but he rebuilt the latter and soon became again a successful and prominent citizen of Covington.[14]

General and Mrs. Henderson reared their children in the former Cary Wood residence, and there the four daughters spoke their wedding vows. Robert and Laura (Wood) Henderson were the parents of Cary Wood; Mary Ruth, who was married to Lodowick J. Hill of Washington, Georgia; Claudia, who became the wife of Edward Y. Hill, younger half-brother of Lodowick J. Hill, also of Washington; John Francis (*see page 127*); Charles, William; Robert and Clifford, who died early in life; and Isaac Purnell Henderson, 2nd. In his old age General Henderson retired from his varied activities and moved to Atlanta, where he died on 3 February 1891. Mrs. Henderson, who was born on 2 May 1829, died on 26 September 1889. They are buried in Covington.[15]

In 1883 the Hendersons had moved from their Floyd Street residence after executing a deed to Peyton W. Douglass in exchange for his promissory note. Dr. Douglass defaulted in his payments, however, and soon moved to Madison; later he married Mrs. Susie Davison of Woodville. Dr. Douglass arranged for the Wood-Henderson house to be transferred to Thomas C. Swann upon payment by the latter to the Hendersons of the sum of $2,775. Thus, on 27 December 1884, was the original Cary Wood home sold for the only time in its more-than one hundred and forty years.[16]

Thomas C. Swann, the new owner, was a newcomer to Covington who a few years earlier had entered into a general mercantile business with J. A. B. Stewart and D. A. Thompson

Courtesy of Mrs. William B. Williford

T. C. SWANN and his son are shown (fifth and sixth from left) on the porch of his mercantile establishment, southeast corner of the Square and Monticello Street, in this 1893 photograph. Others pictured include J. Glass, John B. Davis, Capt. N. C. Carr, J[osiah?] Perry, F[ranklin?] Wright, J. Aron, and J[ames L.?] Whitehead.

under the firm name of Swann, Stewart & Thompson. Subsequently Joseph A. Stewart replaced Mr. Thompson in the firm and the name was changed to Swann, Stewart & Co. The business was housed in a building at the southeast corner of the Public Square and Monticello Street which had been erected by Cary Wood as the second site of his general store. The new owners subsequently expanded into an adjoining building nearer the middle of the block facing the Square. Later Mr. Swann acquired sole ownership of the business and

of the "Store room . . . [and] stalls, stables and buggy house
. . . on the rear of the lot" extending along Monticello Street
to the corner of Reynolds Street. For some years he operated
under the name of T. C. Swann, Merchandise, but later the
business was known variously as T. C. Swann Company and
Swann-Davis Mercantile Company.[17]

A native of that part of Newton County which was for a
short time a part of Henry County, where his father was an
original settler when the latter was created from Creek Indian
lands, Thomas Chalmers Swann was born on 1 January 1849.
After completing his education he taught school in Texas for
one year. Returning to Georgia, he engaged in a general
mercantile business at Conyers for seven years beginning in
1872. He traveled frequently to Augusta to buy goods for his
store, and while there used a portion of his profits to specu-
late in cotton futures. He prospered at the former and was so
successful at the latter that when he moved to Covington in
1879 he already had the nucleus of what eventually became a
substantial fortune.[18]

Mr. Swann was a public-spirited man who soon emerged as
one of Covington's leading citizens. Active in all phases of the
community's life, he was generous in the time, effort and
financial support which he devoted to its activities and institutions. He was a member of the Board of County Commissioners for six years, the last four of which he served as
chairman. A member of City Council for some twenty years,
he was elected mayor of Covington in 1899. He served also as
a county school commissioner and as a member of the Covington Board of Education. He was a trustee of Southern Female
College and was a liberal benefactor of the local Methodist
church.[19]

T. C. Swann's widespread business interests brought him the
presidency of the Covington & Oxford Street Railway Company, of the Bank of Newton County, and of the Eagle
Mining Company of Logan, Idaho. His most notable achieve-

ment, and the one which brought the most lasting benefits to Covington, was the organization in 1900 with John F. Henderson, William C. Clark, Oliver S. Porter, Tyra A. Starr and N. S. Turner of the Covington Cotton Mills. The new corporation was the outgrowth of a small yarn factory which Messrs. Swann and Porter had started several years earlier. A disagreement subsequently caused Mr. Porter to withdraw from the more ambitious venture and to devote his entire efforts to his own mill at Porterdale. The Covington Cotton Mills, begun with a capitalization of $100,000, started operations with 320 looms and 5000 spindles. Under the guidance of Mr. Swann as president the enterprise brought employment and security to large numbers of Newton County families and wealth to those whose vision and ability conceived and directed their operations.[20]

On 14 May 1901 *The Georgia Enterprise*, which had stated editorially a few years earlier that Covington needed just such an industry, reported jubilantly:

THE NEW FACTORY STARTED

The new Covington cotton factory was started to running at 10½ o'clock on yesterday.

Miss Olive Swann, the beautiful daughter of President T. C. Swann, "pressed the button" ... which turned on the steam and started the driving wheel of the ponderous engine ...

A large number of our citizens was present to witness the starting of the big mill ...

May it run continuously, successfully, and forever.

Several years later the same newspaper's announcement on 27 January 1905 of the forthcoming opening of the new Bank of Newton County said in part:

Mr. T. C. Swann, the President is, and has been for many years, so conspicuous a figure in Covington commercial and political life that his name is known throughout the entire county in connection with the success and progress of the city. He has a marvelously clear and keen insight into affairs, good judgement, steady nerve and great foresight. His business ability is clearly shown by the prosperous condition of the two institutions which he has financed for the past several years, namely: the Swann-Davis Co. and the Covington Mills. The success of the Bank of Newton County will be greatly benefitted by having so strong a man at its head.

On 1 September of the same year the *Enterprise* gave further evidence of Mr. Swann's remarkable business acumen:

Mr. T. C. Swann, who, it is said, refuses the presidency of a corporation every month, started on a pleasure trip through the Rockies, Colorado, Oregon, and in passing through Utah was taken from the train and given the presidency of a gold mine . . . His reputation for financiering companies and being a leader [had] preceeded him . . .

The promising career of Thomas C. Swann was ended abruptly on 8 March 1906 when he died suddenly in the prime of life. One of the many tributes paid to his memory said that he "was a man of impregnable sincerity and integrity and . . . his passion for honesty, for fair play, for straight dealing was the key to his personal character and business success. The enterprise and pluck with which he built up the Covington cotton mills . . . indicated his tenacity of purpose and his distinctive initiative ability, and the enterprise which he thus founded stands as a monument to his aggressiveness and honest dealing . . ." [21]

Mr. Swann had been married on 14 January 1873 to Miss Sarah Elizabeth Stowers, who was born in DeKalb County, Georgia, on 24 March 1844 and reared in Oxford, Mississippi. Their children were Stella, who died in childhood; Nancy Olive, who became the wife of James H. Porter (*see page 235*); and Thomas C. Swann, Jr. In reporting Mrs. Swann's death on 21 January 1922 *The Covington News* stated that she was "one of Covington's wealthiest and . . . most esteemed citizens . . . She was a rarely beautiful woman and possessed a poise and strength of character [that was] truly admirable . . ." [22]

In the years between Mr. Swann's purchase of the Wood-Henderson house and Mrs. Swann's death, several changes were made in the structure. Most of these were made under the direction of Miss Olive Swann following her graduation in 1893 from Lucy Cobb Institute, a fashionable finishing school in Athens. Wishing to make the interior of the house more contemporary in appearance, she had the original wide pine floors downstairs covered with hardwood flooring, the hand-carved mantels replaced by mirrored cabinet mantels, and a landing and cushioned seat installed near the foot of the stairway in the reception hall. Her parents had earlier added a bedroom at the rear of the upper floor and a galleried porch across the back of the house. Under Miss Swann's direction a portion of the porch next to the downstairs bedroom was enclosed for use as a sleeping porch and another sleeping porch

Courtesy of Mrs. William B. Williford

MR. AND MRS. T.C. SWANN and their daughter Olive are shown on the veranda of their home, *circa* 1887.

was installed upstairs. The latter was built over the breakfast room which had been made from a portion of the latticed porch downstairs, which had supplanted the earlier "lean-to" at the rear of the dining room. The kitchen was moved close to the house and connected to it by an extension of the galleried porch. It was in this same period that Miss Swann named the family home *Swanscombe* after the Swanns' ancestral seat in England.[23]

Following Olive Swann's marriage and her mother's death, the former's much younger brother, Thomas C. Swann, Jr., lived alone in the house, cared for by his faithful valet Will. The young man, who was born 10 August 1887, had been educated at Georgia School (now Institute) of Technology and the Eastman Business College in Poughkeepsie, New York, after which he served in the United States Army as a quartermaster sergeant in World War I. As an heir to the largest block of stock in Covington Mills, he set out one day with a lunch bag under one arm and entered the world of looms, spindles and cotton. That one day was enough; never again in his lifetime did he put in a full day at work. He owned several farms which he left mostly to the care of overseers, and in later years when he became president of the mills he seldom spent more than an hour at a time on the premises— making it necessary for lesser officials to track him down to get his signature on checks and other documents. By virtue of his holdings in the Bank of Newton County, of which he had been a director since 1914, he was persuaded to serve as president of that institution from 1925 until 1930. Otherwise Thomas Swann devoted his time to the pleasurable pursuits of fox hunting, driving fine automobiles (in an age when that was *something*), reading, and engaging in long and knowledgeable conversations on an astonishing variety of subjects. When the handsome and eligible bachelor was approaching forty he disappointed a great many young ladies and their ambitious parents by eloping on 3 July 1923. The object of his affections was the former Julia Benton, a vivacious native of Monticello, who was a recent graduate of what is now known as Georgia College at Milledgeville.[24]

When she arrived at *Swanscombe* after a honeymoon to Michigan and Niagara Falls, the new Mrs. Swann found the outside blinds closed and the furniture inside swathed in white dust coverings. Her sister-in-law Mrs. Porter prevailed upon her close friend Neel Reid, distinguished classical architect of Atlanta, to direct the redecoration of the house. Under his skillful guidance the old place acquired a beautiful interior which displayed to advantage the Swanns' early Victorian and eighteenth century English furniture. In later years Mrs. Swann had the cabinet mantels removed and most of them replaced by the original mantels which had been stored in the attic of the carriage house at the rear of the property. She also had the stairway returned to its original straight lines, a second upstairs bathroom installed, and the downstairs sleeping porch enclosed for use as a sun parlor. As a finishing touch she installed the quaint lanterns from the old Swann family brougham on each side of the front door, and hung the

Courtesy of Mrs. William B. Williford

Dashing man-about-town Thomas Swann is shown in the National automobile which he bought off the racetrack after it had won the 1912 race at the Indianapolis Speedway.

windows with rosepoint lace curtains beneath gold-trimmed green damask draperies.[25]

In the years which followed *Swanscombe* was the scene of many elegant social functions and the center of a happy family life. Here Mr. and Mrs. Swann reared their only child, Thomas Swann, 3rd, whose good looks and charm endeared him to all whom he met. After being graduated from the Darlington School at Rome and enrolling at Georgia Tech, he was drafted into the army at the age of eighteen. Six weeks later he landed on Normandy Beach in the World War II invasion of Nazi-occupied France. Almost immediately his tank was destroyed and he wandered aimlessly for days before being hospitalized, first in France and later in England, as an unidentified victim of amnesia.[26]

The strain of not knowing their son's whereabouts exacted a heavy toll of Mr. and Mrs. Swann. The father suffered a severe heart attack shortly before a letter finally arrived from his son, but it was too late; he died on 26 March 1945. A few days later *The Covington News* stated editorially that "Few men were better known or more widely loved than was Mr. Swann . . ." The son returned home a few months later, telling his mother that the one thing which had sustained him in his terrible ordeal was the memory of the happy, rose-filled home which he had left behind. A scant four years later, on 15 May 1949, Thomas Swann, 3rd, was killed in an automobile accident as he and three fellow students at the University of Georgia were driving towards Highlands, North Carolina. "Tom, as he was affectionately known to his friends," the *News* commented in an editorial tribute, "had attained in the short span of twenty-four years what it takes some of us a lifetime to gain — a thorough appreciation of life through Christian living." [27]

For a long time after the flowers were removed from *Swanscombe's* front door for the second time in four years, it seemed that the lovely house would be forever shrouded in

CARRIAGE HOUSE
at *Swanscombe*. During the post-World War II housing
shortage Thomas Swann 3rd had it converted into a cottage, and since then it has been occupied continuously
by Mr. and Mrs. George Elliot.

sadness. Memories of the days when it had been a joyously
happy place seemed small consolation indeed to the grief-
stricken woman secluded within.[28]

After a while Mrs. Swann took up part-time residence with
a close friend in Kenilworth, Illinois. There her gay and witty
nature eventually asserted itself and, without realizing it, she
began to make a new life for herself. Still young, she nevertheless was incredulous when happiness again entered her life
in the person of Frank Milford Miller, a widowed Chicago
corporation executive. They were married on 12 October 1951
and established residence in Chicago, where they lived until
Mr. Miller retired from business several years later.[29]

During her ten-year residence in Illinois Mrs. Miller maintained *Swanscombe* with a staff of servants and she visited it
several times a year. When she and Mr. Miller moved into it as
their full-time home in 1959 they made certain improvements
to make the house more comfortable and convenient. The
kitchen was completely modernized, the porch connecting it to
the breakfast room and that room itself were combined to
make a delightful morning room, another portion of the rear

porch was converted into a powder room and a dressing room, and the sun parlor at the rear of the house was made into a charming extension of the downstairs bedroom. In the reception hall beautiful imported wallpaper was installed and an elegant black-and-white tile floor was laid. As a finishing touch the stately sixteen-room house was freshly painted both within and without. The outside shutters were painted a black-green which Mrs. Miller had seen on houses in the old Maine town of Damariscotta. These were so greatly admired in Covington that soon it seemed that every white frame house in town had them, and a national paint manufacturer whose paint Mrs. Miller had used even brought out a paint which was named "Swanscombe Green."[30]

Mr. and Mrs. Miller had planned to spend the spring and fall of each year in Covington and to travel extensively during the other seasons. After only three years, however, this pleasant arrangement was abruptly terminated when Mr. Miller became seriously ill. His wife and his only child, Edward F. Miller of the University of Pennsylvania, were at his bedside when he succumbed on 5 April 1963.[31]

The gardens at *Swanscombe*, in which Mr. Miller had taken an especial interest, received only the most basic maintenance in the six years immediately following his death. Then, on 23 June 1969, his widow was married to William Bailey Williford, an Atlanta author and publisher, who soon was enthusiastically engaged in making the grounds more beautiful than ever. Now, with occasional visits from his son Lawrence, a student at the University of Georgia, a semblance of the old carefree atmosphere has returned to the historic property.[32]

In her nearly half a century as chatelaine of *Swanscombe* Mrs. Williford has at various times been identified as a leader of society and as an active participant in Covington's civic, cultural, and patriotic affairs. She was a charter member of the Covington Book Club and has been president of the Covington Garden Club, president of the Parent-Teacher

SWANSCOMBE
Residence of Mr. and Mrs. William B. Williford.

Association of the old Covington Public School, and a member of the United Daughters of the Confederacy. She is a member and former regent of the Sergeant Newton Chapter, Daughters of the American Revolution; a charter member of the Newton County Historical Society; a patron of the Atlanta Art Association; and a former member of the Advisory Council of Oxford College. She is a communicant of The Church of the Good Shepherd (Episcopal). [33]

When the Covington Garden Club sponsored the first public tour of Covington's ante-bellum homes in 1948, a writer for an Atlanta newspaper reported:

> *Swanscombe* is a beautiful . . . home with wide halls and elaborate furnishings. Its chief features are long mirrors between the tall windows, crystal chandeliers, antique rosewood furniture, huge, heavy-postered bed with pale-green canopy, and a pierced brass firescreen from New Orleans. The overhead beams in the hall are elegant with carved detail, and boxwood borders the walk in front, inside the iron fence.[34]

Nearly a quarter of a century later, when the house was opened for a candlelight tour sponsored by the Newton County Historical Society, of which the master of *Swanscombe* was chairman of the board of trustees, hundreds of persons from every part of the United States and several foreign countries admired the classic beauty of the old house. Two of the costumed hostesses on that occasion excited special interest: Mrs. Lamar Callaway, a great-great-granddaughter of builder Cary Wood, and Mrs. JD Smith, niece of Mrs. Williford, the latter of whom wore a black lace gown which had belonged to the elder Mrs. Thomas Swann. [35]

Today the tall white columns of *Swanscombe* rise serenely from a park-like setting only a block and a half from the busy heart of Covington. The house, like other beautiful old homes in the city, is admired annually by thousands of visitors to Covington. In the spring its gardens are breathtakingly beautiful with the blossoms of dogwoods and azaleas, and a large bank of salmon-pink azaleas is one of the most beautiful sights in all of Newton County. The "Queen of Floyd Street" has an elegance which has been enhanced by time and generations of loving care, and residents of Covington and visitors alike hope her stately beauty will continue to grace the lovely old city for another century and a half.

IV

THE NEAL-SANDERS HOUSE

One of the most beautiful houses ever built in Covington was situated in the middle of the Church Street block bounded by Conyers, Elm and Reynolds streets. This classic edifice, whose central facade has been preserved to the present time, was erected for one of Covington's wealthiest pioneer citizens and was subsequently the home of other families which have been important in the history of the city.

McCormick Neal was born in Warren County on 3 January 1799, and in 1819 and 1820 served as captain of a company of Georgia militia in his home county. He presumably resigned his commission in the latter year and moved to that part of Henry County which would soon form a part of Newton County, for on 10 March 1820 he purchased slightly more than three acres of land from Sarah (Mrs. Joel) Flanegan for $11.125. On 24 December 1824 he bought from Cary Wood Lot number 9 in Square D, and on 5 June 1827 he bought at public outcry twelve acres "on the lot upon which the Town of Covington is Situated ... lying on the west side of Dryed Indian Creek ..." There were to be many more transactions during the remainder of his relatively brief life.[1]

The first two transactions mentioned here brought McCormick Neal the two lots of land upon which his house was built and the two lots to the rear of it upon which he had stables and a garden. Nearby, on the site of the present Newton County Library and the softball diamond, he later built a cotton gin house.[2]

The graceful white-columned house which was erected for McCormick Neal and his wife, the former Sarah Ann Batts, probably was constructed around 1830. The Library of

Congress noted after photographing and measuring the structure in 1934 that the central portico might have dated from as early as the 1820s. It is a matter of historical record, however, that the home of Cary Wood, the man from whom Mr. Neal purchased a portion of the site for his house, was the first clapboard house in Covington. Thus we may assume that the Neal house was erected within a year or two of completion of the Wood house in 1828. The elegance of the Neal residence, both within and without, clearly reflected the cultivated tastes of its owners. The beautiful furniture, paintings, silver and china subsequently passed into the possession of the couple's children, and although some of it was sold later to outsiders, descendants still own enough of the furnishings to give one an impression of the beauty of the home as it must have appeared in the halcyon days prior to the Civil War.[3]

Young Mr. Neal took an active part in the business and political affairs of his adopted home. In 1829 he began the first of four consecutive one-year terms as Newton County's representative in the General Assembly, and in 1833 he served as state senator. Soon after settling on the site which later became Covington he entered into a partnership with his wife's brother McAllen Batts. An 1828 deed refers to them as "Merchants trading under the firm and style of Neal & Batts."[4]

Mr. Batts (*15 December 1805–17 February 1839*) lived in a handsome house at the southeast corner of Church and Conyers streets. He and his wife, Sidney, had several children, one of whom married Atlanta merchant prince E. W. Marsh; the latter couple's son McAllen Batts Marsh was one of the dashing, rich *beaux* of Atlanta society at the turn of the century.[5]

In 1855 McAllen Batts' widow, who was then living in Chattanooga, sold the family residence to John Randolph Camp (*3 July 1832–31 October 1858*). A son of Covington pioneer Gerard Camp (*see page 217*), he had married on 13

BATTS - CAMP HOUSE
Erected *circa* 1835 for McAllen Batts and sub-
sequently for half a century the home of Mrs.
Virginia Beach Camp. (Demolished.)

December 1855 Lucinda Jane Martin (*26 December 1837–15 July 1907*). Following Randolph Camp's death his home was acquired by his brother Septimus C. Camp (*10 May 1842–10 August 1867*), who had married a northern lady named Virginia Beach. In 1867, when nearly everyone was impoverished by the Civil War, Mrs. Camp, or "Miss Jennie" as she was known locally, started a private school. Soon widowed, she spent the remaining years of her life in the house she had shared with her husband. As she became elderly she ventured forth only rarely, and when she did appear in public it was in the long and somber clothing of an earlier era. Following the death of Mrs. Virginia Beach Camp (*20 June 1837–4 March*

Beautiful *bas relief* marks the grave of pioneer citizen McCormick Neal.

1928), the house was purchased by S. A. Ginn (*see page 198*), who demolished it and erected upon the northern half of the lot an attractive brick cottage which is now the residence of Mrs. Godfrey Trammell.[6]

Mr. and Mrs. McCormick Neal were the parents of numerous children, including: George and McAllen, who died in childhood; Louisa, first wife of Osborn T. Rogers (*see pages 146-147*); Corrine; Nellie; Sarah, who married Colonel Robert G. Harper, one-time law partner of L. Q. C. Lamar; Lula, later the wife of Richard Henry Harris; and McCormick Neal the younger. There must have been other children between the birth of Louisa in 1825 and the death of McAllen in 1830, for on the latter's tombstone appear the poignant words "Another shaft is sped, Another son is gone ..." Even more sorrow was ahead for Mrs. Neal: her husband died on 16 July 1834, three days following the death of George at age six, and in less than five years her brother McAllen Batts was dead.[7]

The young widow bought from the administrator of her husband's estate, his brother John Neal, on 9 November 1835, "all those lots in the town of Covington known as Numbers 6, 7, 8 and 9 in Sqaure D." Thus she acquired ownership of the two city blocks upon which were situated her beautiful home and the adjacent outbuildings. When, on 9 December 1839, she became the wife of the Reverend Charles H. Sanders, she continued to live in the Church Street mansion.[8]

Charles Haynie Sanders (whose name was spelled sometimes *Saunders*) was a Methodist preacher and a founder and original trustee of Emory College. He was born 27 February 1798, and probably was a son of the Bretton Sanders who represented Oglethorpe County in the General Assembly in 1810–'11. His first wife, the former Georgianna Cook, had died and left him four children to rear: Ophelia Jane (later Mrs. John H. Hicks), Eugenia Adelaide, Georgianna Cook, and Julia Eliza. By his marriage to Mrs. Neal he became the father of three more offspring.[9]

Emma Batts Sanders, only daughter of the Reverend Mr. Sanders and his second wife, was married on 5 August 1862 to Captain Lorenzo F. Luckie, CSA, who was a member of another prominent pioneer family.[10]

The Luckie family was established in Covington by Hezekiah Luckie, whose will was probated on 4 January 1836. He had represented Newton County in the State Senate in 1827, 1828 and 1829. The tombstone of the patriarch's widow, Mrs. Jane Luckie (*22 May 1777–17 May 1856*), may still be seen in the old Methodist portion of Covington City Cemetery. Nearby are the graves of their son William D. Luckie (*2 September 1800–3 January 1870*) and his wife, Eliza Buckner Luckie (*13 October 1807–11 May 1856*). William D. Luckie was the first

judge of the Court of Ordinary of Newton County, and he
served in the General Assembly in 1835. His brother Alexander F. Luckie (*1798–1854*) served in the General Assembly
in 1834, after which he moved to Atlanta. Subsequently he
was honored when that city's Luckie Street was named for
him.[11]

In the present century one of Alexander Luckie's great-
granddaughters achieved international notoriety because of her
pro-Nazi radio broadcasts during World War II. Using the name
"Lady Haw Haw," she allegedly told Americans via broadcasts from Berlin that their war against Hitler was "a futile
cause" and that Hitler was "an immortal crusader of God."
Arrested at the end of the war, she was imprisoned at Salz-
burg, Austria, for several months before a Federal Court dismissed treason charges against her.[12]

"Lady Haw Haw" was born Jane Foster Anderson, daughter
of Robert and Ellen (Luckie) Anderson of Atlanta. In 1911,
when she was ten years of age, her mother died and she went
to live with her maternal grandmother, who by then was Mrs.
George W. D. Patterson, wife of Demorest's most prominent
physician. She was educated at Piedmont College, where one
of her classmates was Mei Ling Soong, who later became
world-renowned as the spirited and beautiful second wife of
Generalisimo Chiang Kai-shek of Nationalist China. Jane Anderson left Georgia at an early age and soon thereafter was
married to Deems Taylor, noted music critic and composer.
After serving as a war correspondent during World War I she
became the wife of the Marquis de Cienfuegos of Spain.[13]

An earlier and more reputable feminine member of the
Luckie family of Covington was Mary Ann (*3 February
1816–9 October 1848*), daughter of Mr. and Mrs. Hezekiah
Luckie. She became, on 4 February 1834, the first wife of
Columbus Delaware Pace (*9 January 1810–21 August 1834*),
founder of another fine old Covington family. The latter represented Newton County in the General Assembly at the session

of 1847. His handsome home on Pace Street occupied an entire block just north of Usher Street. Judge Pace married (2) Martha E. [Denton?] and (3) Mary Elizabeth Dutton (*see page 91*), the latter ceremony taking place on 17 January 1867.[14]

Captain James McAllen Pace (*2 August 1835–7 September 1912*) was the most distinguished of Judge Pace's children. He was awarded the Bachelor of Laws degree by the University of Georgia in 1861; served as a captain on the staff of his brother-in-law General John B. Gordon in the Civil War; was a member of the Constitutional Convention of 1877; represented Newton County in the General Assembly (1898–'99); was several times mayor of Covington; practiced law with distinction and success; and served as professor of law and a trustee of Emory College. His wife, Leonora (*1841–1915*), whom he married 28 May 1861, was a daughter of General Hugh Haralson of LaGrange and sister of three famous beauties who were the wives of General Gordon, of Chief Justice Logan Bleckley, and of Governor-Nominate Basil H. Overby. Captain and Mrs. Pace made their home in an attractive frame house at the southeast corner of College and Elm Streets which had been built for Captain Pace's uncle Judge William D. Luckie.[15]

One of Judge Luckie's sons was William D. Luckie, Jr. (*14 August 1842–3 April 1885*), a prominent Atlanta businessman who in 1880 was elected Grand Commander of the Knights Templar of Georgia. The W. D. Luckie Masonic Lodge in Atlanta was named in his honor.[16]

Another son of William and Eliza (Buckner) Luckie was Captain Lorenzo F. Luckie (*27 May 1838–10 July 1864*), a hero of the Civil War. Three days prior to the second anniversary of his marriage to Emma Batts Sanders (*see page 37*) he died of wounds received in battles at Malvern Hill and Petersburg, Virginia.[17]

Young Mrs. Luckie, a widow at nineteen, subsequently became the third of the four wives of Colonel William A. Hemphill, founder of *The Atlanta Constitution*. They were

married in a formal ceremony at the Methodist church on 7
March 1871 and thereafter made their home in Atlanta. There,
too, lived Mrs. Hemphill's dashing bachelor brother Osgood
Sanders, who was a founding member of the exclusive Nine
O'Clocks and of the Capital City Club, and whose name is
perpetuated in the Osgood Sanders Day Nursery. Charles H.
Sanders, Jr., third child of the Reverend Mr. Sanders and his
second wife, became a prominent resident of nearby Madison,
where his granddaughter Mrs. Nathan Hunter now lives. There
are no descendants of Mrs. Neal-Sanders living in Covington
today.[18]

During the era in which the Methodist Church in the United
States was split asunder because Bishop James O. Andrew,
president of the board of trustees of Emory College, owned a
slave by inheritance and was not permitted by law to set her
free in Georgia, his friend and associate the Reverend Charles
H. Sanders also was a slave owner — probably on a large scale. In
1849 the Reverend George White's *Statistics of The State of
Georgia* noted that "Charlotte, belonging to Rev. Mr. Saunders
[*sic.* The original spelling of the name], died in 1847, at the
age of 120 years." [19]

If the Reverend Charles H. Sanders were outstanding as a
man of the cloth and as a public-spirited citizen of Covington,
he was brilliantly successful as a businessman. It is doubtful
that any other man in the city's history has ever owned so
much of its prime real estate. The surveys and sales which Mr.
Sanders' executors made of his property fill page after page in
the official records of Newton County. At his death his
holdings included farm lands and such extensive tracts of city
property as that extending from his home on Church Street
eastward along Conyers Street to the present Dearing Street.[20]

At his death on 6 August 1851 he bequeathed to his widow
"the house and lot on which we now live, with all the
appurtenances, the garden lot, and Stable lots and the Gin
house lots, and forty acres of land to be laid off from my

land which lies South from the lots of land on which the Male Academy stands . . ." [21]

The reference to "the house and lot on which we now live" refers to the house and lot which Mrs. Sanders had purchased from the estate of her first husband. In those days Georgia law did not permit married women to own property, so title to the former Mrs. Neal's property was vested in Mr. Sanders following their marriage. It was fitting and proper that among his bequests to her should be the house in which she had lived with her first husband as well as with him. [22]

NEAL - SANDERS HOUSE

Erected for the elder McCormick Neal, *circa* 1830, and occupied by his widow until shortly before her death in 1866. Demolished *circa* 1925. The central facade is preserved in the former Ramsey house (*see page 48*).

On 3 March 1866 Mrs. Sanders, apparently conscious of the approaching end and realizing that her minor son and her widowed daughter would not require so pretentious a residence as she occupied, sold her long-time home to Enoch Steadman for $5500. The property was described as being "lots number Six (6) and Seven (7) and Eight (8) and Nine (9) and twenty five in Square D, being the lots formerly owned and Occupied by McCormick Neal (Senior) in his lifetime, and at the time of his death . . ."[23]

Two months earlier Mrs. Sanders had purchased the Harris-Corley house at the southwest corner of Monticello and Conyers streets (see page 71). In her will, dated 17 July 1866 and probated more than a year after her death on 18 September 1866, she directed that this house not be sold until her son Osgood Sanders reached the age of twenty-one. She stipulated that he and his sister Mrs. Emma B. Luckie were to live there during his minority at no cost to themselves.[24]

Enoch Steadman, buyer of the Neal-Sanders house on Church Street, was born in Hopkinton, Rhode Island, on 25 April 1819 and died in Covington on 7 November 1883. He moved to Covington in 1863 and bought large tracts of land in the vicinity of Cedar Shoals, where he established a twine mill which later became one of the Porterdale properties of Oliver S. Porter. Colonel Steadman, as he was called, served in the State Senate for the sessions of 1871–'72 and 1873–'74 and was a trustee of Southern Masonic Female College. He and his wife, Mary, had (possibly among others) a daughter, Lizzie, and a son, E. S. Steadman. The former became the wife of Charles Vincent Sanford of Covington. This union produced one of Georgia's most distinguished sons: Dr. Steadman Vincent Sanford, president of the University of Georgia (1932–'35) and chancellor of the University System of Georgia (1935–'45). He was born in Covington on 24 August 1871 and spent his early years here.[25]

There is filed in the Newton County Courthouse a deed record which shows that on 30 January 1867 Enoch Steadman transferred to Purmedus Reynolds for $4000 "those tracts or parcels of land . . . in the Corporate limits of the City of Covington . . . recently sold by Mrs. Sarah Sanders to the said E. Steadman[,] it being the lot on which the Said E. Steadman now resides . . . Also the lot . . . known as the Garden lot and Stables and Horse lot . . ."[26]

Purmedus Reynolds (*see also page 11*) is listed in the United States Census for 1860 as a native-born Georgia farmer who lived in the village of Oxford and who had real estate and personal property valued at $20,000 each. He was born 20 December 1805 and died 19 March 1873. Generally referred to as "Judge" because of his service as a judge of the Inferior Court of Newton County, he served in the General Assembly (1838–'40, '43–'50, '53–'54) and in the State Senate (1857–'58). He was a delegate to the Southern Commercial Convention at Montgomery in 1858, a member of the Secession Convention of 1861, and a delegate to the State Convention of 1865.[27]

Judge Reynolds and his wife, the former Nancy Foster Kolherm, reared a large family whose members included Nannie (Mrs. Robert F. Maddox, of Atlanta), Ada (Mrs. J. F. Alexander, of Atlanta), Martha (Mrs. J. M. Russell, of Columbus), Emily, Katherine, Frances (who married Coleman C. Brown and Dr. Gustavus A. Meritt of Covington. *See page 11*), Mary Ann (Mrs. Walker), Fletcher (of Marietta) and John Reynolds (of Savannah).[28]

The Reynolds family lived in the Neal-Sanders house only a short time. Whether the Judge defaulted on his payment is not clear from an examination of official deed records. It is known that his last years were spent in a large brown Victorian house which was built for him in the middle of the block bounded by Hendricks, Washington, Brown and Reynolds streets. Subsequently the latter house was the home of

Charles Hardeman White (*1855–1925*) and his wife, née Lelia Stephenson (*1866–1946*). There the Whites reared their six children and lived out their lives before the house was demolished at about the time of World War II.[29]

In some way ownership of the Neal-Sanders house reverted to Enoch Steadman, for on 22 November 1868 he sold to David W. Spence for $5000 "Lots Number Six (6) and Seven (7) and Eight (8) and Nine and Twenty Five (25) in Square D being the Lots formerly owned and Occupied by McCormick

RESIDENCE OF MR. AND MRS. THOMAS GREENE CALLAWAY,
southwest corner of College and Oak streets. Erected in 1909 for the well-known Covington merchant (*7 December 1869–7 January 1951*) and his wife, née Ackie White (*23 October 1886–8 May 1952*), daughter of Mr. and Mrs. Charles Hardeman White. Here were reared their children, Miss Sarah White Callaway, present owner of the house, and the late Thomas Greene Callaway, Jr. (*21 March 1910–23 June 1972*). The latter served as Newton County's representative (1941) and state senator (1947–'48, 1953–'54) and married as his first wife Mrs. Martha (Candler) York, granddaughter of Coca-Cola tycoon Asa G. Candler. He married (2) Miss Helen Austin of Newnan. The Callaway house was erected on the east half of the block which formerly had been occupied solely by the Luckie-Pace house (*see page* 39).[30]

Neal (Senior) in his lifetime and at the time of his death. Lots Numbers Six and Seven being the Lots on which the Dwelling house and Kitchen are situate and Eight and nine the garden and Stables and Number Twenty five was formerly known as Neal's Gin house Lot adjoining the Grave Yard and Mrs. Camp's horse Lot . . ." [31]

David W. Spence, the buyer, was a prominent Covington dry goods merchant who lived in the original McCormick Neal house from the time of its purchase until his death on 13 September 1875 at the age of 59.[32]

Mr. Spence and his wife, Sophia, were the parents of Caroline F., Anderson H., Adaline (Mrs. James T. Van-Horne, of Monroe), Laura (Mrs. J. F. Rosser, of Toccoa), and the Reverend Charles C. Spence (of Demorest). The first-named child moved with her parents to the Neal-Sanders house when she was a little girl and spent the remainder of her life within its hospitable walls. She was married on 17 January 1879 to William B. Shepherd (*see page 230*), member of an old Covington family. Following the death of eighty year-old Mrs. Sophia C. Spence on 7 October 1903, her son-in-law Dr. James T. Van-Horne, as executor, sold her home and other real estate at public outcry. The house was sold to her daughter Mrs. Callie S. Shepherd on 7 November 1904 for $5592. Included in the purchase were all of the lots which originally comprised the residential property of McCormick Neal, except the north half of the two lots in the block at the rear of the house.[33]

Mr. Shepherd, a veteran of service with the 10th Georgia Regiment, CSA, in the Civil War, was a prominent and influential Covington businessman. He and Mrs. Shepherd were noted for their hospitality, and although their handsome home began to show signs of neglect in their later years, its doors were always open to a large circle of friends. Here they reared their family, which included daughters Ethel and Birdie and sons Ralph, a veteran of World War I; Willie Beck; and Charles. In his last years Charles Shepherd's dwindling funds forced him to turn from daubing paint on canvases to painting the sides of houses, which he did with skill and an artist's feeling for colors.[34]

In her old age financial reverses caused Mrs. Shepherd to sell the lots which for a hundred years had adjoined her still-regal old home. Eventually she mortgaged the house itself, for which she obtained a loan of $3500 from Mrs. Emma Jones Fears of Clarke County on 16 December 1924.[35]

Nine years later, Mrs. Shepherd having died leaving an unpaid balance of $2000, Mrs. Fears foreclosed on 4 April 1933 and acquired clear title to the old house and the city block in which it was situated. Shortly thereafter, on 23 May 1923, she sold the property to V. C. Ellington for $2500.[36]

A few years later Mr. Ellington demolished the old landmark to make way for a brick cottage which he had erected on the southern portion of the property. The new house was sold by him on 6 March 1934 to Leon Cohen, who with Mrs. Cohen (neé Callie Harrison of Arlington) still lives there. The

ROSSER-COHEN HOUSE

Leon Cohen, owner of Covington's oldest retail store, lived in this house for several years after he arrived from Monticello in 1916 to work for his uncle Wolfe Cohen. The latter owned both the house and the department store which had been founded in 1892 by his brother Abe Cohen. The elder Cohens were two of six brothers who came from their native Prussia and settled in Madison, from which they scattered to Eatonton, Elberton, Monticello and Covington.

The house was built for E. B. Rosser, who purchased its site from William W. Clark and James M. Pace for $850 on 23 February 1869. On 15 June 1883 Mr. Rosser sold the house and the city block in which it was located to A. B. Simms (*see pages 55-63*) for $1200. Following the latter's untimely death in 1887, the property was sold in separate parcels to several owners, with the house going to Dr. N. Z. Anderson (*see page 180*). The latter sold it for $1500 on 23 January 1907 to Wolfe Cohen, who subsequently reassembled the entire original lot.

During his years of ownership Mr. Cohen had the house turned around from its original position facing Clark Street so that it would face Washington Street. After he sold his business to his nephew Leon Cohen and moved to Baltimore in 1920, Mr. Cohen sold the house to Dr. N. Z. Anderson and N. Kaplan on 18 January 1924 for $4500. Mr. Kaplan and his family lived there for several years before moving from Covington, after which the house, *sans* the adjoining acreage, was owned by Mr. and Mrs. J. O. Allen. Since the former's death and his widow's removal to Acworth, the house has been let to roomers.[37]

---

other half of the two lots upon which the Neal-Sanders house had stood for so long is now occupied by the residence of Mrs. James Morgan (*see page 191*).[38]

It was fortunate indeed for Covington and for lovers of beautiful old things that before the stately old house was torn down its facade was rescued by Coe David Ramsey (*15 September 1874–4 April 1939*), a local furniture dealer. He had the central facade moved to the two-story Victorian house on Floyd Street which he had bought from the R. W. Milner family (*see page 212*). There, behind its stately columns, he and Mrs. Ramsey, née Susie Cunningham (*22 August 1874–12*

October 1960), reared their children: Martha, Mary Sue (Mrs. J. B. Maddox of Rome), George, Spence, and C. D. Ramsey, Jr.[39]

In recent years the house has been used by St. Augustine's Roman Catholic Church and, since the summer of 1971, it has been the sanctuary of Bethany Assembly. Its aged timbers and graceful lines add a touch of beauty and romance to an area

Courtesy Library of Congress

THE BEAUTIFUL FACADE of the Neal-Sanders house is shown after it was reassembled at the Floyd Street residence of Mr. and Mrs. C.D. Ramsey.

filled with small and unpretentious houses. As long as its facade survives, Covington will treasure memories of the various persons who loved the original house and whose lives enriched the city in which they lived.

V

THE GRAHAM-SIMMS HOUSE

The first ante-bellum house on present-day Floyd Street is numbered 1155 and is known as the Ginn Apartments. Although the original square columns were removed many years ago, it still is a handsome structure whose exterior simplicity is pleasing to the eye.

The house dates from the early 1830s and in its long history has sheltered generations of distinguished visitors. Perhaps the most historic event ever to take place within its elegant rooms was the first meeting of the trustees of the new Emory College on 6 February 1837. The host on that occasion was one of the trustees, Dr. William P. Graham, who also had been an original trustee of Emory's predecessor, the Georgia Conference Manual Labor School, when it was chartered in 1834. The house in which Emory College's trustees met for the first time had but recently been erected for Dr. Graham and his wife, the former Frances Graves. They and their children lived there only a few years, however, before the physician's untimely death sometime between 1842 and 1847.[1]

Mrs. Graham, who was the daughter of Solomon Graves of *Mt. Pleasant*, was left a widow at an early age. She and her brother Iverson L. Graves, as administrator and administratrix of Dr. Graham's estate, sold to William D. Conyers on 24 August 1849 "lots number fourteen and seven in Square A." The property was bounded on the west by the residence of William P. Anderson (now the site of the sanctuary of the First Baptist Church), on the south by the street leading from the courthouse to Madison, on the east by an alley dividing subject property from the property of Robert O. Usher, and on the north by a street running parallel to the street

49

MT. PLEASANT

The original portion of this house, which remained in one family for a century and a half, was built in 1818 for Solomon Graves. The present structure dates from 1835. In the latter part of the nineteenth century a two-story columned portico was removed to permit the addition of a protrusion to enlarge the library.[3]

Solomon Graves (*1 April 1766–October 1830*) was a North Carolinian who became a prominent and influential man in Newton County. His descendants continued the tradition started by him of service to the community and of lavish hospitality to a large circle of friends and relatives.[4]

Mr. Graves and his first wife, the former Miss Frances Lewis, were the parents of Frances (Mrs. Graham), Iverson, Barzillia, William, Sidney, and Dr. John L. Graves. The first-named son married (1) Miss Williams and had a daughter, Fannie; he married (2) Sarah Ward Dutton of Champion, New York (*see page 91*), and had Henry, Cornelia and Dutton Graves. Henry Graves married Henrietta Milligan of Augusta, a niece of Judge A. B. Longstreet, who was the second president of Emory College and a frequent guest in the Graves Home. A son of the last marriage also was named Henry; he married Mrs. Irma (Toland) Stokes of Atlanta and was the last member of the family to live in the ancestral home.[5]

Mt. Pleasant passed from the Graves family when the house and 426 acres were sold in 1958 to Mr. and Mrs. Walter C. Emmel, who came from Montana and who a few years later moved to Oregon. During their brief period of ownership this couple demolished the last remaining portion of the 1818 house and spread the ridiculous stories that a pony had been hidden in a closet during the Civil War and that *Mt. Pleasant's* original 7,000 acres had been a grant to the Graves family from King George III. As a member of the family remarked with caustic amusement, the American Revolution had been over for *years* when Solomon Graves moved to Georgia.[6]

Next owner of the plantation house and of some of the surrounding acreage was Robert W. Hamilton, Jr. (*see page 232*), who in 1970 sold the house and some 300 acres to Mr. and Mrs. James H. Dupre and others. They, in turn, sold the house and 23.14 acres six months later to Mrs. Adele Fortson Cleveland. Mrs. Cleveland and her husband, King Cleveland, lived at *Mt. Pleasant* two years, during which time they expended much time and money in restoring the old house. In 1972 they moved back to Atlanta, where Mr. Cleveland is chairman of the board of the National Bank of Georgia.[7]

Owners of the property since mid-1972 are Mr. and Mrs. Oby T. Brewer, formerly of Atlanta.[8]

bounding the lots on the south. On the same date and for the same sum of money, $1537, Dr. Conyers transferred title to the property to Mrs. Graham in her individual right.[2]

The Graham residence was a fitting addition to the stately houses which lined both sides of Floyd Street. Its large square columns lent an air of solid dignity to the neighborhood, and the beautiful doorway with its glass side panels and fanlight opened into a hallway dominated by a gracefully curving stairway. The latter was copied from a stairway at *Mt. Pleasant*.[9]

The drawing room at the Graham house had a beautiful chandelier, elaborate cornices, and a handsome mantle. In this room Fannie and Margaret, the two young ladies of the household, entertained their *beaux*. A frequent caller was Lucius Lamar, a bright and charming young lawyer of Covington, who had recently been graduated by Emory College. He was deeply in love with Margaret, and she reciprocated to some extent. But the young lady fell madly in love with a music teacher from Columbus, much to the displeasure of her family. Love was victorious, however, for on 8 October 1846 she and John D. Goneke were united in marriage by the Reverend Doctor Alexander Means, who later became president of Emory College (*see pages 76, 114*).[10]

Young Mr. Lamar was a trustee of the Male Academy in 1849, and in 1853–'54 he represented Newton County in the General Assembly. Subsequently he became nationally famous as L. Q. C. Lamar — lawyer, university professor, Georgia legislator, Confederate army officer, Congressional representative and senator from Mississippi, Secretary of the Interior, and Associate Justice of the Supreme Court of the United States. He married as his first wife Jennie Longstreet, daughter of the versatile and beloved Judge Augustus Baldwin Longstreet (*see page 77n*), who later became president of the universities of Mississippi and South Carolina. The couple often visited their old friends the Graves family at *Mt. Pleasant*. On these occasions

Mr. Lamar invariably closeted himself in the parlor with a daguerreotype of Margaret Graham, while his hosts tried feverishly to divert his wife's attention so that she would not be aware of what he was doing.[11]

Margaret's happiness was of short duration. She died in childbirth in 1851 and, her remains having been brought to *Mt. Pleasant* by wagon, was buried by torchlight in an eerie ceremony in the family graveyard. Her husband died the following year, and her brother John and sister Fannie when they were in their early twenties.[12]

Following the death of Mrs. Frances L. Graham in October 1850, the Floyd Street house was sold by her brother Iverson L. Graves, who was administrator of her estate. On 4 November 1851 he conveyed title to the property to Richard L. Simms for the sum of $3170.[13]

The new owner was a native of Charles County, Maryland, where he was born on 1 June 1795. His parents were James Simms and the former Mrs. Sarah Elinor Ann (Lee) Key, and through his mother Richard Lee Simms was a great-great-grandson of the Honorable Richard Lee of Virginia. James Simms moved his family to Georgia shortly after his son's birth and settled in Columbia County. He represented the newly-created county in the General Assembly of Georgia from 1796 to 1806.[14]

Richard Lee Simms was graduated from college in South Carolina.* He opened a law office in Athens, Georgia, and within a short time had become solicitor of the Athens judicial circuit. After a few years he moved to the newly-created county of Newton and established a law practice in Covington. In 1833 he took his seat as Newton's representative to the General Assembly of Georgia. On 26 October 1834 he married Miss Jerustha Bonner, daughter of Allan and Lucy (Awtry) Bonner of Clarke County.[15]

---

*His granddaughter Mrs. Charles S. Thompson of Atlanta told the author on 11 January 1971 that "he was graduated by Columbia University in South Carolina." Quite probably the institution was the College of South Carolina, at Columbia (now the University of South Carolina).

The young lawyer was one of the original commissioners of both Covington (1822) and Oxford (1839). During his relatively brief residence in the new seat of Methodist higher education his home was located at the northeast corner of Wesley and Clarke streets. At about the time of Oxford's incorporation Mr. Simms became a judge of the Inferior Court of Newton County. He was always referred to thereafter as "Judge." [16]

Young Richard Simms was a consistent investor in Newton County real estate from the time of his arrival until the year of his death. Early deed books are replete with the records of his transactions. One of the most interesting of these pertains not to property in Newton County nor even in Georgia, but in the then-Western state of Alabama. On 16 August 1844 he bought from Arthur L. Simms, who probably was his brother, a tract "lying and being in the State of Alabama and on the east side of the Bay known and Called Mobile Bay containing three thousand and four hundred acres more or less . . ." The price was $600. One's imagination is staggered by speculating upon the current value of this property. [17]

Late in 1851 Judge and Mrs. Simms and their five children moved into the former Graham residence on Floyd Street in Covington. It was an ideal location; one which afforded easy access to the father's law office on the Square, to the Southern Female College which the eldest daughter was attending, and to the society of such nearby friends as the Woods, the Floyds, and the Ushers. The spacious grounds surrounding the house contained a detached kitchen, a carriage house, a smokehouse, a fuel house (for wood and coal), a bathhouse, a greenhouse, and "an unmentionable convenience." [18]

The Simms family had less than five happy years in their new home before Judge Simms' death on 28 May 1856. His passing brought expressions of regret and sympathy from a large circle of friends who had known and admired him, and a

Courtesy of Mrs. Charles S. Thompson, Atlanta

RESIDENCE OF JUDGE AND MRS. R. L. SIMMS
This handsome house was built in the early 1830s for Dr. William P. Graham.

touching tribute to his memory was adopted by his fellow Masons in Golden Fleece Lodge No. 6. Judge Simms was buried in the cemetery at Oxford, where his beloved wife joined him on 7 January 1866.[19]

Judge and Mrs. Simms were the parents of two daughters and three sons. These were Sarah Lee, who married (1) Thomas Jefferson Comer of Monticello and (2) E. Pritchett of Jasper County; Lucy Jane, who married Edward Heard of Covington (*see page 98*); James Phillip, who married Mary Lucy Bates, of Covington; Richard Lee, Jr., who married Lucy Hyde Branch of Tampa; and Arthur Benjamin, of whom more later. The only descendants of Judge and Mrs. Simms now living in Covington are Mrs. Earl N. Page, granddaughter of

Mr. and Mrs. Thomas Jefferson Comer, and her daughter Mrs. C. Ben Stanton.[20]

Less than five years after Judge Simms' death Covington and the entire South were catapulted into the Civil War. There were, to be sure, voices of moderation which cautioned against such precipitate action, but by and large the people of Covington, of Georgia, and of the entire southern tier of states responded as though they were embarking upon a holy war in which the only certainties were the rightness of their "Cause" and the inevitability of a speedy victory.

Alas for the Simms' and dozens of other prominent local families! The road ahead was to be one of fear, privation, suffering, sorrow, and defeat. The conflict would erase permanently the gracious, leisurely life in a clearly stratified society which they had known and replace it with a quite different kind of world.

In the beginning it was all very exciting. Dashing young men in resplendent new uniforms were escorted to the railroad station (or *depot*, as it was then called) by admiring friends and relatives, while a fife and drum corps played stirring martial music. Then as the train pulled out mothers, wives and sweethearts wept while fathers, brothers and friends cheered lustily.[21]

Mrs. Richard Lee Simms' family was one of the first to be affected by the war. Her three sons, all "Emory men," left their Floyd Street home to serve with local military companies which soon joined companies from other towns to form larger units and head for the seat of battle.

James Phillip Simms, the eldest of the three sons, was elected second lieutenant of Captain Henry T. Henry's Company of the "Newton Anderson Guards" on 21 October 1861. This local unit was a part of the 6th Regiment, First Brigade, Georgia State Troops, of which Colonel John T. Henderson of Covington was regimental commander. Lieutenant Simms, who was born in Covington on 16 January 1837, was a practicing attorney at the time he joined Captain Henry's company. A year earlier, on 25 April 1860, he had married Miss Mary Lucy Bates, one of the lovely daughters of Dr. Horace J. Bates of Covington (*see page 137*). On 31 January 1862, by which time Simms had been promoted to first lieutenant, the company was called into the service of the State of Georgia by Governor Joseph E. Brown, who acted under the provisions of an Act of the Legislature passed 18 December 1860. In April 1862, the six-month period for which he had volunteered his services having expired, Lieutenant Simms was mustered out. On the second day of the month following, he was elected captain of Company E, 53rd Regiment, Georgia Volunteer Infantry. Promotions to major and to colonel followed within a few months.[22]

Richard Lee Simms, Jr., who was born in Oxford in 1839, volunteered his services soon after the commencement of hostilities. He served as first lieutenant in Wofford's Brigade, McLaw's Division, Longstreet's Corps. While on military leave he married Miss Lucy Hyde Branch, of Tampa, Florida.[23]

Arthur Benjamin Simms, youngest of the three brothers, enlisted as a private soldier in "Cobb's Legion" on 1 August 1861 and soon was promoted to sergeant. Upon the expiration of his enlistment he volunteered for service with the 53rd Georgia Regiment in which his brother James was serving. Eventually he was assigned to the latter's staff. A native of Oxford, Ben Simms was born on 15 March 1841.[24]

With her sons absent from home and her daughter Sarah (Mrs. Thomas Jefferson Comer) living in Monticello, Mrs. Richard Lee Simms and her daughter Lucy joined other women of the community in doing what they could to support their absent menfolk. The Women's Sewing Society was organized for the purpose of making underclothing and, later, knapsacks and haversacks. At first the Confederate government provided the material, but after a while the ladies had to

secure it from whatever sources they could. After the last
male tailor had left for military duty, members of the Sewing
Society undertook the making of coats and pants.[25]

In addition to their activities in behalf of the Confederacy,
many women in Covington undertook the management of their
husbands' and brothers' business affairs. The sometimes-good,
sometimes-bad war news was a barometer of their feelings on
any given day. As casualty lists grew longer, more homes were
affected by the reality of the grimness of the struggle in
which all were involved.

The Simms brothers were unfailing in their determination to
write to their mother, sisters, and James' wife as often as
possible. Sometimes their missives were penned on stationery,
sometimes on scraps of wrapping paper, and sometimes criss-
cross on letters received from home.

On 16 January 1862 Major James P. Simms wrote to his
sister Lucy:

> My Dear Little Sister
>
> This morning I received your letter and hasten to reply. In the
> first place my dear Sister tell me where in the world you found
> paper of so small a size. I don't recollect of ever having seen any
> before so small. You ought to write long letters for your own
> improvement . . .[26]

Later in the year it was Jim's sad duty to inform his
mother of the death of Richard Lee Simms, Jr., who was
killed in an engagement at South Mountain, Maryland, on 14
September 1862. Nine days later he wrote again, this time
from Winchester, Virginia:

> My Dear Mother
>
> I wrote you a letter when I was at Rapidan Station, informing
> you of the reported death of my dear brother. I then had a very
> faint hope that it might prove to be untrue, but as I proceeded on
> my journey to this place I met wounded men belonging to Cobb's
> Legion who had been taken prisoners & paroled. Amongst them
> was George Pierce; they all substantiated what had been told me,

that Dick was killed on the field & buried there. John Floyd[1] has the ring which was upon his finger. Ben was unhurt, but taken prisoner & carried to Baltimore with the rest who were not wounded. Billy Conyers[2] was wounded in the Side Slightly. John Floyd was not wounded as was reported; Charley Saunders[3] was not hurt. Col. Lamar[4] died the day after he was wounded.

I know my dear Mother that it is hard for you to give up your Son. I feel that I cannot reconcile it to my feelings to give him up, but we must remember that it is the will of God & Submit to his will for if we would — we cannot change his unalterable will.

Bennie[5] will soon be with you again. Mr. Pierce reports that the prisoners were treated very kindly, the Yankees not making any distinction between our wounded men & their own.

I heard today that Coleman Brown[6] was killed last Wednesday. Our army has suffered terribly up here, but not so much as the Enemy. We have lost a great many men; this town is full of our wounded.

I expect you have heard by this time all that I know as Mr. Neal[7] has gone home & Mr. Pierce also. I requested Mr. P. to write you a letter which I expect he has done—

Your Affectionate Son

J. P. Simms[27]

---

[1] John C. Floyd was a 22-year old son of Judge John J. Floyd (*see page 92*). A first lieutenant in the "Lamar Infantry" (Company A, Cobb's Legion, Georgia Volunteer Infantry), he was wounded and captured at Crampton's Gap, Maryland, 14 September 1862; exchanged; captured again in April 1865; released on parole at the end of the war.[28]

[2] Major William Denson Conyers, Jr. He and James P. Simms had married sisters (*see page 137*).

[3] Charles H. Sanders, Jr. (*see page 40*). A lieutenant in the "Lamar Infantry," he was captured at Crampton's Gap, Maryland, 14 September 1862; paroled and exchanged 6 October 1862; elected captain of his company 3 July 1863; captured at Fort Royal, Virginia, 16 August 1864; released at Fort Delaware, 17 June 1865.[29]

[4] Jefferson Mirabeau Lamar, younger brother of the noted L. Q. C. Lamar, who was a lieutenant colonel in "Cobb's Legion." He was killed while leading his command in the engagement at Crampton's Gap, Maryland, in September 1862. He was supposedly the most brilliant member of a family noted for dazzling intellect.[30]

[5] Bennie and Ben: Arthur Benjamin Simms, brother of the writer.

[6] Coleman Brown: See page 11.

[7] McCormick Neal (Jr.), older half-brother of "Charley Saunders." *See pages 36, 71, 203.*

Major Simms continued to advance in the CSA and was given assignments of increasing responsibility. He fought at Fredricksburg as colonel in command of the 53rd Georgia Regiment, and participated also in the Gettysburg campaign. After distinguished service at the battle of Cedar Creek he was promoted to brigadier general on 8 December 1864. Captured during the retreat from Richmond on 6 April 1865, he was released from imprisonment at Fort Warren on 24 July 1865.[31]

As the war moved toward its final drama with the inexorability of a Greek tragedy, Mrs. Richard Lee Simms struggled to manage her various properties, and to secure adequate foodstuffs to feed herself and those of her former slaves who had not taken advantage of President Lincoln's emancipation proclamation.

As the fighting drew nearer and the bombardment of Atlanta got underway in July 1864, a detachment of Federal troops under the command of Brigadier General Kenner Garrard entered Covington. They foraged for foodstuffs and generally frightened the townsfolk, but there were no casualties during their overnight stay. Mrs. Simms, fearful that her silver would be "appropriated," entrusted it to a Mr. Hayes.[32]

Prior to the widely heralded invasion by General Sherman and his men she was sequestered at the family plantation in Jasper County, a circumstance which caused some concern to her son Ben. "If Ma has her silver in the Country with her," he wrote to his sister Lucy, "it is in much more danger than it would be in town, from the fact that most depradations are committed by stragglers, and stragglers are restrained more around town . . . that is the reason I was sorry to see Ma quit home . . ."[33]

Mrs. Simms apparently heeded her son's warning and returned to Covington before the arrival of General William T. Sherman's forces, for two of her granddaughters recall a family story which indicates that she was in her Floyd Street home at that time. According to them, several local men who were home on furlough sought a hiding place to avoid capture by the Federal troops. Mrs. Simms led them to the second floor of her home, where a trap door in the hallway ceiling opened into the attic. The men climbed into the small space under the roof and remained there several days until the last Yankee soldiers had left the town.[34]

Sherman's forces passed through Covington on 18 November 1864. A small contingent camped for one night on a stretch of lawn between the Simms residence and a carriage house near the home of Mr. and Mrs. Robert Usher, but no damage was done to the property.[35]

The March to the Sea signalled the imminent conclusion of hostilities. Soon after General Robert E. Lee surrendered to General Ulysses S. Grant on 9 April 1865, Covington's gallant sons began to return home. Some came by train and some on stretchers, but most of them walked all or a portion of the way from the place where they had surrendered and been pardoned, or from the prison where they had been confined.

When General James P. Simms returned to Covington he resumed the practice of law. Arthur Benjamin Simms studied law under the distinguished Judge John J. Floyd, passed the bar, and then joined his brother in establishing the firm of Simms & Simms. From offices on the north side of the Square they soon had a practice which by post-war standards was lucrative. James P. Simms established his wife and children in a home on Herring Street which had previously been the summer residence of William F. Herring and his wife, the former Miss Chloe Conyers of Covington (*see page 80*), before they moved to New York.[36]

Following the death of their mother, Arthur Benjamin Simms bought his sisters' and brothers' interest in their parents' Floyd Street residence. Here he brought his bride, the former Sarah Shelton Terrell Jackson, native of Greene County

and graduate of Southern Masonic Female College at Covington, whom he had married at sunrise on 3 January 1878. The
couple maintained their home in much the same manner as
had Judge and Mrs. Simms, and it was here that all of their
children were born. These were Arthur Benjamin, Jr., who
married Miss Eva Hurt, daughter of Atlanta financier Joel
Hurt; Sarah Jackson, who was married to Charles Seymour
Thompson, an organizer of the Bank of Covington; and
Jerustha Bonner, who became the wife of Ralph Leslie Turner,
head of the First National Bank of McDonough. Mr. and Mrs.
Thompson lived in Covington for some years before moving to
Atlanta. Their home here was the large brick residence which
still stands at the southwest corner of Floyd and Elizabeth
streets — the latter street being named for their daughter of that
name.[37]

The Simms brothers took an active part in all phases of
community life. James P. Simms represented Newton County
in the General Assembly in 1865–'66 and again in 1877, and
A. B. Simms served in the same body in 1873–'74. The latter,
a trustee of Southern Masonic Female College, served also as
mayor of Covington, "making a most popular and efficient
officer." The brothers were respected professionally and politi-
cally, admired and popular socially, and greatly beloved by
their families and close friends.[38]

Thus Covington was deeply shocked and saddened when the
two men died suddenly within a week of each other. James
Phillip Simms died shortly after midnight on the morning of
30 May 1887 and Arthur Benjamin Simms answered the final
call in the early evening of 6 June 1887.[39]

The stunning loss of two of its most prominent citizens,
coupled with the deaths within the same week of their sister
Lucy Heard's infant son and of three daughters of Isaac Henderson, caused Covingtonians for years to come to refer to
this period as "Black Week."[40]

In those days there was no such thing as local telephone

service; radio and television were undreamed-of miracles; and then as now the Covington newspapers were published only once a week. Thus the prompt communicating of important news was not an easy matter. The local undertaker solved the problem of imparting news of deaths and funeral arrangements by going from house to house and wordlessly displaying a crepe-draped blackboard with black ribbon streamers. Upon it was written the name of the deceased and the time and place of the funeral.[41]

Local newspaper accounts of the funerals of the Simms brothers indicate that they attracted large contingents of local and out-of-town dignitaries. The bar association of Newton County adopted a lengthy and beautiful Resolution in their memory which said in part:

> It does not often happen that any community is called to mourn the concurrent death of two such superior men ... These devotedly attached brothers, so joined in their lives, were not divided in their deaths ...
>
> Born in this community, living here and dying here, types of our best civilization and most advanced culture, actively and nobly illustrating both of these in their private walks and public careers ... their honorable fame invested the county with respect and dignity. Sprung from uncommon stock, not haughty, but of elevated pride of character, cradled in the lap of competence, their early advantages were ample, and their education liberal ... Their warp and woof was all heroic stuff ...
>
> As citizens, neighbors and friends, they were unsurpassed among men ...
>
> The courtesies of their lives were broad and generous, always polite and genial, kind and tolerant, and bearing everywhere, and at all times, a conspicuous inbred sense of lofty honor.
>
> Their private lives deserved and received all admiration — tender and blameless in social relations — devoted to their friends, affectionate in their families, simple, upright ...
>
> But the crowning glory of their lives was their Christian faith ...[42]

Mrs. A. B. Simms continued to live in the family home during the early years of her widowhood. There her son and daughters grew to adulthood and there they maintained the tradition of gracious hospitality which was historically associated with the house. The girls, Sarah and Bonner, received their *beaux* in the staid parlor furnished in the height of Victorian and Empire style. The floor of this room, as well as the floors of the library and reception hall, was covered with a handsome French Wilton carpet. A "very good tapestry curtain" divided the reception hall from the back hall. When his sisters and their admirers were not ensconced in the parlor, young Ben Simms entertained his friends at such functions as a reception and smoker for members of the Covington Tennis Club. In reporting upon the last, *The Georgia Enterprise* stated that "a royal feast was served." [43]

One of the most beautiful affairs ever held at the Simms residence was the reception following the wedding of Sarah Simms and Charles Seymour Thompson on 22 June 1910. The young couple had spoken their vows in a brilliant ceremony at the Methodist church, which was decorated for the occasion with huge cathedral candles and masses of white flowers and greenery. At the reception afterwards the beautiful bride received many compliments upon her wedding gown of charneuse satin trimmed with lace she had brought from Brussels. Her bouquet was of orchids and valley lilies. A fashionable assemblage of Southern society which had converged upon Covington for the wedding and reception showered the bridal couple with rice and rose petals as they left the family home for a honeymoon trip to San Francisco and other points of interest in the West. [44]

On 1 February 1919, after almost seventy years in the Simms family, the Floyd Street house was sold. Mrs. A. B. Simms transferred title to it to S. C. Steadman, grandson of the Enoch Steadman who had once owned the Neal-Sanders house (*see page 42*). On 17 January 1922 S. C. Steadman executed a deed to his mother, Mrs. Maggie S. Childs, "to correct" the earlier deed. The new document stated that in the transaction between Mrs. Simms and Mr. Steadman, Mrs. Childs had put up $1090 cash "arising from the sale of her Anderson Avenue property," plus $2000 received from her son in repayment of a debt, and the assumption by her of an indebtedness by him to the Bank of Covington in the amount of $1340. Thus it appears that the title should have been in Mrs. Childs' name all along. One assumes that she had lived in the house from the time Mrs. Simms sold it.[45]

A native of Covington, Mrs. Childs was the former Maggie Clarke (*see page 212*). On 19 November 1888 she had become the bride of E. Stoney Steadman, a Covington native who died in 1898 at the age of thirty-five. He had been editor of the *DeKalb New Era*. In April 1903 Mrs. Steadman had been married to Walter Childs, a widower who was a member of a prominent Newborn family. Her children were Sanford Clarke Steadman and Hugh and Walter Childs, Jr. Twice widowed, Mrs. Childs died 4 September 1955 at the age of eighty-five and was buried beside her first husband in Covington City Cemetery.[46]

The Graham-Simms house was sold by Mrs. Childs on 23 May 1923 to W. A. Andrews for $5,000. Mr. Andrews, his wife, their daughter Gertrude, and the latter's husband Mr. Kilpatrick moved to Covington from Thomaston. During their relatively few years in the city Mr. Kilpatrick was employed at Norris Hardware Company on Monticello Street. Mr. Andrews was retired from business.[47]

The house passed to another new owner on 18 November 1925 when W. A. Andrews sold it to Rucker Ginn for a consideration of $3200 cash and the "Annie Rainey Home Place" on Monticello Street (now the house immediately behind the Episcopal Church).[48]

Tinsley Rucker Ginn was one of the early automobile dealers of Covington. A native of Royston, Georgia, he had achieved fame as a baseball player at the University of Georgia, from which he was graduated in 1914. He played professionally for the Cleveland Indians for a year or two and served as a major in World War I. After marrying Frances Davis of Athens, he moved to Covington and opened one of the first automobile dealerships in the city. Mr. Ginn and his lovely wife were prominent in community affairs and enjoyed unusual social popularity.[49]

The Ginns refurbished the Graham-Simms house, and under Mrs. Ginn's discriminating direction it was furnished with a handsome assortment of period pieces. For a few years the old house was filled with friends of the popular young couple and with the playmates of their two youngsters. The happy time came to a tragic and abrupt end in 1931, however, when Mrs. Ginn died on 16 April. The distraught thirty-nine year-old widower seemed to his friends to lose all interest in living. Four months later, on 30 August 1931, he too was dead of natural causes. Reunited in death, Rucker and Frances Ginn were buried side-by-side in his native Royston.[50]

The two children of the couple, Mary Ellen (now Mrs. Ginn McCord of Ft. Valley) and Rucker, Jr., continued to live in their parents' home for a short time. Their uncle and aunt, Mr. and Mrs. S. A. Ginn, became their guardians and lived with them until the whole family moved into a new house (*see page 36*). Subsequently the beautiful old house was converted into four apartments. Years later young Rucker Ginn and his bride, the former Sally Duggar of Atlanta, lived for a while in one of the units. Today, still owned by Rucker Ginn and his sister through the T. R. Ginn Estate, it is known as the Ginn Apartments.[51]

GINN APARTMENTS
The historic Graham-Simms house as it appears today. The two-story columns which originally graced the facade were removed in the 1920s.

VI

"EDWARDS HOUSE"

An unpretentious two-story house at the southwest corner of Monticello and Conyers streets has been home to several of Covington's most prominent families during its long history.

The site of the house was designated in the original plan of the city as Lot 16 in Square C. It was sold on 7 December 1831 by Winfred W. Brown to John Harris for $600. The deed included a reference to "appurtenances," which suggests that a house of sorts was already on the property. Probably it was a simple log cabin similar to others in the village, at least one of which was incorporated into a house which is still standing.[1]

Mr. Harris apparently enlarged the existing structure considerably, or perhaps built an entirely new house, for when he sold it on 15 September 1853 it brought him $2500. The seller by then was living with his family in a lovely Greek Revival house which had been built for him just beyond the original southern boundary of Covington (*see pages 158-159*).[2]

The new owner of the house was Dr. Jeptha Melton Cody, who was born in Warren County on 15 January 1823. His father was Michael Cody, a native of Halifax, North Carolina, who had moved to Georgia in 1790. Among the children of the latter and his second wife, née Rebecca Rogers, were Jeptha Melton and Madison Derrell (*see page 104*). A daughter, Louisa Amanda, became the wife of James Madison Wellborn, who with his brother Marshall H. Wellborn amassed a considerable fortune and lived opulently in Warrenton. James Cody, a son of Michael's first marriage, married Mary McCormick, and his own sister Elizabeth married Thomas Neal; both spouses were relatives of the original McCormick Neal of Covington (*see pages 33-37*).[3]

Dr. Jeptha M. Cody married on 16 January 1845 Missouri Eliza Cheely, who died on 26 October 1849. His second marriage was to Amanda Melvina Carr, daughter of John P. Carr of Covington (see page 104), on 11 March 1851. Several years later, during which time Dr. Cody's brother Madison Derrell Cody had married Mrs. Cody's sister Frances Carr (see page 104), the couple moved from Warrenton to Covington. With them came a son and a daughter who had been born of Dr. Cody's first marriage. The former, L. L. Cody, subsequently became a well-known figure in Macon.[4]

The family's first home in Covington was a house on one of the numerous tracts which had belonged to the estate of the Reverend Charles H. Sanders (see page 40), located at what is now the northeast corner of North Emory Street and Highway 278. On 15 September 1853 Dr. Cody sold the property to John Harris for $1350 and on the same date bought the latter's former residence at the southwest corner of Monticello and Conyers street (see page 158).[5]

From the front windows of their new home the Codys could see land being cleared for the beautiful edifice which was soon to be erected for the Covington Methodist Church. In that house were born their daughters Frances and Mary Rebecca, and there on 21 January 1858 Mrs. Cody expired. The once-happy family was dispersed, with the children of Dr. Cody's first marriage going to live with their aunt Mrs. Wellborn in Warrenton.[6]

In the following year Dr. Cody married as his third wife Julia A. Latimer, who became the mother of Jeptha Benjamin Cody. In that same year he bought a 10-acre tract of land southeast of the bridge on Railroad (now Emory) Street and had a charming two-story house erected upon it. In the present century this house was the home of the late Mr. and Mrs. Robert I. Weaver, and now the site is occupied by the Snapping Shoals Rural Electrification Association office building.[7]

METHODIST CHURCH

There has long been uncertainty concerning the precise date of construction of this beautiful church with the classic facade. A memorial tablet on the interior commemorates the faithful attendance of Robert Bass Livington (*see page 209*), "Who for 28 years, from the dedication of this church to his death, was rarely out of this seat at any service." As Mr. Livington died on 11 May 1888 at the age of seventy-four years, the date of the church's construction can therefore be pinpointed as 1860.[8]

The church originally had a gallery at the rear which was used by slaves for a short period before the Civil War. During the latter part of that conflict the building was used as a hospital for wounded Confederate soldiers. Subsequently it was used for a number of years as the site of Emory College's commencement exercises.[9]

In 1954 the Methodist church was used in the filming of the motion picture version of *A Man Called Peter*. The local Presbyterian church was not used in this biography of its former pastor because its architecture was not considered typical of the Old

South. The Reverend Peter Marshall had served the local Presbyterian church from 1931 to 1934, during which time his charm
and his Scottish brogue endeared him to the community. Many
residents recalled a memorable Sunday when he wore his kilts to
church. Later he became a national figure in his capacity as
chaplain of the United States Senate.[10]

Among the prominent men who served as pastor of the
Methodist church were the Reverends Samuel Anthony (1838),
Eustace W. Speer (1857), William J. Parks (1861. *See page
92*), and Lundy H. Harris. The last of these served also as a
professor at Emory College, and his widow, Mrs. Corra W.
Harris, was a noted newspaper columnist and author (*The
Circuit Rider's Wife*, etc.).[11]

On 25 August 1859, four years before his death on 24
January 1864, Dr. Cody sold his Monticello Street house to
Matthew R. Stansell for $2000. The new owner presumably
died within a few years, for on 20 January 1866 it was sold
to Mrs. Sarah A. Sanders for $2500. The seller on that
occasion was Francis Marion Jones of Charleston, who may
have been Mr. Stansell's son-in-law.[12]

Mrs. Sarah Ann Sanders was the widow of wealthy pioneer
citizens McCormick Neal and Charles H. Sanders (*see pages
33, 37*). She bought the Harris-Cody house shortly before selling
her magnificent Church Street residence and only eight months
before her death on 18 September 1866.[13]

Under the terms of Mrs. Sanders' will the house was to be
used by her son and daughter, Osgood Sanders and Mrs.
Emma B. Luckie (*see page 39*) until the former attained his
majority. Accordingly, on 1 December 1869, McCormick Neal
the younger, as executor of his mother's estate, sold the house
to J. T. Corley for $1500. The deed specified that Mr. Neal
acted only after his half-brother had reached the age of

twenty-one and stated further that all heirs of Mrs. Sanders were in accord with the transaction.[14]

James T. Corley, a well-to-do Covington merchant, lived in the house until he purchased the former Carr-Cody residence on what subsequently was known as "Corley's Hill" (*see pages 106-107*). One assumes that one of his numerous sons and daughters lived in the Monticello Street house after he acquired the other property in 1878. It is interesting to note that Mr. Corley lived in two houses which had previously been the homes of the brothers M. Derrell and Dr. Jeptha M. Cody.[15]

On 15 November 1887 James T. Corley sold to Mrs. A. M. Edwards for $7500 Lot 16 in Square C, "being the lot whereon the said James T. Corley resided for a number of years . . ."[16]

The new owner of the house was the former Amanda M. Bryan, a sister of Dr. Samuel Bryan of Covington. They may have been grandchildren of Dr. Jasper Bryan (*18 June 1801–7 November 1863*), a native of Baldwin County, Vermont, who was a prominent pioneer resident of Covington.[17]

Old records testify that Miss Addie M. Bryan became the wife of Colonel E. F. Edwards in Newton County on 13 October 1868. The bridegroom was born in Oglethorpe County on 24 September 1842, a son of Samuel Edwards, who later was a member of the former's household in Covington. Ellijay Flournoy Edwards served in the Civil War with the famous "Troup Artillery," after which he studied law under Judge John J. Floyd (*see pages 90, 97*). He married as his first wife Miss Mary E. Evans, who apparently died soon after they were united on 5 August 1866.[18]

Colonel Edwards practiced law for some years in partnership with John P. Harris (*see page 159*), with offices at the northwest corner of the Public Square and Pace Street. Between 1881 and 1888 he served as judge of the Court of Ordinary of Newton County, and he represented the Twenty-

EDWARDS HOUSE
Prominent occupants of this landmark at 1184 Monticello Street included Judge John Harris, Dr. Jeptha M. Cody, James T. Corley, and Judge E. F. Edwards.

Seventh District in the State Senate at the session of 1892–'93. He served also as mayor of Covington and as chairman of the Newton County Board of Commissioners.[19]

In 1898 Judge and Mrs. Edwards journeyed to Macon for the brilliant ceremony at Christ Episcopal Church which united in marriage their son William Annesley Edwards of Washington, D.C., and Miss Annie Foster Napier. They were accompanied home by their daughter Mamie and her husband Dr. P. D. Mahoney, who paid them an extensive visit before returning to their home in Florida. Dr. Mahoney was murdered at Alexander City, Alabama, late in 1899. Another of Judge and Mrs. Edwards' daughters, Ida, had become the wife of Wade H. Gray of Asheville, North Carolina, on 8 July 1896. A third daughter, Minnie, was then Mrs. Fiske of Grovetown, Georgia.[20]

Judge Edwards, "one of the most prominent citizens of Covington," died on 22 May 1902 and was buried in Covington City Cemetery. His residence, whose appearance he had enhanced by the addition of a front porch supported by four square columns, was occupied by his widow until her death, after which it passed to their daughter Mrs. Gray. When the latter died at Greenville, South Carolina, on 27 December 1935, her body was sent to Covington for interment. The local funeral service was held in the lobby of the Hotel Delaney, southwest corner of Monticello and Reynolds streets. Mrs. Gray's survivors included three daughters in South Carolina and California; her brother Will Edwards of Edwards' Pike, Colorado; and her sister Mrs. Mamie Patterson of Los Angeles.[21]

Three years before Mrs. Gray's death her girlhood home was sold by, presumably, her daughter, Mrs. *[sic]* Esther C. Gray. The deed identified the property as "the Mrs. Addie Bryan Edwards home place . . ." and specified that it included all of Lot 16 in Square C except the portion which had been sold by Mrs. Gray to trustees of the Methodist church.[22]

The Methodist trustees had purchased what had once been Mrs. Edwards' rose garden as an ideal site upon which to erect a new parsonage. Shortly thereafter an attractive two-story red brick house was erected upon the property and the old frame parsonage at the southwest corner of Monticello and South streets was sold.[23]

The new owner of the Edwards house was Ferdinand Augustus Briscoe (*13 August 1867–1 October 1935*), who acquired it for "$10 and other valuable considerations." A resident of Covington since 1907, he owned and operated Briscoe Monumental Works. His wife was the former Mary Alice Mann (*23 February 1871–18 August 1957*) of Rockdale County. Their children were Otto Thomas Briscoe, who followed his father in operating the monument business, and Kate Etta Briscoe, who became the wife of the Reverend Samuel Davidson Cherry.[24]

On 17 October 1935 Otto T. Briscoe transferred to his

sister his interest in their late father's home, this being a part of the equal division of the latter's real estate. Subsequently Mrs. Cherry, who made her home in Decatur after she was widowed, converted the house into several apartments.[25]

Bereft of the upper-echelon society, the political leaders and the interesting persons who frequented it during the lifetimes of Judge and Mrs. Edwards and their predecessors, and inexorably faded by time and the comings and goings of many tenants, the old house is a reminder of times that are no more. It still has a simple dignity, however, and is a conspicuous landmark in the heart of a community which is fast changing from a sleepy village to a bustling suburb of Atlanta.

VII

"CLARK'S GROVE"

A wooded tract of land west of Dried Indian Creek was selected in 1834 as the site of a manual labor school to be operated under the auspices of the Georgia Conference of the Methodist Episcopal Church. Here, on four hundred acres of land extending roughly between the McDonough and Stone Mountain roads, the first students arrived early in March 1835. They found "a Steward's hall, two houses for the Offices of the school, and six dormitories . . . together with a kitchen, smoke-house, and etc." In the next year two of the students' rooms were converted to recitation rooms and another was prepared for "the apparatus" — facilities for studying the solar system, mechanical properties of the atmosphere, and the science of electricity.[1]

Stretching beyond the buildings was land upon which the students were expected to work three hours each day in raising cotton, corn, oats, wheat, and potatoes. It was confidently expected by Dr. Alexander Means, the superintendent, as well as the trustees and the Conference, that through such activity could the major portion of the institution's operating expenses be financed. Such was not to be the case, however, for to lighthearted school boys such drudgery was unthinkable when there were rabbits to chase, balls to be hit, and instructors to be outwitted. Consequently, the Manual Labor School was soon in serious trouble.[2]

It was declared to be a great success as a social institution. On this point the authorities reported:

"It is . . . a fact worthy of observation, that all classes of our Students — the rude and the cultivated, the poor and the rich, mingle without distinction in their common labor and engage alike in whatever duties are assigned them . . ."[3]

One student at the Manual Labor School, L. Q. C. Lamar (*see page 52*), recalled later:

> We all had to work three hours every day at the ordinary work of a plantation — plowing, hoeing, cutting wood, picking cotton and sowing it, pulling fodder, and every item of a planter's occupation. When we left that school we could do not only this ordinary drudgery in the best way, but the most expert could shoe a horse, make an ax helve, stock a plow, or do any plain bit of black-smithing and carpentry. It was great training for us all, for we became perfectly versed in the details of the work of a farm. Many of Georgia's most distinguished men were reared there.[4]

To Dr. Ignatius Few, who had been the prime mover in the establishment of the Manual Labor School and who continued as a trustee, goes the dubious distinction of being the person in authority who ignored the onrushing financial crisis while he grandly planned an even more ambitious undertaking. The result was the creation of Emory College, which was chartered on 10 December 1836, and which Dr. Few served as president until succeeded in 1840 by the remarkable Judge Augustus Baldwin Longstreet.* The new institution, which was in reality an outgrowth of the Manual Labor School, was located on a new campus north and northwest of Covington. There, on 1452 virgin acres purchased on 8 October 1836 from Covington pioneer Cary Wood (*see pages 16-17*) for $10,000, the Methodists built not only a college but an entire new town as well. The former was named in honor of the late Bishop John Emory (*1789–1835*) of Maryland, and the latter after the

---

*Augustus Baldwin Longstreet (*22 September 1790–9 July 1870*) was a native of Augusta and a Yale graduate who achieved distinction as lawyer, jurist, educator, and clergyman. He was known also as an accomplished politician, orator, farmer, and newspaper editor. His *Georgia Scenes*, a collection of humorous and homespun tales of post-Revolutionary Georgia, still retain their freshness and appeal nearly a century and a half after they were first published. Judge Longstreet served as president of Emory from 1840 to 1848, during which period his daughter Virginia became the first wife of L. Q. C. Lamar (*see page 52*).

English university where John and Charles Wesley had been educated.[5]

With the discontinuance of the Manual Labor School, the land which it had occupied was gradually sold to several Covington residents. The tract upon which the school buildings were located was acquired by Allen Turner, who had attracted attention at the Methodist Conference held in Washington, Georgia, in 1834 by insisting that Georgia Methodists should cease contributing to the support of Randolph-Macon College in Virginia and start a college of their own. After planting the seed from which grew both the Manual Labor School and Emory College, "Uncle Allen" apparently fell upon hard times. On 6 January 1853 Green B. Turner, who must have been either his father or his brother, executed a deed transferring title to "the place Known as the Campus" in return for the purchaser's promise that he would not present any claims against Allen Turner for "merchantile business" debts dating from 1840. Green B. Turner, "one of the earliest settlers of Newton County . . . one of its prominent citizens . . . [and] an esteemed member of the Methodist Church . . . ," died in 1869 at the age of 82.[7]

Purchaser of the "Campus" property was William W. Clark (see page 112), who paid $1000 for an unspecified acreage. In addition to his promise regarding Allen Turner's debts, Mr. Clark was required to agree also that "if any person shall sell or permit [to be] sold any intoxicating liquors or play or permit to be played any game of hazard on said premises the said premises [are] to revert to the trustees of Emory College . . . "[8]

William White Clarke was one of Covington's wealthiest and most distinguished citizens. Prominent for decades as a member of the bar, he represented Newton County in the General Assembly (1841, 1842), and in 1861 was elected to the Confederate Congress. He was a trustee of Southern Female College for many years and was a director of the Georgia

Railroad and Banking Company. When the latter subdivided a large tract of land in DeKalb County in 1882 and started a new town it was named Clarkston in his honor.[9]

"Colonel" Clark, as he was deferentially referred to after the current fashion for so addressing distinguished members of the bar, practiced law in Covington for more than forty years. His office was located, from 1840 until his death, in a building in Lot No. 1, Square D. This property extends along the south side of Floyd Street from the Square to Elm Street. The house which earlier occupied this site had been owned by Hamilton Burge, a brother of Thomas Burge of *Burge Plantation* (see page 93).[10]

William White Clark married on 22 April 1846 Temperance Boddie Conyers, daughter of Dr. William D. Conyers of Covington. The bride had spent her girlhood at *Natural Grove*, the Conyers residence which occupied the southern portion of the Conyers Street block bounded by Monticello, Hendricks and Reynolds streets. (Subsequently W. H. Pickett built a Victorian house at the southeast corner of the property which was supplanted in 1935 by the present Post Office; the northeast corner later was occupied by the old Delaney Hotel.) The site for this handsome residence was purchased on 17 October 1832 for only $50. It had been owned since 1826 by Joseph Henry Lumpkin (*1799–1867*) of Oglethorpe County, brother of Governor Wilson Lumpkin, graduate of Princeton, and first chief justice of the Supreme Court of Georgia.[11]

Dr. William Denson Conyers (*13 February 1794–25 February 1868*) was born in North Carolina, but removed at an early age to Greensboro, Georgia, with his parents, Ross and Betsey (Denson) Conyers. After serving as a soldier in the War of 1812, he became one of the pioneer settlers of Newton County. Minutes of the Inferior Court for the period 1822–1838 contain numerous documents bearing his signature as a justice of the Inferior Court. He owned a large plantation which extended into what later became Rockdale County.

When the Georgia Railroad was being built westward to Atlanta in 1843, he kindly deeded the necessary right-of-way through his property, a generous act which resulted in the present county seat being named for him.[12]

Dr. Conyers' first wife was Elizabeth Perry (*10 February 1798–31 January 1841*), whom he married in Franklin County, North Carolina, on 6 November 1822. A daughter of Colonel Jeremiah Perry of that county, she was a sister of Temperance (Perry) Williamson, of Mary (Perry) Kolb,* and of Doctors Wiley and A. C. Perry — all of whom settled in Covington. On 10 March 1859 Dr. Conyers married as his second wife Mrs. Amanda Belle (Chipley) Slaughter (*24 October 1808–17 December 1892*), a native of Louisville, Kentucky, and widow of Dr. Martin G. Slaughter of Marietta.[13]

Dr. Conyers' children, all born of his first marriage, were: William Denson Conyers, Jr. (*see pages 137-139*); Elizabeth Denson Conyers (*19 August 1827–died age 69*), who married, 29 December 1853, Colonel John Randolph Dyer, a native of Rhode Island.** She was one of Georgia's most brilliant and attractive women of ante-bellum days; Chloe Perry Conyers (*born 16 June 1835*), who married, 5 November 1861, William Francis Herring*** (*see page 61*), a native of Fayette

* Mary Perry (born 29 April 1801) was the wife of Captain Martin Wiles Kolb, who represented Newton County in the General Assembly in the sessions of 1824–'25, 1826, 1827, and 1828.
**Their daughter Mary Harrison Dyer married Isaac Purnell Henderson 2nd, son of Robert J. and Laura (Wood) Henderson (*see page 20*). The only son of the younger couple, Isaac P. Henderson 3rd, thus was a descendant of Covington's most prominent pioneers: Dr. William D. Conyers, General Robert J. Henderson, Isaac P. Henderson, and Cary Wood, and was a relative of the Carr, Clark, Floyd, Harris, Lee, Neal and Williamson families.
***The Atlanta home of William F. Herring's parents, Mr. and Mrs. William Herring, and of his sister and brother-in-law Major and Mrs. Austin Leyden, was a magnificent structure on Peachtree Street which during the Civil War was used successively as headquarters for General John B. Hood, commander of the Army of Tennessee, CSA, and for General George H. Thomas, commander of the Army of the Cumberland, USA. The fourteen Ionic columns from the house now adorn an apartment building in Ansley Park and the site itself is occupied by Davison's department store.

CLARK'S GROVE, residence of Col. and Mrs. William W. Clark. This house was the only one of the dormitories erected in 1835 for students at the Manual Labor School which was not subsequently moved to the new campus of Emory College. In later years the Clark family added a veranda with square two-story columns across the front. (Burned.)[15]

County who amassed a fortune as a cotton broker in Augusta and Philadelphia and spent his last years in New York City; and Temperance Boddie Conyers (*born 5 November 1824*), who became the wife of William White Clark.[14]

Clark's Grove, the beautiful estate of Colonel and Mrs. William White Clark, was the scene of a senseless Civil War tragedy which orphaned three young women. It happened that on 22 July 1864 Captain George Hewitt Daniel of Covington was at home briefly from service with the 8th Regiment of Infantry, Georgia State Guards, which had been called into active service and was embroiled with the Union forces in the Atlanta campaign. He went to the Georgia Railroad depot to meet one of his daughters who was returning from a visit in Conyers. Captain Daniel carried his gun with him, and when some of Union General Kenner Garrard's men saw him they placed him under arrest. After a drum-head court-martial he was sentenced to be shot. Two Union men escorted him to *Clark's Grove*, where he was peremptorily dispatched.[16]

Confederate Sergeant Walter Clark, a former Emory student who was hospitalized in the converted chapel at his *Alma Mater*, wrote that "Geo. Daniel . . . had been out bird hunting that morning and on his return was captured by the Yankees, who were enraged by the killing of two of their men by [Presley] Jones . . ." Clark wrote that Jones had killed two Union soldiers and wounded another two with his squirrel rifle by the courthouse, for which he was shot and mutilated. (This is at slight variance with the more frequently quoted version of the Jones affair cited on page 153).[17]

The victim of this unhappy affair was a cultured, forty-seven year-old native of England. He had lived in Newton County since about 1835 and had engaged in the grocery business and in farming. Twice a widower, he had married into two well-known county families; the first union being formed with Mary Webb and the second with Huldah Battle Colley, daughter of Elder Joel Colley (*see page 7*).[18]

The shooting of George H. Daniel was made possible by General Sherman's order to Brigadier General Kenner Garrard, commander of the Second Cavalry Division, that he destroy railroads leading into Atlanta. In an after-action report submitted on 24 July 1864, General Garrard wrote in part:

> The depot and considerable quantity of quartermaster and commissary stores at Covington were burnt. . . . One train (platform) was burnt at Covington, and a small train (baggage) at station near the Ulcofauhachee captured and burnt . . . Over 2,000 bales of cotton were burnt. A large new hospital at Covington, for the accommodation of 10,000 patients from this Army and the Army of Virginia, composed of over 30 buildings besides the offices, just finished, were burnt, together with a very large lot of fine carpenters' tools used in their erection. Also a large lot of new hospital tents burnt at Covington . . . . [19]

When the war and the Reconstruction period had become

only grim memories, the Clark family made several changes in their secluded home. The most apparent of these was the substitution of a veranda supported by four simple two-story columns for the earlier one-story front porch, and the addition of porches on the south side of the structure and of a two-story addition on the north side. Here the family entertained handsomely and kept the welcome mat out for friends from near and far.[20]

When William White Clark died in a Baltimore hospital on 6 August 1883, his obituary in a Covington newspaper stated:

> [He] was a remarkable man [who] had won fame and fortune as a lawyer. He never betrayed a trust or denied a friend ... He was a straight-forward man and had no cant or hypocricy in his nature. What he considered duty he never flinched to perform ... A stern, unswerving devotion to the principles of right and justice won for him the admiration of all who knew him well ...[21]

Upon the death of Mrs. Clark on 1 August 1902, she was eulogized as "one of the best known and most highly respected women in Covington ... a woman of broad culture and refinement ..." She and her husband are buried on an iron fence-enclosed plot in Covington City Cemetery, where also are the graves of their daughters Mary Elizabeth, Tempe White, and Sarah Isabella; their son William Conyers Clark and his wife; and the latter couple's daughter, May Belle Clark Brookes. There is also a memorial to the W. C. Clarks' son William White Clark 2nd, who died in the Phillippine Islands.[22]

Following the death of their mother the three unmarried Clark daughters continued to live at *Clark's Grove*. In summer their brother and his family spent a month or two in the cool, tree-shaded rooms of the spacious house. William Conyers Clark (*19 October 1852–19 January 1932*) had married Sallie Strong Echols (*1863–1 June 1929*) in a ceremony at her mother's home on 21 January 1885. For some years thereafter they lived in an ornate Victorian house opposite her girlhood home in Midway (now North Covington), which is said to have been a wedding gift from the bride's mother.[23]

William Conyers Clark was for many years a wealthy, prominent, and influential resident of Covington. While still a young man he organized Clark Banking Co., originally a private institution, which occupied a building at the southwest corner of Clark Street and the Square. The structure had previously housed the grocery store owned by Dr. Archibald Camp (see page 218), and the site had been owned earlier by Judge Richard

HOME OF MRS. SARAH JANE ECHOLS

(1832–1913). A daughter of Charles Strong (20 December 1802–10 October 1870), a pioneer resident of Newton County who was a trustee of Newton County Academy, she had been married on 19 June 1854 to John H. Echols. Mrs. Echols bequeathed her home to her son John, who received also her father's plantation of 568 acres. To her daughter Mrs. W. C. Clark she left a 600-acre plantation which had belonged to Covington pioneer Cary Wood (see page 16) and, later, his daughter Mrs. Osborn T. Rogers (see page 147). Another Echols daughter, Mrs. Addie Turner, and son Charles Echols were jointly bequeathed a farm on the Alcovy River and property in Covington. A third daughter, Leila, died early in life.

The Echols home was bought from a Mr. Lackey after the columned mansion on the family's plantation burned in the 1870s or '80s. Located at the northeast corner of Echols and North Emory streets, it is now an apartment house owned by E. E. Callaway.[24]

L. Simms (*see page 53*), who purchased it in 1836 from pioneer citizen Cary Wood (*see page 16*). Mr. Clark was also associated with T. C. Swann in the establishing of Covington Mills, of which he was secretary and treasurer and a director.[25]

In later years Mr. Clark suffered financial reverses which resulted in Clark Banking Co. being merged into the new Bank of Newton County. Mr. and Mrs. Clark moved from Midway into a columned house on Floyd Street, where they spent their last years.[26]

ADAMS-CLARK HOUSE

Erected *circa* 1920 for L. D. Adams, a local merchant, who was a brother of Charles F. Adams and of George C. Adams. The latter, while serving as Newton County school superintendent, organized a Corn Club which was the forerunner of the national 4-H Club; later he served as Georgia Commissioner of Agriculture (1933–'35).[27]

The site of the Adams house had earlier been occupied by the columned home of R. B. Livingston, which burned. Later the land was owned by T. J. Shepherd.[28]

L. D. Adams constructed his home as a cottage, later raising it to accomodate another floor and adding columns across the front. After moving to DeKalb County Mr. Adams sold it to Mrs. William C. Clark for $7,000 on 14 January 1928.[29]

After the deaths of Mrs. Clark and her husband the property was purchased by John H. Wood (*1879–1960*), a Covington merchant, who converted it into apartments. Now known as Wood Apartments, it is owned by his son Edgar Wood.[30]

Mrs. William C. Clark was a memorable personage in the annals of Covington. In addition to being a leading figure in society from the days of her young ladyhood, she was the first woman in Newton County to register to vote. Her last years were spent in circumstances far removed from the opulence and ease she had known previously, but to the end she held her head high and never let anyone forget that she was born a lady, in the now-outmoded original sense of that word. Wearing outdated silks and carrying a faded parasol, "Miss Sallie" walked around town with the same regal dignity as when she had been driven by a top-hatted coachman in a handsome carriage. In her era if one were a lady neither wealth nor the absence of it, nor serene happiness as contrasted to searing heartache made any difference – and Mrs. Clark knew something about all of those conditions. The only one of her children to survive her was Walton C. Clark, a consulting engineer in Washington, D.C.[31]

A glimpse at the code by which the Clarks and their kind lived, and a rare testament to the sense of *noblesse oblige* which was an integral part of their character, may be obtained from the following extract of a document executed on 14 February 1884:

> Whereas during the late war between the Confederate States and the United States, Wash Conyers, col[ored], was with Maj. Wm D Conyers as his special Servant = and whereas after the termination of the war and during the last illness of Dr. Wm D. Conyers, he [the] said Wash, col, was faithful in his attentive[ness] and Services to his old master, and whereas Wm W Clark my father the son in law of Dr Wm D Conyers & brother in law of said Maj Wm D Conyers intended to and did give to said Wash Conyers col, and his children fifty acres of land in the County aforesaid, upon which the said Wash, col, now lives = but died before making to said Wash and his children a Deed to said land = Now, therefore this Indenture . . . between W. C. Clark, executor of the last Will of Said W. W. Clark deceased, . . . doth hereby convey to the said Wash Conyers, col, and his lawful children, Fifty acres of land . . . belonging to the estate of W. W. Clark . . . part of what was known

as the old Smith place . . . bounded on the West by the land occupied by Maj. A. H. Lee . . . [32]

Clark's Grove passed out of the family when William C. Clark sold it on 15 January 1925. The purchaser was Covington Mills, which paid $6500 for the property.[33]

In the ensuing years the house was used as headquarters for the local unit of the Ku Klux Klan, which made the second floor available for private dances and parties. Many gay affairs were held in the upper rooms of the old structure, one of the most memorable being a costume ball attended by everyone who was anyone in Covington society. Participants remembered years later beautifully gowned Dolly Bolton* arriving with handsome Tommy Callaway (*see page 44*), the latter wearing a dashing, red-lined blue cape.[34]

The gala parties on the second floor and the dark activities of the hooded order on the first floor came to an end when the building was destroyed by fire *circa* 1930. On 2 March 1932 the property was sold at public outcry to Covington

CLARK'S GROVE TODAY
Residence of Mr. and Mrs. Robert R. Fowler.

*Dolly Bolton, now deceased, became the first wife of Dr. Duane Beam, a prominent Philadelphia physician. She was the daughter of Mr. and Mrs. Louis D. Bolton, and a great-granddaughter of the inimitable Dolly Burge of *Burge Plantation* (*see pages 92-93, 129*).

Mills to satisfy a judgement for payments in arrears. At that time the seller was identified as something called the Social Advancement Club, which may have been a euphemism for the Ku Klux Klan.[35]

On 1 November 1938 there was another change of ownership when Covington Mills sold the property to Mrs. Louly Turner Fowler. For $2000 she acquired a tract of 10.59 acres which had been the campus portion of the lands owned by the Georgia Conference Manual Labor School.[36]

Mrs. Fowler, a daughter of the late N. S. Turner (*see page 168*), was educated at Shorter College. On 18 October 1933 she became the wife of Robert R. Fowler, Jr., who now is president of the Bank of Covington. He is a native of Covington and was educated at Emory and Yale universities.[37]

The younger Mr. and Mrs. Fowler built upon the site of the former Clark residence a handsome two-story brick house with square columns. They moved into the white-painted structure in 1941, and it was there that their three children were reared. These are Louly, Florence (Mrs. James L. Peacock), and Robert R. Fowler, 3rd. The first-named daughter is the wife of Samuel Burney Hay, Jr., a member of one of Covington's pioneer families. His parents are the Reverend Mr. Hay, former pastor of the local Presbyterian church, and the former Frances Dearing, and his grandparents are the late Mr. and Mrs. John M. Dearing (*see page 189*).[38]

Today *Clark's Grove* is secluded from the busy activity of a growing city by a heavy growth of trees and underbrush. Beyond the gently curving drive the new house with the ageless appearance is serene in its setting of old trees. Nearby, the original brick kitchen which is all that remains of the Clark family's additions to the property is used as a playhouse for the Fowlers' grandchildren. Time and fire and man have brought many changes to the one-time Manual Labor School campus, but it still is one of the most interesting and historic of Covington's landmarks.

VIII

"THE FLOYD HOUSE"

From a slight rise in the second block of Floyd Street a stately columned house rises impressively above other lovely old homes in the neighborhood. It is the one-time residence of the man in whose honor the street was named — Judge John J. Floyd, distinguished pioneer of Covington and long one of the town's most respected citizens.

A native of nearby Madison, John Julius Floyd was born on 7 March 1809, a son of Major John Burford Floyd and the former Ann Stewart of Virginia. He was graduated by Franklin College (now the University of Georgia) in the class of 1828. Following the custom of the time, John Floyd probably read law in the office of an established lawyer in Madison before setting up his own practice. On 31 October 1834 he married Miss Mary Butler Colbert of Morgan County.[1]

The exact year in which the young couple moved to Covington is not known, but John Floyd is listed as a purchaser of Newton County property as early as 1833. On 13 October of that year he bought from the estate of John J. Beatie of Greene County a lot designated as Number 80 in the 9th District of what had formerly been Henry County, for which he paid $120.[2]

The beautiful Greek Revival house which was erected for the Floyds on what was then designated as "the Madison Road" and sometimes "the Alcova Road" is generally accepted as dating from the early 1830s. It has been lovingly cared for in all the years since it was built and looks today the same as in the halcyon days "before the war." The major changes, both made early in the present century, were the removal of the kitchen from its original location in the back yard to connect with the back of the house, and the sale of strips of property to the east and south of the house — with the consequent elimination of the carriage house and other outbuildings.[3]

The Floyd House, as the property is still known, reflects the cultivated taste of its first owners. The classic colonnade features four round Doric columns set between two square columns of the same order, and arranged *in antis* to the pilasters at each end of the portico. The interior features a fine circular staircase, beautiful wainscoting and stencilled wallpaper, and hand-carved mantels ornamented with Greek scrolls and medallions.[4]

John J. Floyd's outstanding talents as a lawyer soon established him at the forefront of his profession. He began his career of public service by representing Newton County in the State Senate for the terms of 1835 and 1836. In the latter year, in his capacity as captain of a company of state militia, he was called out to meet an Indian uprising. In 1845 he donned the black robe of the judiciary when he ascended the bench as judge of the Flint Judicial Circuit. He chose to follow the nomadic life of a circuit judge only four years before resuming the practice of law, but some years later he returned to the bench.[5]

Originally a member of the Whig party, to which the better educated and wealthier citizens usually belonged, Judge Floyd worked long and diligently to further its influence. He was the party's unsuccessful candidate for Congress from the Fourth District in 1844. Six years later, having concluded with other prominent Georgians that the Whig party was dying, he was elected president of the new Constitutional Union party. Although this political organism was short-lived, it endured long enough to nominate Howell Cobb governor by acclamation and to help him carry all but ten counties in the election.[6]

A prominent judge of a later era wrote that Judge Floyd was
a tall-well-proportioned man; his complexion rosy, with large blue

eyes. He read Blackstone's *Commentaries* once every year as long as he lived, and he read his Bible, too, for he was a great hand to quote Scripture in his arguments ... [He was] almost irresistable before a jury. [A contemporary] said "His tongue dripped honey" ... and [he was]a very attractive personality ... [7]

Judge Floyd and his gracious wife were popular additions to Covington's ante-bellum society. Their handsome home was the scene of lavish dinners and elegant "collations," and always its hospitable doors were open to friends and relatives. Guests often arrived with a small trunk and remained for several weeks at a time.

One of the first social affairs held in the Floyd residence was the wedding and reception of Miss Sarah Ward Dutton and Iverson L. Graves (*see page 51*) on 29 October 1834. The bride, a native of Champion, New York, was one of the first graduates of the Emma Willard School and had come to Covington to teach at Southern Female College. Her sister Elizabeth subsequently became the third wife of Judge Columbus D. Pace (*see page 39*).[8]

A good friend from Madison who lived with the Floyds for

HOME OF JUDGE AND MRS. JOHN J. FLOYD

a time was destined to achieve posthumous fame as a diarist. This was Mrs. Dolly Sumner (Lunt) Lewis, widow of Dr. Samuel H. B. Lewis. After the death of her husband and their child far from the couple's native Maine, she taught school in Madison and, briefly, in Covington. In 1850 she was married in Madison to Thomas Burge, a patrician planter whose first wife had died several years earlier. Thereafter Dolly lived on the Burge plantation only nine miles east of Covington. The diary* which she kept from shortly after her first husband's death in 1843 until several years after the death in 1873 of her third husband, the Reverend William J. Parks of Emory College, has become justly celebrated for its portrayal of daily life in the momentous years it covers.[9]

It is probable that Dolly Lewis taught at Southern Female College (*see pages 112-118*) during the time she lived in the Floyd home. Judge Floyd was vitally interested in the college from its earliest days, and served for some years as a trustee of the institution. In 1855 he enrolled in the preparatory department his youngest daughter, Florida (later Mrs. George H. Hammond of Decatur). Other children of Judge and Mrs. Floyd were Frances Ann, who married the younger McCormick Neal (*see pages 201-207*); Mary Louisa, later the wife of Dr. William A. Shelby of Orlando; Sarah Elizabeth, who died in childhood; William B., a bachelor who moved out West; Stewart; and John Colbert Floyd, who married Louisa Allen of Bainbridge, lived many years in Columbus, and died in retirement at Chipley (now Pine Mountain), Georgia.[10]

A frequent visitor to the hospitable home of Judge and Mrs. Floyd undoubtedly was his young grandniece Rebecca Latimer, who attended school in Oxford. Despite at least one published statement that the young lady attended Southern Female Col-

*Dolly's diary has been published in two versions, the second considerably longer than the first: Dolly Sumner Lunt, *A Woman's War-Time Journal* (New York: 1918; Macon: 1927), and James I. Robertson, Jr., editor, *The Diary of Dolly Lunt Burge* (Athens: 1962).

BURGE HOME

For many years the residence of Thomas Burge (*8 August 1806–10 December 1858*), a native of Hancock County and a graduate of the University of Virginia. Probably erected at about the time of his marriage on 25 October 1830 to Mary Clark (*24 December 1813–27 August 1848*), by whom he had five children: Margaret Louisiana, Rebecca, Eliza C., Thomas and Wiley C. Burge.

On 22 January 1850 Mr. Burge married as his second wife Mrs. Dolly Sumner (Lunt) Lewis (*29 September 1817–26 October 1891*). Their only child, Sarah Cornelia (Mrs. J. D. Gray, *11 December 1855–8 June 1892*) inherited the property, but died soon afterward.

Many years later Mrs. Gray's daughter Dorothy (Mrs. Louis Davant Bolton, *7 November 1880–29 June 1964. See page 129*) returned to live in her ancestral home, and upon her death. the property passed to her son John Gray Bolton (*see page 130*. He died in Pennsylvania in 1971). The latter eventually transferred title to it to his second wife, Elsie, who on 20 May 1969 sold it to Mrs. Julia R. Hamilton (*see page 233*). In 1971 Mrs. Hamilton and her husband, Robert W. Hamilton, Jr., sold the house and some of the original Burge land to Mr. and Mrs. H. T. Newsome of DeKalb County.[32]

lege, she herself recorded that she graduated at Madison
Female College in 1852. The commencement speaker on that
occasion was Dr. William H. Felton, a physician who later
served in the Georgia legislature and in the Congress of the
United States. The widowed Dr. Felton and young Miss
Latimer were married in 1853. In her great old age, after she
had become famous as an author and as a vital force in
Georgia politics, Mrs. Felton became for one day in 1922 the
first woman member of the United States Senate.[11]

When the firebrands of South Carolina, enthusiastically
encouraged by a small but vocal group of influential Georgians, finally rent asunder the union which had been forged by
the patriots of 1776, the Floyd family was affected along with
all others in Covington. Twenty-one year-old John Colbert
Floyd, who had been a student at Emory College, enlisted as
a private in the "Lamar Infantry" (later Company A, "Cobb's
Legion" of Georgia Volunteer Infantry) in August 1861. Within
a few months he had been elected first lieutenant. On 14
September 1862, during the bloody engagement at Crampton's
Gap, Maryland, in which many fine Covington men were killed
or captured, he was wounded and imprisoned. Later
exchanged, he was captured again as the Confederacy drew its
last gasping breaths in April 1865.[12]

In the first year or two of the war there was a display of
confidence and even gaiety in Covington and elsewhere in the
Confederate States of America. The departure for war or the
return on leave of local men inspired a round of parties and
picnics, with blushing maidens casting admiring glances at male
friends resplendent in their new grey uniforms. Visitors
continued to arrive for lengthy stays, and the Floyds
undoubtedly had many friends and relatives under their hospitable roof. One such visitor was Anna Maria Green, a friend
of Florida Floyd, who had boarded with the family while
attending Southern Female College. She came from her home

in Milledgeville on several occasions, always recording in her diary that she had heard a sermon by the Reverend Thomas F. Pierce, pastor of the Covington Methodist Church. Young Miss Green's diary* indicates that both Florida Floyd and her cousin Florence Usher (*see page 125*) had become her good friends.[13]

During the months and years when anxiety and sorrow became bosom companions to the women and the few men left in Covington, Mrs. John J. Floyd worked tirelessly to help the Confederacy's soldiers and the families they had left behind. She and her daughters were among the prominent local women who banded together in 1861 as the Women's Sewing Society. Mrs. Floyd served as president of the group throughout the war, and under her guidance the weekly ses-sions at the Covington Hotel resulted in an impressive quantity of warm clothing to be sent to the men on the battlefields.[15]

Judge Floyd, who had returned to the bench of the Flint circuit for a second four-year term beginning in 1861, organized and equipped a cavalry company of the Georgia State Guards. Known originally as "Floyd's Newton Cavalry," it subsequently was designated Company K, 2d Regiment, Georgia Militia. Judge Floyd was elected captain on 4 August 1863 and colonel on 5 September of the same year.[16]

When it became known on 22 July 1864 that Union troops were nearing Covington, Judge Floyd hastened to his home and found that his family had already fled to the home of relatives in Madison. Seeing smoke billowing above the new

---

*Anna Maria Green (*1844–1936*) later became the wife of Samuel Austin Cook of Albany. Graduating from Southern Female College with first honors in 1862, she kept a diary during the war years which was edited by James C. Bonner and published under the title *The Journal of a Milledgeville Girl 1861–1867* (Athens: 1964). In her old age Mrs. Cook authored *The History of Baldwin County, Georgia* (1925).[14]

soldiers' hospital, he quickly mounted his horse and set out to join his family. At *Burge Plantation* he reigned in to warn his old friend, saying "Mrs. Burge, the Yankees are coming... Hide your mules and carriages and whatever valuables you have..." That lady noted in her diary that she and her young daughter thereupon divided their meat, silver and best clothing among the servants, who secreted the articles in their little cabins. "I shall sleep no more to-night," she concluded.[17]

It was to be a long time before anyone in Newton County would sleep as peacefully as he had prior to 1861. With the cessation of hostilities in April 1865 a defeated and impoverished Georgia was placed under the rule of a Reconstruction government. Sons, brothers and husbands were dead or maimed; stores and factories were in ashes; cattle and crops were appropriated; homes had been plundered of furnishings and family treasures; slaves had been freed, leaving no "hands" for next year's crops — yet with it all people picked up the shattered pieces of their lives and looked ahead.

Gradually economic conditions began to improve, and ten or fifteen years after the war Covington and Newton County began to share the vision of the imaginative men who would lead the city and the county into a new era of prosperity. A great wave of railroad building swept across the reunited nation, and Georgians were just as eager to have the advantages of cheap transportation as were their brethren in all parts of the country. One of the many railroad ventures sponsored within Georgia by its own citizens was the Loganville Railroad Company, of which John J. Floyd was an incorporator.[18]

From the days of his young manhood until the day of his death, Judge Floyd was an active participant in things political. Although he apparently never sought public office after ascending the bench, he continued his avid interest in politics and served on numerous occasions as a delegate to conventions, assemblies and party gatherings. Of especial importance was his wise counsel in the days immediately following the Civil War. In 1865 he was a delegate to a special convention called by Provisional Governor James Johnson for the first Wednesday in October. In 1868, the year in which Atlanta succeeded Milledgeville as the state capital, Judge Floyd journeyed to the former in his capacity as a vice president of the State Democratic Convention and participated in the selection of a presidential elector.[19]

As he grew old with grace and dignity, Judge Floyd wore his years lightly and was admired and respected by his fellow citizens in Covington and Newton County. He had long since been honored by having the street upon which he lived named Floyd Street. He had been chairman of the Grand [Masonic] Lodge of Georgia's Committee on Southern Masonic Female College. And, as throughout his life, he continued to be an active and influential member of the local Methodist church.[20]

Death came to the distinguished former jurist on 12 March 1883. In commenting upon this sad event *The Georgia Enterprise* said in part, "He was well known to the people of Georgia and for years had been considered one of the best criminal lawyers in the State. He ... wore the ermine with honor to himself and satisfaction to the public." [21]

Mary Colbert Floyd, who was born on 27 February 1817, survived her husband by twenty-five years, dying on 3 February 1908. She was laid to rest beside him in the "new" cemetery adjoining the old Methodist graveyard on Elm Street.[22]

Mrs. Floyd apparently sold her stately home soon after she was widowed, for a deed made on 11 December 1884 by General and Mrs. Robert J. Henderson transferring the former Cary Wood home to T. C. Swann stated that the property was bounded on the east "by lot of Edward Heard." [23]

The new owner of the Floyd residence was a son of Fitz Herbert Heard and the former Emily A. Davis of Covington. His paternal grandfather, Joseph Heard of Morgan County, was a grandson of Revolutionary patriot and Georgia Governor Stephen Heard of Elbert County. Joseph Heard and his three wives are buried on Little River, ten miles west of Madison.[24]

Edward Heard was born on 24 November 1847 and died on 13 March 1919. He was a retail merchant in Covington, being associated in the dry goods business with Messrs. Charles White and D. A. Thompson under the firm name of Heard, White & Thompson. On 2 November 1882 Edward Heard took as his bride Miss Lucy Jane Simms, youngest daughter of the late Judge and Mrs. Richard Lee Simms (*see page 55*), who had been born in Covington on 11 December 1845. When the Heards moved into the former Floyd home they were joined there by Mrs. Heard's widowed sister-in-law, Mrs. R. L. Simms, Jr., and the latter's only child, Richard Lee Simms, 3rd. Mrs. Simms, the former Lucy Hyde Branch of Tampa, had lived with her late husband's family since his death in the Civil War a few months after their marriage. Many years later she became the wife of Dr. Frank Pharr of Decatur.[25]

Edward and Lucy (Simms) Heard became the parents of four children: Edward, Jr., Herbert Simms, Benjamin Simms, and Lucy Hyde Heard. The daughter, who was named for Mrs. Heard's beloved sister-in-law, was known throughout life as "Hyda." She inherited the family home upon the deaths of her mother and father, in 1919 and 1920 respectively. She lived there infrequently, however, as she spent many years as a missionary to China and later maintained a home in North Carolina. She died in the latter place on 9 June 1960 and was buried in Covington.[26]

A month after "Miss Hyda's" death her old family home was sold by Ralph Leslie Turner, executor, to Dr. William Kirk Swann. The stated consideration was $10, but it was pretty generally known around town that $12,500 had been

asked for the property. On 2 August 1960 Dr. Swann transferred a one-half undivided interest in the property to his wife
"for love and affection." [27]

Dr. Swann was a native of the Newton-Rockdale area and
was a distant relative of the T. C. Swann family whose
extensive grounds adjoined his own. He had previously practiced medicine in Monroe, but he foresook his profession upon
moving to Covington. Mrs. Swann, the former Stella Upshaw.

THE FLOYD HOUSE RETAINS ITS ANCIENT ELEGANCE

was for many years a teacher in the local public schools. She had kinsmen in Newton County and was an aunt of Berrien K. Upshaw, first husband of *Gone With The Wind* author Margaret Mitchell. Mrs. Swann was a bright and animated person, and her exceptionally keen mind made her an interesting conversationalist on almost any subject.[28]

On 1 June 1949 the Swanns' beautiful home was the scene of the reception which followed the wedding of their daughter Mary Arnall Swann and William Thomas Rainey, Jr., of Fayetteville, North Carolina, at the First Methodist Church. On this occasion the house was decorated with arrangements of pine, magnolias and white gladioli.[29]

Dr. and Mrs. Swann were the parents also of Dorothy (Mrs. Robert Wharton of St. Simons Island), Eleanor (Mrs. Reid Childers of Griffin), Paul Swann of Dalton, and Dr. W. Kirk Swann, Jr., of Knoxville, Tennessee. The father died soon after purchasing the Floyd-Heard house and his widow died in 1966. In the latter year the Swanns' sons, as executors of their mother's estate, sold the property to John Riley Thompson.[30]

For several years the new owner and his wife, the former Mary Ann Lambert of Atlanta, occupied one of the two apartments into which Miss Hyda Heard had subdivided the house. The other unit was, and still continues to be, occupied by Mr. Thompson's mother, Mrs. W. H. Thompson. A native of Virginia, where she was born Jessie Bennett, Mrs. Thompson formerly was a teacher in the Covington public schools. Since her retirement she has devoted her time to traveling and to maintaining the beautiful old house in which she lives.[31]

As it has for nearly a century and a half, *The Floyd House* continues to dominate Floyd Street from the slight knoll upon which it was built. Its classic facade adds grace and dignity to a street which is known far and wide for its beautiful homes.

IX
THE CARR-CODY-CORLEY HOUSE

One of the loveliest of Covington's ante-bellum houses was erected for John Pace Carr. The date of its construction is not known, but an examination of early deeds suggests that the house probably dates from about 1836. The tract of land upon which it was built was bought by Mr. Carr on 6 October 1835 from William Brown, administrator of the estate of Joseph Bishop. In the course of a sale at public outcry, Mr. Carr obtained for $340 a tract of land described as being on the west side of Dried Indian Creek at the point where the road from Covington to Decatur crossed the creek and north of a line extending along what is now Clark Street to the lands of the Manual Labor School. Mr. Carr subsequently made substantial additions to the property by purchases over a period of several years.[1]

The house constructed for John P. Carr had a beautiful facade of four wooden Ionic columns supporting a pediment projecting from the central portion of the gable roof. A balcony projecting to within a foot of the columns was hung by two metal rods, and the balustrade featured a criss-cross deisgn. The entrance doorway was Palladian in style, with both sidelights and fanlight.[2]

The interior of the house featured a beautiful stairway and handsome woodwork. The detail of the base panels and dado rails, as well as of the mantels, was especially fine. As was customary at the time, the kitchen was a separate building set some distance behind the house. At a greater distance were the slave quarters, the carriage house and barn, a smokehouse, and a summer house. A beautiful lawn bordered with box-wood led down to a private bridge which spanned Dried

Indian Creek. The entire grounds had been skillfully planned by a landscape architect from New York.[3]

John Pace Carr (*1797–1875*) was a native of North Carolina who moved to Warren County, Georgia, with his parents, Benjamin and Cebelle (Matthews) Carr. There the elder Carr was lieutenant in a company of militia in 1814 and a justice of the peace from 1813 to 1817. The son may have been the J. P. Carr who is listed as an original settler of DeKalb County in 1822. If so, he did not tarry there long, for his name appears in Newton County deed records as early as 1835. Mr. Carr and his first wife, the former Martha Turner, were the parents of — possibly among others: Benjamin Franklin Carr (*18 December 1822–22 November 1888*), who married, 22 February 1849, Mary Elizabeth Henderson (*see page 158*), and George T. Carr (*see page 152*). The children of Mr. Carr and his second wife, Mary Turner (*2 May 1810–10 October 1850. Sister of first wife?*) were: Amanda Melvina (*born 6 January 1832. See page 69*); Frances (*see page 104*); Nathan Collier (*11 January 1836–24 January 1921*), who married Angeline McCalla; Lizzie (*1838–1869*), who was wed to Captain James S. Hargrove; Florella (*1847–1896*); and John W. Carr. As the 1860 U.S. Census lists William Pace, an eighty-two year-old native of North Carolina, as a member of the widowed Mr. Carr's household, it is likely, considering Mr. Carr's middle name, that Mr. Pace was his uncle.[4]

John P. Carr's grave in Covington City Cemetery is not on the plot with the grave of his second wife nor on the plots of any of his known children except Florella. Thus it may be that the two other persons buried on the plot with him and Florella may be children of a third marriage, or perhaps they were grandchildren. These are Clarence Holt Carr (*1868–1883*) and Anna Belle Carr (*1873–1883*).[6]

On 19 March 1863 John P. Carr sold to Madison D. Cody for $5000 a fifty-five acre tract "on which the said John P. Carr formerly resided[,] and bounded ... on the west by land belonging to W. W. Clark and James Roberts[,] on the north by lands belonging to George Berry[,] Nix Freeland[,] Georgia Rail Road & Banking Company[,] and Harry Camp[,] on the east by land belonging to Harry Camp and by Dried Indian Creek[,] and on the south by land belonging to the said John P. Carr and W. W. Clark . . ." The land thus described corresponds roughly to the property now bounded on the west by

CARR - CODY - CORLEY HOUSE

This picture was made a century after John P. Carr built his home atop what later became known as "Corley's Hill."

West Street, on the north by Stone Mountain Street and the Georgia Rail Road tracks, on the east by Dried Indian Creek, and on the south by Washington Street.[7]

Madison Derrell Cody (27 September 1824–25 January 1875), purchaser of the property, was Mr. Carr's son-in-law. He and Frances Carr (1835–1872) had been married in Covington on 24 February 1852*, a year after the marriage of his brother Dr. Jeptha M. Cody to her sister Amanda Carr (see page 69).

In 1861 M. Derrell Cody had been a delegate to the Secession Convention from Warren County, where his family was both wealthy and prominent. He must have become a judge of the Inferior Court of Newton County following his removal to Covington shortly after the beginning of the Civil War, for he was often referred to as "Judge." [8]

The house which Derrell Cody bought from John P. Carr was described many years later by one of his nephews in these words:

> The old Carr Homestead ..,. was perhaps the most conspicuous location in Covington, situated on the brow of a high hill west [of town]. A row of stately Lombardy poplars surrounded the commodious dwelling, then large fruit orchards, and beyond these [were] cultivated fields and meadows. [Judge Cody's] wife was a beautiful and charming woman. They had one son, Claude Carr, who graduated at Emory College [in] 1875 with first honors and [later became] dean of Southwestern University . . . [in] Texas . . .[10]

Following the death of the widowed Judge Cody in 1875 his home was owned successively for brief periods by Benjamin H. Hill, Augustus H. Lee, and John Neal. The first of these may have been the Jasper County native who amassed a fortune as a lawyer and who was elected to the United States Senate in 1877. The second man was a Newton County native who married on July 1850 Martha Walker Henderson, daughter

---

*Madison D. Cody (Jr.), an 1848 graduate of the University of Georgia, was killed in a Civil War battle at Crampton's Gap, Maryland. Whether he was a son of M. Derrell Cody by an earlier marriage, or of his brother Dr. Jeptha M. Cody is not known.[9]

CARR - CROWE HOUSE

The attractive Church Street residence of Mr. and Mrs. Wendell Crowe is said to be one of the oldest houses in Covington. In years past it was often referred to as "the old Carr place," leading many persons to believe that it was one of the several local houses erected for Captain Nathan C. Carr (*see page 102*). Upon the death of Alfred Cureton, however, he devised this house and one on the opposite side of Church Street (or "what I call *East* Monticello Street") to his granddaughters Annie Cureton Carr and Clara Cureton Carr, "children of E. P. Carr and my deceased daughter Clara Carr." When the girls had grown up and married, the latter (then Mrs. Crawford Jenkins of Columbus) elected to take full ownership of the house on the east side of the street and her sister (Mrs. William N. Rainey) chose the house on the west side. The latter structure is now the first house behind the Episcopal church and is the home of Mrs. C. C. Estes.

Mrs. Jenkins' house subsequently was owned by a Mr. Gray, Thomas G. Barnes, and John H. and W. Edgar Wood. In 1943 it was acquired by Mrs. Crowe, the former Thankful Bickmore of Denver, for $7,500.

The most prominent of the earlier owners, Alfred M. Cureton (*1813—1888*), was a wealthy merchant who married Amanda Perry (*1824—1879*). Their daughter Clara married Edward Pace Carr, son of Captain Nathan C. Carr. The possibility that the younger Carrs lived in the house would seem to explain why it was long identified with their name.[5]

of Isaac P. and Ruth (Shepherd) Henderson (*see page 158*) and served in the Civil War as major in the "Young Guards" (Company H, 3rd Regiment, Georgia Volunteer Infantry). He subsequently became a large-scale Newton County landowner. Mr. Neal, the third owner, apparently acquired the property on a mortgage. He quite probably was the by-then aged man of that name who had served as executor of the estate of his brother McCormick Neal (*see page 37*). John Neal, a native of Warren County, lived briefly in Bibb and Pike counties and in Louisiana before moving in 1858 to Atlanta, where he built one of the city's notable Greek Revival mansions on what is now the site of Atlanta's City Hall. The house served as headquarters for General William T. Sherman during the Battle of Atlanta. Upon Mr. Neal's death he left a small bequest to his nephew McCormick Neal the younger.[11]

The Carr-Cody house came into the possession of James T. Corley on 3 November 1884 when he acquired title to it from John Neal for $3000. Actually Mr. Corley had purchased the property from Augustus H. Lee on 12 December 1878, but there appears to have been a loan on it made to the latter by Mr. Neal in the amount of $5910. In the 1878 deed Mr. Lee relinquished his former residence occupying the block bounded by Reynolds, Brown, Conyers and Lee streets as well as "my house and lot . . . whereon I now reside, containing about thirty-five acres . . ."[12]

James T. Corley (*4 December 1830–31 October 1895*) had formerly lived in the Harris-Cody house on Monticello Street (*see page 72*). He was engaged in a general mercantile business in a building located in the middle of the west side of Monticello Street between Washington and Reynolds streets. In later years his four sons were associated with him. Mr. Corley invested heavily in real estate, buying and selling both farm lands and city property. At one time he operated a gold mine on his land which had a vein "about as wide as the finger," and which produced gold worth $3.50 per seven and a half pounds of ore. He was a county commissioner when the present courthouse was constructed in 1884, and during the pastorate of Dr. J. M. Brittain he was superintendent of the First Baptist Church's Sunday School. At his death *The Covington Star* commented that "Mr. Corley was a man of sterling integrity, and was always found on the moral side of every question of public interest." [13]

James T. Corley and his wife, neé Skinner, were the parents of seven children: Will; John J., who married Annie Bradshaw; Tom, who married Leonora Anderson; Mary, later Mrs. Davis Melson; Martha Vashti, who became the wife of B. H. Buchanan; Walter T., who married Kate, daughter of Captain Silas Henry Starr, Jr., of Starrsville, and his first wife; and Emma, who wed Colonel Lucius Lamar Middlebrooks, a distinguished Covington lawyer.[14]

During the lifetimes of Mr. and Mrs. Corley the driveway leading up to their home from Railroad (now Emory) Street was made a public street and named for Mr. Corley. Following their deaths the still-handsome house passed into the possession of W. H. Pickett (*see page 14*). His wife had thought

FADED GRANDEUR

she would enjoy living there, but she decided against it because of the extensive repairs which would be required. Also, the neighborhood which had grown up on the once-beautiful grounds was unattractive and deteriorating. Subsequently the house changed hands several times, and in 1936 it was owned by a Negro undertaker named Nelson. It has long since been divided into quarters for numerous low-income families.[15]

Fortunately for posterity, a picture of the house (*see page 103*) and measured drawings of it were placed in the Library of Congress many years ago. They remind us reproachfully of the elegance and beauty which once graced one of Covington's most commanding sites. The interior of the house has been stripped of stairway, paneling, mantels, chandeliers and ornamentation, and the outside is sagging and jaded. The old structure teems with the numerous families which are crowded into its ancient rooms.

One may still detect something of its former glory, but today John P. Carr's proud mansion is a rebuke to the community which failed to appreciate, rescue, and preserve an architectural treasure.

X
"THE PRESIDENT'S HOUSE"

One of the attractive old houses in Covington is known as *The President's House*. Sitting sedately beneath giant oak trees on what is now known as Davis Street, it has been associated with many of the prominent pioneer figures in the city's history.

In its earliest form it occupied what originally had been two land lots and the site of a proposed street. The former were acquired by John N. Williamson sometime prior to 13 March 1837. On that date he registered, *ex post facto*, a deed of sale to him by three justices of the peace for "a Street running east and west between lots number 20 and 21 owned at present by the Said Williamson and lots number 22 and 23 in Square D . . ." [1]

John Napier Williamson was one of the most distinguished of Covington's pioneer citizens, and through blood or marriage he was related to several of the prominent local families of his time. [2]

A native of Virginia, he had served as a general in the United States Army during the Indian War of 1839. "He was an honest lawyer, an enlightened statesman, a faithful friend, and a good man . . ." He represented Newton County in the State Senate at the sessions of 1834, 1837, 1838, 1839, 1840, 1841, 1847, and 1853–'54. General Williamson died on his fifty-fifth birthday, 4 May 1857, and, as he had quite positively directed in his will, was buried at *Longwood*, the estate between Covington and Oxford where a sturdy house had been built for him *circa* 1836. [3]

General Williamson and his first wife, Louisa, whom he probably married in Virginia, were the parents of Zalema

109

Williamson (*1826–1868*), who became the wife of Dr. John B. Hendrick of Covington (*see page 136*). On 3 November 1831 John N. Williamson married as his second wife Lorena Luckie of Newton County. In his will he left a bequest of slaves to the children of William D. Luckie (*see page 37*), which suggests that the two men were brothers-in-law. General Williamson's third wife was Temperance ("Tempe") Perry (*see page 80*), who was born in North Carolina on 11 March 1805. Children of the last union were John P. and Wiley B. Williamson. The father's will directs that his brothers-in-law Doctors Wiley and A. C. Perry should counsel with his wife concerning the boys' education, and directs that the sons are to "read law one year for the purpose of learning <u>their rights partic-ularly</u> . . ." The *Longwood* estate was sold by Dr. William

LONGWOOD, home of General John N. Williamson. Now numbered 5155 N. West Street, it is presently the residence of Mr. and Mrs. James Oglesby.

D. Conyers, General Williamson's brother-in-law and executor of his will, to Andrew J. Miller on 7 July 1859, after which the widowed Mrs. Williamson returned to her native North Carolina.[4]

John N. Williamson had sold his home in Covington to Charles E. T. W. Campbell on 27 February 1837. The buyer paid $2133 for both lots number 20 and 21 in Square D and "a parcel of land Known and distinguished in the plan of Covington as a street running east and west . . . upon which Allen Turner now has his dwelling house and resides . . ." [5]

Allen Turner (see page 78) presumably had rented the Williamson house after the General moved to his new home north of town. The former quite likely was, in its original form, a modest cottage. That it was situated on the site of the house which still stands is made clear, however, by the deed's statement that the house was situated upon the premises of what had originally been planned as a street.[6]

Charles E. T. W. Campbell was a man whose name was seen fairly often in early records of Newton County. It appears that he later moved to Jasper County, for on 12 October 1866 his wife, Mrs. E. W. Campbell, petitioned Jasper County Superior Court for permission for him, in his capacity as trustee for herself and her children, to sell lands which had been given her by her father, S. H. Gay. The court granted the desired permission, whereupon Mr. Campbell sold 25 acres in Newton County to James Harwell for $1250.[7]

On 6 August 1839 Mr. Campbell sold his Covington home to Manson Glass for $1700. Judge Glass retained the house only a few years, after which he moved to Newborn. Years later he served as one of Newton County's delegates to a state meeting at which secession from the Union was discussed. When Judge Glass died in 1892 at the age of 81 *The Covington Star* stated that he "was a real gentleman of the old Southern type and was respected by the people of this county."[8]

Next owner of the house and surrounding acreage was William W. Clark, who acquired it on 1 December 1846 for a consideration of $1000. The price represented a steady decline in the value of local real estate, for General Williamson had sold the property to Mr. Campbell for $2133; Campbell had sold it to Glass for $1700; and now the latter had sold it for a mere $1000.[9]

William White Clark, the new owner, was born near Augusta on 23 September 1819, son of John and Sarah (White) Clark. He entered the Manual Labor School at Covington in 1838, but later was forced to withdraw when the death of his older brother left him with no resources. Thereafter he studied law and was admitted to the bar. In 1858 he formed a partnership with Jefferson Mirabeau Lamar (*see page 59[n*]*), which was terminated only by the latter's death in 1862. Five years later Mr. Clark entered into a partnership with James M. Pace, and thereafter he won both fame and fortune as a lawyer of remarkable abilities.[10]

On 16 December 1859, after living there for thirteen years, William W. Clark sold his house in Square D and soon thereafter moved to the former site of the Manual Labor School (*see pages 76-78*). The deed of sale reveals that by then Mr. Clark had acquired the entire block, for it states that for the sum of $5,000 he transferred to Southern Masonic Female College title to "the premises formerly occupied by me, being the Square East of the Female College . . . consisting . . . of four lots and a Street. The lots being numbers twenty (20), twenty-one (21), twenty-two (22), and twenty-three (23) in Square D and the Street . . . between . . . " It is probable that during his years in the house he had enlarged it to accommodate his growing family.[11]

The Clark residence was bought by the college for use as a home for its president. Chartered on 17 January 1850 as Southern Female College, largely through the efforts of General John N. Williamson, the institution offered a two-year preparatory course and four years of college work. It was an outgrowth of Southern Female Academy, a preparatory school which was in operation as early as 1839.[12]

From its earliest days the college's board of trustees was composed of some of the most distinguished men in Georgia. In 1855, for example, the members of this body were Honorable Howell Cobb, wealthy lawyer and planter, formerly congressman and governor of Georgia, who would become Secretary of the Treasury, president of the Confederate Convention, and major general in the Confederate States Army; Honorable William Schley, former congressman and governor of Georgia; Robert Randolph Cuyler, president of the Central Railroad & Banking Company of Georgia and of the Southwestern Railroad; and Colonel Timothy Mathews Furlow, wealthy Americus planter and former legislator. Covington's representatives were, relatively speaking, men of comparable stature: William P. Anderson, Dr. W. D. Conyers, John Harris, Dr. J. B. Hendrick, Colonel Thomas F. Jones, Columbus D. Pace, and the Reverend Creed Fulton, president of the college.[13]

The site of Southern Female College had originally been designated in the plan of Covington as lots number 12 and 13 in Square D. The property was first used as a muster or parade ground for local militiamen. Following the creation of the college, which was incorporated in the 1851–'52 session of the General Assembly, the Inferior Court ordered the street bisecting the property to be closed and relinquished all rights, title, and interest in it.[14]

In 1854 the Reverend George White wrote:

The Southern Masonic Female College . . . was adopted by the Grand [Masonic] Lodge of the of State Georgia . . . [in 1853]. The College edifice is a chaste, beautiful, and durable brick building, flanked in front by two elevated quandrangular towers, with an open portico or verandah between, and situated in a retired grove. It is well supplied with philosophical and chemical apparatus . . .[15]

In 1858 Georgia Masons subscribed $40,000 for the college, of which $6,000 was to go toward "extension of the real estate belonging to the Institution and the erection of some buildings and the improvement of the College edifice." After paying $5,000 for the former Clark home, the college had only $1,000 left to accomplish the objectives set forth by the Grand Lodge.[16]

When the Grand Lodge acquired the college its president was Dr. Alexander Means (6 February 1801—5 June 1883), a native of North Carolina who formerly had practiced medicine in Covington. A licensed Methodist preacher, he had been the superintendent of the Manual Labor School when it opened in 1834. In 1854 he became president of Emory College.[17]

As a resident of Covington prior to becoming president of Southern Female College Dr. Means undoubtedly already had a home in the little town. Subsequently he bought an old cottage in Oxford which he enlarged and made elegant with tall white columns.[18]

It is safe to assume that Dr. Means' successor, the Reverend Creed Fulton, AM, moved his family into the former Williamson-Clark house. But in 1858 President Fulton offered his resignation for reasons of health. The Reverend Charles Cooper succeeded him in 1861, but the college closed its doors in the summer of 1862 because of the Civil War.[19]

From that time until July 1864, reported Judge John J. Floyd (see page 92), who was then chairman of the Grand Lodge's Committee on Southern Masonic Female College, "the College buildings were for the greater part of the time occupied by the Confederate Government as a hospital . . . the buildings were appropriated . . . In July, 1864, they were abandoned and left in bad condition, and the Board had no funds to make necessary repairs . . . " [20]

As the building was in use as a hospital when Federal troops reached Covington, it was spared. The fine library and laboratory, however, were destroyed.[21]

SOUTHERN MASONIC FEMALE COLLEGE.

In 1865, John Harris (*see pages 158-163*), who by then had become Grand Master of the Grand Lodge of Georgia, reported that after being closed three years "on account of the condition of the country," the college had resumed operation on a limited scale. Professor James L. Jones, who had long been a member of the board of trustees, guided the institution until the Reverend James L. Pierce was elected president in 1866.[22]

In the latter year Trustee Samuel Lawrence of Marietta lamented, "The institution . . . is languishing, from the pecuniary condition of the country. That class of citizens from whom our colleges [formerly] received their principal support, being reduced from wealth to poverty, are rendered unable to educate their sons and daughters by sending them off to school . . ." [23]

In 1868, the Executive Committee reported that, "Two thousand dollars of the money appropriated last year was expended in payment of the President's salary . . . and the remaining one thousand in enclosing the ground and [in] repairs upon the buildings . . ." [24]

The college's president during this difficult period was a distinguished educator named Gustavus J. Orr.* He was succeeded in 1870 by the Reverend James Neel Bradshaw, to whom the trustees carefully explained that he was to look solely to the pupils' tuition for his compensation, and was "to have and

hold, by lease, free of rent, the College and all College property, subject only to insurance . . . and . . . if repairs and improvements be needed, of general character, there must be a special contract, in writing, . . . otherwise the said J. N. Bradshaw is to make the repairs at his own option and hold no legal claims upon the Board for such outlay." [26]

PRESBYTERIAN CHURCH.   Erected in 1926
to replace an earlier structure which had burned.

The Reverend Mr. Bradshaw was a Presbyterian minister who had transferred from the Knoxville Presbytery to the Good Hope Presbytery in 1866. He was instrumental in the reorganization in 1877 of a church of that denomination in Covington, where an earlier church had existed between 1827 and 1847. A house of worship for the new congregation

*Gustavus John Orr (9 August 1819–11 December 1887) was born in South Carolina and educated at Franklin College (now the University of Georgia) and Emory. He served as professor of mathematics at the latter from 1849 until 1867, except for time out for non-military service to the Confederacy. He was president of Southern Masonic Female College from 1867 until he resigned in 1870 to become professor of mathematics at Oglethorpe College. In 1872 he was elected Georgia's first State School Commissioner, in which capacity he "was . . . truly the father of public education in Georgia . . ." [25]

was consecrated on 6 October 1878, and for several years thereafter Mr. Bradshaw served as supply pastor.[27]

He moved from Covington some years later to serve other Presbyterian churches, and died at Madison, Florida, on 21 January 1895. His body was returned to the scene of his earlier labors and rests today in Covington City Cemetery beside that of his wife, Anna, and members of their family. Among the Bradshaw children were Annie, who was the wife of John J. Corley (see page 107), and Sarah Margaret, who was married to David A. Thompson (20 August 1847–27 June 1931). The latter was a brother of Sam Thompson (see page 152).[28]

The "Dave" Thompsons lived for many years in a handsome galleried house on East Street, facing College Street, which is said to have been built for Dr. John J. Dearing (see page 189). Subsequently the property was owned by Mrs. Thompson's nephew, Oliver Bradshaw. Now stripped of much of its original acreage, the house is owned today by Mr. and Mrs. Arthur D. Jordan and is identified as number 2107 Anderson Avenue, S.E.[29]

In 1878, the year in which he participated in the consecration of the local Presbyterian church, the Reverend J. N. Bradshaw experienced mounting problems at Southern Masonic Female College. Late in the year the Grand Lodge of Georgia advised the college president that because of the acute financial condition of the institution, it had resolved to make no more appropriations for it. The Masons voted, however, to pay $525 to be used in making repairs to buildings and fences. In 1880 a committee was named "to dispose of the interest the Grand Lodge of Georgia has in said Southern Masonic Female College . . . "[30]

Two years later the committee reported that, the Trustees having sold all of the property purchased from William W. Clark with the exception of the president's house and lot (which they valued at $2,500), it was "unanimously decided that the only honorable [way] the Grand Lodge could dispose of ... [all of the College] property was to reconvey the College building and lot with the personal property therein to the Trustees of Southern Female College ... or their successors ... and to make a deed of gift conveying said President's house and lot to said Trustees ..." Accordingly, the report continued, a deed of title had been executed on 26 November 1881 by which the property was conveyed to John J. Floyd, C. D. Pace, W. P. Anderson, James M. Pace, A. B. Simms, O. T. Rogers, J. M. Levy, John E. Rosser, McCormick Neal, Henry T. Henry and W. W. Clark, as Trustees of Southern Female College. Possession was to be delayed until 1 July 1882, by which time the current academic year would have been concluded.[31]

The re-constituted board of trustees of Southern Female College, not wishing to re-establish the operation of the institution, transferred the college to the North Georgia Conference of the Methodist Episcopal Church, South, on 29 June 1882. It operated briefly thereafter as Georgia Methodist Female College.[32]

A few years later when the City Fathers of Covington inaugurated plans for the creation of a public school system, Captain J. M. Pace, then mayor, asked the North Georgia Conference to permit the city to take over the property. The Conference agreed to this proposal, and on 14 July 1894 the transfer was duly effected. A subsequent inspection of the original college building revealed that a large crack had developed from top to bottom of one wall, so the building was condemned. The debris from it was used to fill a marsh which encroached upon Floyd Street in the vicinity of McCormick Neal's meadow.[33]

The Covington City School Commission, which had been created in 1887, set about in 1889 to gradually merge the public school and the Male Academy, which had operated under private auspicies for many years. Several years later a public school building was erected on the site of the Female college. At that time a local newspaper reported that, "The school building is a magnificent brick structure of the latest designs of Georgia's best architect . . . " A growing enrollment necessitated subsequent additions to the structure, and in 1910 an auditorium was built which afforded living quarters on the first floor for Superintendent J. C. Upshaw. In its last years the by-then outmoded building housed only the lower grades before they, too, were moved to the former site of Joseph S. Anderson's plantation home. In 1958 it was announced that the structure would be razed, and a year later a modern Municipal Building was erected on the site. This attractive brick edifice houses the city's administrative offices, the fire department, and the police department and jail.[34]

The former residence of the presidents of Southern Female College was sold by the City of Covington on 3 July 1906. The purchaser was Mrs. Julia E. Guinn, who paid $2000 for the house, a 130-foot frontage on Davis Street, and 300 feet extending behind it to East Street.[35]

Born Julia Glenn in 1865, she apparently was orphaned at an early age and was reared by her aunt and uncle, General

and Mrs. Winfield Scott of Covington. She was known thereafter as Julia E. Scott. Mrs. Scott's will refers to "my beloved
niece Julia ... who has lived with me since childhood, and
occupied the place of an affectionate and dutiful daughter ... " This document, which was probated on 4 March
1918, left Mrs. Scott's entire estate to her niece. General Scott
(*25 January 1829–5 April 1892*) was lauded upon his death
as "a prominent citizen of Covington for many years [who]
was loved and esteemed by all classes of our citizens. [He]
was a fine type of the old time southern gentleman—
commanding in personal appearance, high toned, genial,
generous, liberal hearted, charitable, quiet in demeanor, and
always pleasant and agreeable ... " General Scott was a Presbyterian, and had served in the Civil War as a member of
Company C, 7th Tennessee Regiment. His title presumably was
awarded by the United Confederate Veterans organization.[36]

Julia E. Scott became the bride of Richard Chessley Guinn
in a fashionable ceremony performed at the Presbyterian
church at 9:25 p.m. on 22 June 1892. Their first home was in
Midway (now North Covington). The bridegroom was for
many years Covington agent for the Georgia Railroad, and was
said by an admirer to be "the best depot agent in the United
States." He was a son of Robert Guinn of Newton County.[37]

During the many years in which *The President's House* was
their residence, Mr. and Mrs. Guinn made numerous changes in
the old structure. They enlarged it from one and a half to
two stories, and added columns and porches across the front.
Here was born their only child, Eugenia, who on 24 March
1921 became the wife of Tandy E. Bush (*see page 213*). Mrs.
Guinn, a charming and delightful woman, died in 1954, one
year after the death of her eighty-six year-old husband.[38]

On 18 July 1963, by which time she and her husband had
moved to Tampa, Florida, Mrs. Eugenia G. Bush sold her
long-time home to Charles D. Strickland for "ten dollars and
other valuable consideration." [39]

THE PRESIDENT'S HOUSE
Residence of Mr. and Mrs. Charles Strickland.

Mr. Strickland, a Covington lawyer, is a native of Meriwether County. He received the BB.A. degree from Georgia State University and the LL.D from Emory University. He married, 19 May 1953, Louise Nichols of Dacula. The couple has one child, David Strickland. They are members of the Presbyterian church.[40]

The Stricklands have maintained *The President's House* much as it was during the lifetime of Mr. and Mrs. Guinn. Its graceful columns and spacious porches are an attractive reminder of the long years of history associated with it, as well as of the outstanding men and women who have called it home.

XI
"USHER HOUSE"

The recent unveiling of what had appeared to be a faded dowager has revealed, to practically everyone's surprise, a handsome middle-aged matron with a sparkle in her eyes. Thus by analogy do we refer to the reappearance of a beautiful old house which had been concealed for years behind two enormous magnolias. While nearly everyone in Covington was bemoaning the loss of the trees, a few discerning persons applauded the owners' courage in returning to public view the graceful ante-bellum *Usher House*.

Erected prior to 1848 for Robert Oliver Usher, the house was built east of Judge R. L. Simms' house and directly opposite the residence of Judge John J. Floyd. As with the other local houses of its period which have survived, the name of the architect — if such there were — is not known today.

In any event, the proportions of the three-story structure, and the quality of its ornamental detail, are pleasing to behold. The facade of six Doric columns is capped by the only original "captain's walk" extant on a local ante-bellum house. A graceful balcony is suspended above the front doorway. The stairway within and what remains of the original paneling are walnut. The entrance hall, drawing room, library and dining room all have elaborate cornices and center ceiling motifs. The original wide floor boards are still visible throughout the house.[1]

Robert Oliver Usher, the man for whom this beautiful house was built, was one of Newton County's pioneer residents. As early as 1842 he was listed as a local merchant. He and his partner, Joseph S. Anderson (*see pages 183-184*), engaged in a general mercantile business in a building which still stands at the northwest corner of the Public Square, at the intersection of Hunter and Clark streets. Originally erected in Oxford in 1837 as a hotel for students at Emory College, it was moved to Covington piece-by-piece and reconstructed on its present site (*see picture, page 185*). The firm occupied the lower floor and the rooms on the second floor were rented to local bachelors. Usher Street, an east-west avenue behind the building, was named for one of the store's proprietors; and Anderson Avenue, an artery leading from Floyd Street to the present E. L. Ficquett School, was named for the other. A later partner's name is perpetuated in the street running along the east side of the building, which was named Hunter Street in his honor.[2]

Mr. Usher was born in England on 25 April 1809 and upon immigrating to the United States he lived in Connecticut for a while. The time of his arrival in Georgia is not known, but as previously stated his name appeared in records of the county as early as 1842. On 17 December 1845 he married Miss Frances Wingfield Colbert of Columbus, who was a native of Morgan County. As they were wed in Newton County, it is likely that the ceremony took place at the home of the bride's sister Mrs. John J. Floyd (*see page 89*), whose house faced the Usher residence across the dusty road to Madison.[3]

The Ushers' many-roomed house was to resound with the happy laughter of their children, grandchildren and great-grandchildren in the ninety years it remained in the family. Robert and Fannie Usher suffered the loss of three small children before the father himself answered the final call on 9 May 1859. He was interred in the Methodist cemetery, where his family plot was marked by an elaborately carved marble monument and surrounded by a handsome iron fence.[4]

The will of Robert O. Usher said "I give and bequeath unto my beloved wife, Frances A. Usher, my house and lots on which we now live in the City of Covington, embracing the whole Square composed of two lots [Nos. 16 and 17, which

QUAINT IRON GATE
guards the final resting place of Mr. and Mrs. Robert O. Usher.

formed a *portion* of Square A] ... also my swamp lot now used as a meadow and which I purchased of William D. Luckie ..." [5]

Within two years of Mr. Usher's death his adopted state was swept into the inferno of the Civil War. Life for his family and for his friends and neighbors took on a new tempo of urgency and anxiety. With the beginning of the bombardment of Atlanta in the summer of 1864, large numbers of wounded men were transported to Covington and Oxford via the Georgia Railroad. Churches, college buildings and other available structures were transformed into hospitals, and the women of Newton County performed valiant services as nurses, letter writers and confidantes. [6]

On the night of 20 July 1864 General William T. Sherman ordered Brigadier General Kenner Garrard's three brigades to proceed from Decatur to Lithonia, Covington and Social Circle. As they followed the commander's orders the troops burned bridges over the Yellow and Alcovy rivers and destroyed the railroad station between Lithonia and the Alcovy. At Covington the Union forces wrought more damage (*see page 82*).[7]

In the fall of that year when Sherman's forces marched past the Usher residence en route to Savannah, the family clustered on the balcony to watch apprehensively. By then neither they nor the most fervent Confederates could fail to recognize that theirs was truly a lost cause.[8]

In the first year following the cessation of hostilities the Usher family knew relatively the same privations as other Southerners. Foodstuffs, clothing and medical supplies were so scarce as to be almost nonexistent. Confederate money and bonds were worthless, freed slaves were little interested in working in fields, and the heel of the conqueror was felt when resentful whites intimidated the emancipated blacks. It was not an easy time in which to live, but at least it was less emotionally unsettling than the four years of war had been.

During the sorrow of her early widowhood and through the anguished years of the Civil War Mrs. Robert Usher continued to maintain her beautiful residence as a home for her surviving children. These were Florence, who later became the wife of Oscar Thomason of Madison; Julia, who was married to John Francis Henderson (*see page 20*); Robert Oliver Usher, who never married; and Fannie Wingfield, who became the wife of W. J. Metcalf (*see pages 163-164*). The first of these children married a man from so wealthy a family that Mrs. Usher specified in her will that her orphaned grandchildren Florence and Usher Thomason should "have no part of my estate as a divine providence furnished them with a grandfather who is amply able to furnish them with all the comforts and necessities of life." Mrs. Usher directed that her daughter Mrs. Metcalf was "to have possession and control of my house and lot ... where I now reside." [9]

Mrs. Robert O. Usher survived her husband by almost forty years. She was born 25 July 1821 and died 15 February 1896. In mourning the passing of this stately lady *The Covington Star* reported that "the very name of 'Fannie Usher' seemed the synonym of all that was lovely and pure and good ... She was greatly beloved by everyone who knew her ..." [10]

The younger Robert Usher and his sister Fannie Metcalf lived out their lives behind the white columns of their parents' home. Known to a circle of devoted friends as "Mr. Rob" and "Miss Fan," they were the personification of the Old South's aristocracy. Robert Usher never worked, but even in old age he walked to the Square once a day to collect his mail at the post office. He used a cane with nonchalance and was always faultlessly attired. His linen invariably was so fresh that the courthouse loungers whispered that he wore a fresh shirt every day — and probably even took a *daily* bath! [11]

"Miss Fan" is remembered by a younger woman whom she welcomed into her small and select circle as "a darling person." During her lifetime it was recalled vaguely that she had been married — witness the fact that she was *Mrs. Metcalf* — but only a few oldtimers were aware of the circumstances. Fannie Usher had been married on 12 December 1876 to William J. Metcalf, who five years later bought the residence of the late Judge John Harris (*see pages 163-164*). Despite her husband's continuing entreaties that she move with him to a distant state, Fannie Metcalf adamantly refused to leave her family. Finally Mr. Metcalf gave up in defeat and left Covington without her. Gradually the bloom of youth faded from her cheeks and in time she became a wrinkled old woman, but she remained to the end of her life "Miss Fan," the darling of her family and friends. [12]

Although Mrs. Usher's will had directed that her daughter Fannie was to have the use of her home, the daughter shared it not only with her brother but also with her sister Julia and the latter's family.

John Francis Henderson, to whom Julia Usher had been married on 22 October 1872, had been reared across the street in the stately house built for his maternal grandfather, Cary Wood (*see pages 18, 20*). A son of General Robert J. Henderson and the former Laura Wood, he was born 25 April 1850. He was educated in the local schools and then engaged in farming operations until he sold his holdings in 1912. His election in 1885 as treasurer of Newton County gave him the experience and the public confidence which would result in his subsequent election to the board of directors of the Clark Banking Company and, later, to the presidency of the Bank of Covington. He was elected a director of the Covington & Oxford Street Railway Company in 1896. In 1900 he and T. C. Swann were the principal financial backers of Covington Mills, of which Mr. Henderson became secretary, treasurer and a director. In 1908 he succeeded Mr. Swann, by then deceased, as president of the Bank of Newton County, a position which he filled with distinction during the remainder of his life.[13]

John F. Henderson served as mayor of Covington in 1899, and he was for twenty years a steward in the local Methodist church. Mr. Henderson was in all respects a model citizen; a thrifty and successful businessman, an able and respected public servant, a devoted churchman, a trusted and kindly friend, and a loving husband and father. Upon his death on 19 April 1917 *The Covington News* stated that "his life was one full of splendid deeds and was at once a noble and worthy example for emulation ... He combined in a rare measure a kindly, pleasing and lovable personality with the strictest integrity in business matters ... Surely Covington['s] ... debt for such a life is incalculable ..."[14]

Mr. and Mrs. Henderson were the parents of Frances, who

married Hugh Wright; Robert Clifford, who married Hattie Hunter and lived in Decatur and, later, in Ormond Beach, Florida; and Florence.[15]

The marriage of Florence Henderson to Albert Sidney Burney of Rome was solemnized in a beautiful ceremony at the home of her parents on 16 August 1899. The bride descended the handsome stairway and was met by the bridegroom at an improvised altar in one of the drawing rooms. The bridal party, the bouquets of summer flowers and the flickering candles in the crystal chandeliers were reflected in gold pier mirrors in each of the front rooms. In reporting the nuptials one local newspaper stated that "Miss Florrie was the pet of the town ... one of our fairest and dearest daughters ... The presents were many, remarkably appropriate, and valuable ..." After a honeymoon at Blowing Rock, the young couple made their home in Rome for the remainder of their lives.[16]

Mrs. John F. Henderson died on 14 June 1917, less than two months after the death of her husband, and her obituary stated that she possessed "all the traits of a lovable character ... and she was indeed a Christian woman ..." [17]

Frances Henderson continued to live in the family home with her aunt and uncle, Miss Fan and Mr. Rob, until they both died in 1936. There she was married to Hugh Wright, originally of Starrsville. His life ended tragically in 1926 when he was drowned at St. Simons Island while rescuing his wife's young cousin, Mary Louise Trotti of Decatur. His heroism brought a posthumous award of a medal by the Carnegie Hero Fund Commission in the following year.[18]

> Mr. Wright was one of the most prominent citizens of Covington, and his death threw a pall of sorrow over the entire city ... All business houses of Covington were closed during the time of his funeral services ...[19]

Hugh Wright's widow, who survived him until 1945, maintained the family residence as a home for her only child,

Hugh Wright Jr., who now is a prominent Atlanta attorney, until she sold it on 8 June 1936 to Mrs. Dorothy G. Bolton for $5000.[20]

Mrs. Bolton was a woman whose roots were deep in Newton County's soil. Born Dorothy Gray, she was a daughter of the Reverend John Davis Gray, a Methodist circuit rider, and the former Sarah Cornelia ("Sadai") Burge. Her mother was the daughter of the redoubtable Dolly Lunt Burge of *Burge Plantation* (*see pages 92-93*).[21]

Orphaned at an early age, Dorothy Gray and her sisters Ida and Fannie, together with their brothers Davis and Joe, temporarily found a home with friends at *Mt. Pleasant*, the 1820-era plantation of the Graves family (*see pages 50-51*). Eventually the boys went to live with relatives in California and the girls were reared in Evanston, Illinois, by their great-aunt Miss Cornelia Lunt and her sister-in-law Mrs. Orrington Lunt. The latter was the widow of Dolly Lunt Burge's brother, who had acquired a fortune after moving to the Midwest from his native Maine. A founder of Northwestern University, he was honored posthumously when the library at that institution was named for him.[22]

Dorothy Gray eventually became the wife of Louis Davant Bolton, and Ida in time was married to Merritt Joseph Morehouse. Their sister Fannie died at age eighteen. The surviving sisters, although living in Grosse Point, Michigan, and Evanston, respectively, during their prime years, always retained a deep affection for *Burge Plantation*. In time they bought their brothers' interest in it and, almost simultaneously, persuaded their husbands to retire and move to Georgia.[23]

Mrs. Morehouse planned to modernize the old plantation house, causing her sister to express apprehension that its authentic ante-bellum charm would be destroyed. A happy solution was reached when Mrs. Morehouse, who really liked the setting more than the house, agreed for Mrs. Bolton to move the original structure across the road. This was done,

MOREHOUSE RESIDENCE

Built for the late Mr. and Mrs. M. J. Morehouse on the
original site of the Burge home at *Burge Plantation* (*see
pages 92, 93*). Now the home of their son and daughter-
in-law, Mr. and Mrs. Dutton Morehouse.

and Mrs. Bolton set about to create gardens appropriate to the
period of the house. Her sister and Mr. Morehouse soon had
built on the original site of the house a classic one-story
structure patterned after a house on the James River in
Virginia.[24]

When Mrs. Bolton purchased the Usher-Henderson-Wright
house on Floyd Street in Covington, she did so to provide a
home for her daughter-in-law, Mrs. Mollie Legare (Reeves)
Bolton and her two children, Louis Davant 2nd and John
Gray Bolton, Jr. The stately house provided a perfect setting
for many of the elegant furnishings from the Bolton home in
Grosse Point which were too formal for the simple old Burge
house.[25]

A thorough redecoration of the house was undertaken by
the new owner. She installed one or two handsome mantels
from the Neal-Sanders house (*see pages 33, 46*), and a magnificent Waterford crystal chandelier in the dining room. The
addition of a kitchen on the ground floor of the house, which
had three floors at the rear, eliminated the need to use the
original detached kitchen. Installation of bathrooms and a

furnace made the house comfortable by contemporary standards.[26]

Usher House, as the younger Mrs. Bolton preferred that it be called, soon resounded once again with the sounds of growing children. The Bolton sons, nicknamed "Nickey" and "Jack," were handsome youngsters who were generous, if selective, in their friendships. Nickey, the older of the two, was an inseparable playmate of his across-the-street neighbors, young Tom Swann and Goodwin Tuck. With the former he worked out a system of signals by which he could be alerted when the Swanns were having peach turnovers for lunch, whereupon he rushed across the street for an extra dessert before returning to the schoolhouse at the rear of *Swanscombe*.[27]

Mrs. Mollie Bolton, petite and pretty, was an animated and witty addition to the Covington social scene. She was too much a Charlestonian, however, to forget *where* she was from. (She had made her bow to society at the St. Cecelia Ball, the oldest and most exclusive social event in the country.) Thus, while loved by a small circle of close friends, she was little known to the mass of Covingtonians. For several years she conducted dancing classes for her friends and their children, and when her contemporaries were gathered for instruction stately old *Usher House* fairly rocked with revelry.[28]

Mrs. Bolton was one of a small group of Episcopalians who met in April 1950 and decided to organize a local congregation. Thereafter they held a service every Sunday evening until Phi Gamma Hall at Oxford College was made available for Sunday morning worship. The first service in that historic structure was held on 11 June 1950, at which time the name *The Church of the Good Shepherd* was adopted. Mrs. R. A. Tribble, who had conceived the idea of the first meeting, was responsible for arranging an appropriate altar setting, and Mrs. Bolton was pianist. The choir practice sessions at the Bolton residence soon became a weekly gathering attended by the entire congregation.[29]

Plans for erecting a church structure originated with Mr. and Mrs. Leslie J. Moore and Mrs. Thomas Swann over a Sunday night supper at the latter's home. A drive for funds was launched, a piece of property adjoining Franklin Wright Park was acquired, and the services of an architect were obtained. The dreams of the determined little band of Episcopalians were realized on 16 September 1951 when the new building was consecrated by The Right Reverend George Henry, Bishop of North Carolina. He was assisted in the service by two future bishops, the Reverends J. Milton Richardson of St. Luke's and John B. Walthour of the Cathedral of St. Philip, both in Atlanta. First rector of The Church of the Good Shepherd was the Reverend Jack Hopper.[30]

EPISCOPAL CHURCH

The new church had the unique distinction of being the first ever admitted into communion with the Diocese of Atlanta as a parish instead of as a mission church. The beautiful new building excited considerable comment in Covington, where the local newspaper said it "adds much to ... our community." Constructed of old brick, it was patterned after parish churches common to rural England. The beautiful stained glass windows were given in memory of Thomas Chalmers Swann, 3rd, by his mother.[31]

After the Bolton boys grew up and went away to college, *Usher House* was a quiet and lonely place for their mother. On 6 November 1957 Mrs. Louis D. Bolton sold the handsome house to Mrs. Lyda Sue Hall for "$10 and other valuable considerations." Shortly thereafter Mrs. Mollie (Reeves) Bolton became the wife of the Reverend William Parkinson, now of Warrenton, Virginia, whose first wife had been a sister of Wendell Crowe of Covington (*see page 105*).[32]

The new owner of *Usher House* was the former Lyda Sue Bower, daughter of Mr. and Mrs. Augustus Rodolphus Bower of Covington. After receiving the AB and MA degrees from Brenau College, she had studied at Emory Univeristy before becoming a teacher. In the course of her professional career she had served at Oglethorpe and Brenau colleges, and for twenty-six years she had been dean of Kirby-Smith School in Jacksonville. An early marriage to a member of a well-known Macon family had ended in divorce.[33]

Mrs. Hall moved into her new home immediately upon purchasing it. There she delighted in entertaining the numerous patriotic organizations of which she was a member. Although she served many groups in one capacity or another, her chief interest was the Daughters of the American Revolution. She had served as regent of a chapter in Jacksonville, and following her return to Covington she became regent of the Sergeant Newton Chapter. Under her auspicies as organizing president, the Sergeant Newton Junior Society of the Children of the American Revolution was born and nurtured.[34]

On 8 August 1959 *Usher House* was the scene of the marriage of Mrs. Hall's niece, Mary Patricia Bower of Winder, and Richard Willis Schermerhorn of Auburn, New York. The bride descended the hand-carved stairway and met the bride-groom at an altar formed before a pier mirror in the living room. Dr. Edgar A. Callaway of the First Baptist Church of Covington performed the impressive double-ring ceremony.[35]

Mrs. Hall died on 11 June 1971 following a long illness. Under the terms of her will her foster son, John H. Hall of Tucker, was to have a lifetime interest in the house, provided he chose to live there. The will provided that ultimately the house was to go to the City of Covington if the latter would maintain it as a museum and pay city taxes if the property were not tax-free. As both Mr. Hall and the city declined to accept the house on those terms, probably because of its neglected condition and a reputedly heavy mortgage, the property was offered for sale.[36]

Admirers of the old and beautiful were relieved when, on 19 January 1972, *Usher House* was purchased by Dr. and Mrs. Robert Lee Faulkner for a reputed price of $38,000.[37]

Dr. Faulkner is a native of McCormick, South Carolina, where he was born on 25 January 1937. He received the BA degree from Emory University in 1957 and the MD from Baylor University in 1961. His wife, the former Priscilla Willis Gainer, was graduated by Agnes Scott College with the BA degree in 1960 and received the MA degree from Emory in 1965. The couple was married at Panama City, Florida, on 19 June 1965 and immediately came to Covington, where Dr. Faulkner established a medical practice.[38]

Soon after they became the owners of *Usher House* the Faulkners began a major renovation of the property. As pre-viously noted, they began by removing two large magnolias which had concealed the columned house for more than a quarter of a century. The removal of ill-conceived additions within, the moving of the old kitchen building from the back yard to connect with the house, and the application of several

USHER HOUSE
Home of Dr. and Mrs. Robert L. Faulkner.

coats of white paint soon had the lovely old house shining like a gem in its setting of summer-green trees. The Faulkners began to acquire with deliberation and discrimination handsome furnishings appropriate to the size and period of their house. Among these were a large poster bed and an interesting secretary from the original Burge plantation house, where a former owner of *Usher House* had spent her last years (*see pages 129-130*).[39]

A few weeks after Dr. and Mrs. Faulkner and their small daughter Priscilla Bonner moved into the house in the summer of 1972, a second daughter, Lucinda, was born. The family inherited the long tradition of grace and hospitality which had been started by Mr. and Mrs. Robert O. Usher and continued by subsequent owners. Covington may take equal pride in beautifully refurbished *Usher House* and in the charming new owners who have preserved it for future generations.[40]

XII

THE BATES-TERRELL HOUSE

One of the pioneer settlers of Covington was Dr. Horace J. Bates, who arrived shortly before Newton County was created on 24 December 1821. He was a native of Herkimer County, New York, where he was born on 10 November 1796. He moved to Georgia in 1813 and settled at Eatonton, where he lived nearly ten years.[1]

Dr. Bates probably was the first physician in the village of Newtonsboro, as Covington was known until its incorporation in 1822. Subsequently he entered into practice with his brother-in-law Dr. John B. Hendrick (*1819–1881*), son of General Hendrick of Butts County and Alabama. Their office was located in what had been Dr. Bates' first residence, a house at the present southwest corner of Clark Street and the Public Square.[2]

One of Newton County's two representatives in the General Assembly for the 1831 term, Dr. Bates was its state senator in 1843. In 1836 he was an incorporator of the Middle Branch Rail Road Company, which unsuccessfully sought to build a line from Madison to the Chattahoochee River via Covington and Decatur. He was a trustee of the local Methodist church as early as 1830, in which year the church was moved from its original location at the northeast corner of Church and South streets to a new site on Washington Street, between Railroad (now Emory) and Lee streets.[3]

During most of his more-than half-century in Covington Dr. Bates was an extensive buyer of real estate. The tract on Monticello Street upon which a one-story house was erected for him was assembled prior to 1840. He owned lots 17, 19 and 20 in Square C, which extended from Monticello west along South Street (then the extreme southern border of the

136

town) to what is now Lee Street, the last of these being purchased on 6 September 1832 for $30.50. Lot 17 was known as his "Barn lot," and presumably the lot between it and the house was devoted to a garden and an orchard.[4]

On 4 January 1831 Dr. Bates married Mary Ann Hurt Hendrick, who was born in Jasper County of 25 December 1816. She was a granddaughter of William Hurt, a Revolutionary soldier who was the progenitor of a large family which became prominent in both Georgia and Alabama. The children of Dr. and Mrs. Bates were Gustavus J., who married Ella Dillard of Selma, Alabama; Martha Jacqueline, who became the wife of Robert R. Wood (see page 174); Mary Lucy, who was wed to James P. Simms (see page 57); and Virginia C. Bates.[5]

The last-named daughter, who had been educated at Southern Masonic Female College, was married on 11 May 1861 to William Denson Conyers, Jr., son of Dr. William D. Conyers and his first wife (see pages 79-80).[6]

"Billy" Conyers had known his bride all his life, having grown to manhood half a block away at Normal Grove, his father's handsome home. Dr. Conyers enjoyed returning to his native North Carolina for visits as often as possible. On one such occasion he took with him his daughter Chloe and his son Billy. The children were excited over the trip and looked forward to visiting the ancestral home of the Perrys, their late mother's family, on the banks of the Tar River. The trip was made in the family coach, a huge conveyance with steps which unfolded to permit one to enter and leave. The coachman's seat was outside the body, which rested upon high springs. At the end of each day's journey the Conyers family group lodged at a convenient house, but they always cooked their meals over camp fires. When they reached a river it was necessary to be ferried across on a rude float.[7]

Back home again, Billy Conyers went off to Georgia Military Institute at Marietta, from which he was graduated in

1858. He then read law under one of the distinguished lawyers for which Covington was noted, after which he began to establish himself as a promising member of the bar.[8]

Virginia Bates and William D. Conyers, Jr., were married less than a month after the guns were fired upon Fort Sumter. The fever of war raged in Covington, as elsewhere, and the young lawyer and most of his friends soon joined local military units. He volunteered on 1 August 1861 and was elected first lieutenant of the "Lamar Infantry," a unit which became a part of the 8th Georgia Regiment commanded by General Howell Cobb.[9]

The young officer was soon in the thick of the fighting. In one of the bloody battles fought in Maryland during September 1862 he was wounded in the side. His home-town friends Lieutenant Richard L. Simms, Jr., and Lieutenant Colonel Jefferson M. Lamar were killed in the same action (*see letter on page 59*).[10]

Shortly thereafter Lieutenant Conyers must have been at home on convalescent leave, for on 19 August 1863 his daughter Willie Rebecca Conyers was born. The baby was named for her father and his spinster aunt who, after the death of his mother, had been "Mother To The Motherless." [11]

As the war became more grim William D. Conyers, Jr., was promoted to captain and then to major. While in the capacity of acting colonel at Spotsylvania Court House, Virginia, he was killed in battle on 12 May 1864. It was his twenty-sixth birthday. His body was returned home and buried in the family cemetery atop "Rivers' Hill," halfway between Covington and Oxford.[12]

Several months later the commanding general of Conyers' brigade in the 1st Corps of the Army of Northern Virginia wrote to one of the young hero's sisters as follows:

Winchester, Va.
Sept. 10, 1864

Mrs. C. P. Herring: —

Dear Madam

Learning from your husband [William F. Herring. *See page 80*] that you were a dear sister to my friend and valued officer the lamented Maj. Conyers I have thought it would be some consolation to you to know how he was appreciated by his companions in arms. Attracted by the conspicuous gallantry of your brother at the battle of Chancellorsville which was the last engagement of the brigade after I had taken command of it we soon became intimate friends and I can say he was one of the best officers and purest patriots in my command. He fell as you have learned on the 12th of May last near Spotsylvania Court House in one of the bloodiest battles of the war and the last time I saw him he was in front of his command stimulating and encouraging them by his example. He was the embodiment of a high toned and gallant officer whose loss was deeply mourned by myself and the officers of the brigade. You and his other relatives and friends have my sincere sympathy.

Very Respectfully Your Friend,
s/   W. T. Wofford[13]

Major Conyers' widow, after the fashion of the time, was known thenceforth as Mrs. Virginia C. Conyers. Although her father-in-law directed that her late husband's proportionate share of his estate should go to Major Conyers' sisters instead of to his daughter, Mrs. Conyers and her child did not suffer. Her father was one of the wealthiest men in Covington; additionally, Willie Conyers (later Mrs. Charles Walford Cook. *See page 167*) received a bequest from her namesake Miss Rebecca Conyers.[14]

Mrs. Conyers was a charter member and the first president of the Covington Chapter of the United Daughters of the Confederacy. This organization, an outgrowth of the war-time sewing and hospital aide group (*see pages 95, 205*), came into being as the Ladies Memorial Association. Its original purpose was to decorate the graves of fallen soldiers of the "Lost Cause." On 5 March 1895 it became a local chapter of the United Daughters of the Confederacy, which had as its

CONFEDERATE MONUMENT
Unveiled on 26 April 1906 by Miss Mattie
Heard, daughter of Captain Grant D. Heard.
Orator for the occasion was Captain J. M. Pace.
Dr. W. D. Travis was marshal of the parade,
which moved from the Public Square to the
local cemetery, where school children decorated
Confederate graves with flowers.[16]

objective the perpetuation of the ideals and the memory of the men and women of the Confederacy. Mrs. Conyers held state-wide office as recording secretary and treasurer of the Georgia Division.[15]

Dr. Horace J. Bates died of pneumonia at his Monticello Street residence on 27 December 1883. *The Georgia Enterprise* said of the eighty-six year old physician that, "By industry and energy ... he ... died an honored and wealthy man ... " His widow survived until 17 August 1900, at which time she was eulogized as "one of the oldest, purest and best women in Covington ... " [16]

Mrs. Virginia Conyers had lived all these years in her parents' home. Following the death of her mother, by which time she had succeeded her brother Gustavus J. Bates (*24 October 1831–23 January 1891*) as executrix of their father's estate, she sold the property to S. P. Pickett in December 1900. The lot in which the residence was located brought $3000.[17]

Mrs. Conyers spent her last years in Atlanta, in which city she died on 18 October 1920. "Beloved by a host of friends

... throughout the south ... [She] was a woman of unusual grace and culture [and was possessed] of a charming personality ..." Interment was on her parents' plot in Covington City Cemetery.[18]

The long-time home of the Bates family was sold by S. P. Pickett on 28 August 1906 to H. D. Terrell. The price paid for the residence lot and the "Barn lot" between Hendricks and Brown streets was $3395.[19]

Henry Denton Terrell, the purchaser, was born 13 July 1854. Starting in a one-room blacksmith shop at Dixie Crossroads, he invented a cotton scraper and scooter which became universally used in cotton fields. He realized enormous sums from the device and later sold the patent for half a million dollars. He was at one time president of the First National Bank of Covington.[20]

On 21 November 1878 Mr. Terrell married Nannie F. Davis (1857–1922), daughter of Fletcher and Carrie (Webb) Davis. They became the parents of Clarence Davis and Joseph Bain Terrell.[21]

Mr. and Mrs. Henry D. Terrell enlarged the former Bates cottage to such an extent that a stranger would have assumed that it was a completely new house. Only the wide heart-pine flooring and the massive hand-carved beams beneath the original structure remained as visible clues to its history. The Terrell home when completed was a spacious, two-story house with magnificent Doric columns across the front. The fan design above the downstairs front windows pretty accurately dates it to approximately 1910.[22]

The Terrell family lived in their sumptuous home for only a few years before selling it on 3 December 1917 for $8000. They apparently moved to Atlanta then, for Mr. Terrell died at his home in that city on 4 March 1928, six years after the death of his wife. They are buried beside their two sons in Covington City Cemetery.[23]

The new owner of the Bates-Terrell house was Charles

Andrew Sockwell, Newton County farmer and dairy operator. A native of Walton County, where he was born 8 July 1870, Mr. Sockwell was the son of J. W. Sockwell and his first wife, née Lucy Cook. Most of his youth was spent at *Harris Quarters*, the former plantation of John Harris (*see page 164*), which his father began buying piecemeal in 1885. After J. W. Sockwell's marriage to Fannie Hurst on 20 January 1889 the family moved into Covington and lived successively in the former residences of Dr. Henry T. Henry (*see page 196*) and S. C. Rheburgh (*see page 191*).[24]

Charles A. Sockwell was married in 1897 to Jessie Upshaw of Social Circle, who was a cousin of Claude Upshaw and Mrs. W. K. Swann (*see page 99*) of Covington. Their only child, Mary, became the wife of James Fletcher Biggers of Covington.[25]

Mr. Sockwell served as mayor of the city, as chairman of the State Milk Control Board, as a director of the Bank of Covington, and as commander of Knights Templar, and he was a Mason and a Shriner. Upon his death on 21 April 1941 it was said that, "He was noted in the County as a philanthropist, having helped numerous young men obtain a college education ... Covington merchants paid final tribute to Mr. Sockwell by closing their establishments during the funeral hours ... "[26]

Mrs. Sockwell (*26 October 1870–21 August 1959*) was educated at Lucy Cobb Institute and Shorter College. Long active in social, patriotic and religious affairs of the community, she had served as president of the Covington Garden Club and of the local chapter of the United Daughters of the Confederacy, had been regent of the Sergeant Newton Chapter, Daughters of the American Revolution, and was for some years a Sunday school teacher at the First Baptist Church.[27]

Mrs. James Biggers, whose husband had died before either of her parents, continued to live in the family home for nearly a decade after her mother's death. She made several changes which modernized it, and otherwise maintained it beautifully. Finally, on 31 August 1968, she sold the house for "$10 and other valuable considerations" and moved into smaller quarters.[28]

The house was purchased by Lieutenant Colonel William Gasper Borella, USAF (Ret.). A native of Newport, Vermont, he was educated at Norwick University and became a career Air Force officer. Retiring in 1967 after a career which spanned both World War II and the Korean Conflict, he subsequently accepted a position with the Veterans Administration in Atlanta.[29]

BATES - TERRELL HOUSE
Erected for Dr. Horace J. Bates, *circa* 1840, and enlarged in this century by Henry D. Terrell. Now the residence of Colonel and Mrs. William G. Borella.

Colonel Borella and his wife, the former Virginia Giddens of Albany, share their handsome home with their youngest daughter, Sally, who is a high school student. Their other children are Suzann (Mrs. Waddell Hagins, of Albany); Terry (wife of the Reverend David Hamrick, a Baptist pastor at Woodstock); John, who is in the Navy; and Julie and Jean, who are college students.[30]

The pristine condition in which Colonel and Mrs. Borella maintain their home makes it one of the most outstanding houses in Covington. Its gleaming white columns in a setting of evergreens are a beautiful reminder of the Bates, Terrell and Sockwell families who lived on the site so long and who were such an important part of "Old Covington."

XIII
"DIXIE MANOR"

The only ante-bellum two-story brick house standing in Covington today is *Dixie Manor*, which occupies a commanding site near the intersection of Monticello and Church streets. Built at a time when, almost without exception, Covington's wealthy pioneer families were moving into Greek Revival houses, it is distinguished by its classic early English Regency architecture.

The site of the house is a gently rolling eminence which originally was just south of the town's southern boundary. The property once was a part of the dowry of Mrs. Sarah Flanegan. Her husband, Joel Flanegan, was listed as late as 1825 as being a justice of the inferior court of Newton County.[1]

Thomas Jones apparently moved into his fine new house prior to 1840, a year in which deeds to several pieces of property described them as "adjoining the lot whereon Thomas F. Jones now lives."[2]

The house itself must have excited even more admiring comment then than it does today. The brick from which it was constructed have been said variously to have been brought from England and to have been made on the banks of the nearby Yellow River. Whatever their origin, they were used skillfully and plentifully in construction of a house which was unique for its time and place.[3]

Thomas Jones was one of the earliest settlers of Newton County, serving as a juror at the first session of Newton Superior Court on 15 April 1822 and as an original trustee of Newton County Academy. Born in South Carolina on 14 February 1775, he may have been the man by that name who is listed as having moved to Walton County from Hancock

145

County prior to 1830. In 1800 he married Rebecca Powell, also a native South Carolinian, who was born on 5 August 1785.[4]

One of the sons of Thomas and Rebecca Jones was Thomas Franklin Jones, born 2 August 1816. On 4 May 1838 he was appointed first lieutenant of the Newton County Militia; on 22 August 1839 he married Elizabeth Scott; in 1858 he was a trustee of Southern Masonic Female College; in 1859–'60 he represented Newton County in the State Senate; and on 10 May 1866 he was appointed judge of the Calhoun County Superior Court.

While serving in the legislature in 1859 the younger Jones offered resolutions calling for a convention to select delegates to the Democratic National Convention to be held in Charleston. As a member of the former he served on a committee which recommended that Howell Cobb be the party's candidate for President. (The then-Secretary of the Treasury, however, was not at that time popular in secession-minded Georgia because of his "extreme Union views," and he was not nominated.) Another son of Colonel and Mrs. Jones was Major P. B. Jones of Early County, at whose home Mrs. Rebecca Jones died on 11 February 1872.[5]

The handsome Jones residence was sold on 13 August 1861 to Osborn T. Rogers for $5000. The transfer of title included fifty-five acres "together with all . . . the . . . appurtenances thereof . . . " Mr. Rogers subsequently acquired additional acreage adjoining this property, one such transaction on 21 March 1867 involving the purchase of two acres for $400.[6]

Osborn Thorn Rogers was born on 7 November 1824 in Monroe County, son of the Reverend Osborn Rogers and the former Mary Spivey. He spent a part of his youth and early manhood in Oxford, where his father was prominently identified with the Methodist Church and Emory College.* On 21

*Henry Morton Bullock, A History of Emory University (reprint, Atlanta: 1972) p. 141, refers to "Reverend O. Rogers" as one of a group of citizens of Oxford who in 1851 organized themselves into a group for the purpose of circulating religious books and tracts. This must have been Osborn T. Rogers, as his father had died in 1837, yet nowhere else has the present author seen the son referred to as "Reverend."

October 1845 he married Louisa Matilda Neal (*5 January 1825–8 July 1857*), daughter of McCormick and Sarah Ann (Batts) Neal (*see pages 35-36*). Children of this union were Anna Corinne (later Mrs. John B. Davis), Sarah (who became the wife of John L. Chancellor of Mississippi), and Osborn T. Rogers, Jr. (who married Fannie Moore).[7]

The widowed Osborn T. Rogers married as his second wife, on 23 July 1861, Mrs. Mary Jane Stokes. A daughter of Mr. and Mrs. Cary Wood (*see page 18*), she was born in Covington on 27 August 1832. Her first husband, Charles William Young Stokes of Madison, and their infant son had died several years earlier. The children of Osborne Thorn and Mary Jane (Wood) Rogers were Mary (who became the wife of Wilbur Fletcher Haygood, son of Bishop Atticus G. Haygood), Louise (later Mrs. Paul Green of Savannah), and Cary Wood Rogers (who died in Savannah on his twenty-first birthday).[8]

When Osborn T. Rogers, his second wife, and his children moved into their imposing brick home in 1861, the South had already embarked upon its disastrous road to ruin. Covington was caught up in the fever of the Civil War. Local men were fighting on distant battlefields, and as the casualty lists lengthened a somber pall hung over the little town.

Courtesy of Dr. J.R. Sams

OSBORN ROGERS HOME

Young Corinne Rogers later graphically recalled the arrival in Covington of a segment of the United States Army:

> One morning we were startled by a horseback rider as he came dashing through town yelling, "The Yankees are Coming, they are at Conyers." We heard the cannon fire, the windows were rattling ... Just a little time afterward [we could see from the windows of our house facing both Monticello and Church streets] ... a surging mass, wagons, buggies, cows, hogs, folk, women and children in terror, screaming and crying, calling for others. Down the hill they rushed, just back of them the "Blue Coats" in a charge ...
>
> This was Stoneman's Cavalry aiming at the railroad to cut off supplies. But ... Little [General] Joe Wheeler overtook them and captured them [before they could reach their objective].
>
> How happy we were when Wheeler dashed into town. We thought him invincible. We gave him and his staff their supper ...[9]

Just after the alarm was given, Ben Camp, fearing capture, appealed to the Rogers family to hide him. They put him in a dry well in the back yard and covered it with a chicken coop. Benjamin Franklin Camp (1830–1923) was a member of the 16th Georgia Cavalry, and presumably he was at home on leave at the time. It appears that he was a son of Harry and Sarah A. Camp and a nephew of Gerard Camp (see page 217), all of Covington.[10]

Corinne Rogers' narrative continues:

> It was not long [afterward that] Girrard's Cavalry came and burned the bridges over Alcova and Yellow rivers, the depot and the cotton bales. Mr. Camp was still in Covington, sick at the time. He remembered us and came again to be protected. Our house had two roofs on it with a space between. Mama thought of that place, had a ladder put to a ventilator which was on hinges for fire protection, and he was safe again, and for a day or two we fed him at night. He always [thereafter] called me the Good Samaritan ...
>
> We all knew we were in the line of Sherman's march to the sea; so as many as could left town. Father carried us to the plantation, Basbun [sic. Should be Barbour] County, Alabama. We had to go to Augusta and cross the state from there to Eufaula. It was a long hard trip. We went through pouring rain. Streams were all out of

banks. We were expecting the Yankees any where. Baby not expected to live. Father's furlough out, and if questioned [he] would be imprisoned, so it was a horrible nightmare.

We got to the plantation just before Wilson's cavalry came to burn the bridges over the rivers . . .

It was two years before we returned to Georgia. Mr. O. W. Porter's mother occupied our house and cared for what was left after the Yankees ransacked [it,] cutting up the carpets for saddle blankets [and breaking] crockery and furniture . . .[11]

The writer of these vivid passages, Anna Corinne Rogers, was married on 12 March 1872 to John Burckett Davis. Born in Newton County on 5 July 1834, he was educated at Emory College, served as a lieutenant in the CSA, represented Newton County in the General Assembly (1871–'72), and was elected clerk of superior court in 1884. After nearly forty years of distinguished service in the last position, he and Mrs. Davis moved to San Leandro, California. There he died on 10 July 1926, just a few years short of his one hundredth birthday. Mrs. Davis survived until 12 August 1942.[12]

Mrs. Davis' father and step-mother, Osborn T. and Mary Jane (Wood) Rogers, were important figures in the religious, cultural, and social life of post-war Covington. Mr. Rogers served as a trustee of Southern Masonic Female College between 1878 and 1882, and both he and his wife were devout and useful members of the Covington Methodist Church.[13]

In later years a person who knew the Rogers family wrote:

Covington, of the ancien regime, . . . [is] a fine old lady, sitting serenely in her old brocade, with a smile of contentment, viewing unmoved the passing years. . . . [Its] splendid old homes . . . tell the story of the refined and advanced civilization that once obtained there, making it one of the most aristocratic social and political centers of Georgia . . .

The best built and the most architectural [sic] of the many old homes of Covington is the old Rogers mansion . . . This splendid old brick house . . . would be a credit to any city . . . Originally the tract comprised fifty-five acres. A spacious lawn surrounded the house . . . [and] the picturesque old English-looking residence stood

on a noble eminence with its well designed loggia, overlooking the
town. A high open brick wall surrounded the house and garden,
which was laid out in formal flower beds. These beds were surrounded by a boxwood hedge, planted by Mrs. Rogers ... [Now]
neighbors have established themselves to the right and left, but the
fine old house still overlooks the city ... The brick used in its
building are said to have cost $10,000, for all the interior walls are
of solid masonry ...[14]

In the financial straits experienced by nearly all Southerners
in the post-war years, Osborn Rogers found it necessary to
mortgage his house. When he was unable to meet the payments, it was advertised for sale at public outcry. On 1
December 1876 his wife obtained ownership of the property
by submitting the highest bid, $2000.[15]

Less than a decade later the Rogers family moved to Savannah. There Osborn T. Rogers died on 22 January 1896. His
widow survived until 9 May 1920 and was buried beside him
in Laurel Grove Cemetery.[16]

When the Rogers family moved away from Covington they
either rented their beautiful house or, more likely, let one of
the Rogers children live there — probably Corinne and her husband, John B. Davis. Finally, in January 1892, Mrs. Rogers
sold the house to A. N. Hays for $2500.[17]

Mr. Hays lost no time in disposing of his purchase at a
handsome profit. On 5 January 1892 he conveyed title to
Clark Banking Co. for $3000. Two years later, on 15 January
1894, the bank sold the house and one and one-quarter acres
of land to Charles Franklin Adams for $1500.[18]

Three years later *The Covington Star* reported:

> We regret to state that Mr. Charlie Adams, who has been ill
> during most of the past summer, is still very low, and not expected
> to live many days.[19]

He apprently died soon thereafter, for his will was offered
for probate on 6 December 1897. This document provides that
his estate should contribute equally with his brothers and
sisters to the maintenance and support of their mother; that

his twin sisters Ella and Emma Adams were to receive $100 each; and that a like sum should be paid to Captain and Mrs. R. E. Wright "for care and expense of my son, Charles Wright Adams, while he was with them." The testator left to "my only son" the balance of his estate, which included a farm and "my house and lot in Covington." Mr. Adams, who was born in 1866, was buried in his family's cemetery on Dixie Road east of Covington.[20]

The will indicates that Mr. Adams was a widower, and his son's middle name and the bequest to Captain and Mrs. Wright suggests that the boy was the Wrights' grandson. He was reared by relatives in Alabama, but after completing his education he returned to Covington as a handsome and well-to-do bachelor. He lived on the farm which he had inherited from his father (now the home of Mrs. Otis Nixon). After many years as a dashing man-about-town he married Ruth Thornton of Jackson. The couple had two children before their marriage was terminated by divorce. Subsequently Mr. Adams moved to Florida, where he died.[21]

In 1901 D. J. Adams, guardian of Charles Wright Adams, petitioned Newton Superior Court for permission to sell the house which the boy had inherited from his father, as it "is a large two story brick structure and expensive to keep up and brings only $150 per annum rent..." John F. Henderson, nephew of Mrs. Mary Jane Rogers, testified that he was acquainted with the house "and that $2000 is a good price for it." Accordingly, on 26 October, Judge John S. Candler directed that the house be sold for not less than $1000 and that the proceeds be invested in the old Purington place,* a farm of two hundred and sixty acres.[22]

*The Purington farm on the west bank of the Alcovy River had belonged to the late Mrs. Cynthia A. Purington (1812–1897), who apparently inherited it from her first husband, William P. Berry. Her second husband was William B. Wright and her third was Elder Joseph L. Purington. Mrs. Purington, who spent her last years in a house on Monticello Street, was a daughter of Elder Joel Colley (see page 7).

On 1 January 1902 the house was sold to Mrs. Corrie C. Wright for $2000. The deed identified the property as "That tract or parcel of land ... Containing one and one quarter acres ... and having thereon a brick dwelling house, and known as the Rogers dwelling house ... and being the same property bought by A. N. Hays from Mrs. M. J. Rogers ... " [23]

The new owner was a native of Covington, being a daughter of George T. Carr (1829–1903) and the former Alethia A. Wilson (1833–1925). Her father was a son of pioneer citizen John Pace Carr (see page 102) and his first wife, ne'e Martha Turner, and her mother was a daughter of Elias Wilson and the second of his four wives, Temperance Saxon. George T. Carr had served briefly with the "Newton Anderson Guards" at the beginning of the Civil War, but soon after that unit became Company E of the 53rd Regiment of Georgia Volunteer Infantry he paid a substitute to take his place and returned home.[24]

The George T. Carr residence occupied an extensive tract on Railroad (now Emory) Street and was for many years one of Covington's most distinctive houses. Here Mr. and Mrs. Carr reared their children: Clara (1855–1886), who became Mrs. C. Y. Henderson; James Wilson (9 November 1861–8 November 1927), J. Carlton (1865–1890), and Corrie. Subsequently the Carr residence became the home of Mr. and Mrs. Sam Thompson, who added a more impressive facade to the house, and later was occupied by their daughter and son-in-law Mr. and Mrs. Count Gibson. In its last years it was the home of A. Belmont Dennis, editor of The Covington News, and Mrs. Dennis. Subsequent to Mr. Dennis' death in 1961 it was demolished to make way for a chain grocery store and a parking lot.[25]

It was said that during the Civil War one of the Carr family's house slaves, a girl named Liza, alerted Covington to the impending arrival of Federal forces by rushing into town screaming, "The Yankees are coming!" A wounded Confederate soldier appealed to the family for help in avoiding capture. He was covered with an old linen duster, concealed in a chimney, and a screen was placed in front of the fireplace. He emerged only after the troops had departed.[26]

The intersection of Railroad and Usher streets was known as "Carr's Corner," and it was here that a local man lost his life in the Civil War. The incident is said to have occurred when one Presley Jones, after declaring that Sherman's army would enter Covington only over his dead body, shot one of the two mounted men who arrived ahead of the main force. The other rider immediately shot the would-be hero and he died a few minutes later.[27] (For a slightly different version of this incident, see page 82).

Several years after Mr. and Mrs. George T. Carr moved to Atlanta their daughter Corrie was married to Dr. Joseph Allen Wright of Covington. The ceremony was performed at the Spring Street residence of the bride's parents on 24 January 1900. Upon their return to Covington the bridal couple was honored at a brilliant reception.[28]

Dr. Wright (1853–1933) was a prominent physician, and he also owned a drugstore at the southwest corner of Clark Street and the Public Square. This emporium had Covington's first — and for many years only — soda fountain. The drugstore was operated by Dr. Wright's brother Tom.[29]

"Miss Corrie," as Mrs. Wright was affectionately called by many Covingtonians, died in 1945 at the age of eighty. She bequeathed her home, which she had named Dixie Manor, to her long-time physician, Dr. J. R. Sams, as an expression of appreciation for "his kind service." The property surrounding the house had been decreased when Mrs. Wright sold a strip along Monticello Street to Guy Robinson, a local pharmacist, who subsequently erected upon it a one-story brick house. After providing certain other bequests, Mrs. Wright's will directed that the residue of her estate be turned over to trustees of the local Methodist church for the purpose of building a Sunday School annex or other appropriate memorial to her son Wilson Carr Wright (*1904–1918*).[30]

Dr. J. Roscoe Sams, the principal individual beneficiary of Mrs. Wright's generosity, was born in nearby Newborn on 30 May 1889. His father, Marion Sams, had left his native Beaufort, South Carolina, in disgust after the Civil War when the family's beautiful home had been lost because the only medium of exchange acceptable to "Carpetbag" officials for payment of taxes was gold — something which few southerners had in any quantity.[31]

Young Roscoe Sams was graduated by the University of Georgia Medical School and later served in France during World War I as a captain in the Medical Corps, 77th Infantry Division. Dr. Sams established his medical practice in Covington after being released from military service, and soon thereafter was married to Miss Clara Pharr of Dacula.[32]

When Dr. Sams inherited *Dixie Manor*, he and Mrs. Sams moved there from the attractive two-story brick house* which had been built for them on a portion of the Church Street lot formerly occupied by the ante-bellum cottage of Mrs. Virginia Beach Camp (*see page 35*). The only structural changes they made in the former Rogers mansion were to use a portion of the huge bedrooms to add closets and to glass-enclose the downstairs back porch. With care and talent Mrs. Sams assembled handsome furnishings appropriate to the period and style of the beautiful house. Her success may be measured by a newspaper story at the time of Covington's first Tour of Homes in 1948, which said in part:

> One of the most magnificent homes on the tour is that of Dr. and Mrs. J. R. Sams, *Dixie Manor*. It has just been re-decorated, but the spirit of its over 100 years of existence has been preserved. It is a large place, furnished with quiet and charming elegance. The green-and-white scenic wallpaper in the hall, the delicate gold-leaf molding and Chinese hand-painted paper in the dining room, the deep turquoise walls and shelves in the library, the kitchen with its

*Now the residence of Mr. and Mrs. James Hutchins.

large fireplace and quaint Dutch tiles of blue . . . the secret stairway from a closet downstairs to a bedroom above . . . the original
mahogany staircase . . . all make this house outstanding. The garden
once was noted for its rare plants from all over the world — and the
last word in refinement, in the days when this house was new, was
to have the outhouse to match. The house is of mellow red brick,
and it still has, far down the garden, its brick outhouse—probably
the quaintest relic on the whole tour . . .[33]

DIXIE MANOR

The handsome English Regency residence of Dr. J. R. Sams has been a Covington
landmark for nearly a century and a half.

Dr. Sams, long beloved as a good man and a kindly physician, was honored on his eightieth birthday, 30 May 1969, when Mayor Walker Harris proclaimed "Dr. J. R. Sams Day." Hundreds of friends and patients crowded the Public Square to honor one of Covington's most distinguished citizens. After a program of band music, Mrs. Jerry Bray, president of the Covington Service Guild, presented Dr. Sams a key to the city. Later he was presented a plaque and a birthday cake by the Kiwanis Club, of which he is a charter member.[34]

Dr. Sams lived alone for several years following the death of Mrs. Sams on 27 January 1970. In that period he sold many of the handsome furnishings in his home to such persons as Mrs. N. S. Turner (*see page 170*) and Mrs. P. W. Pratt, Sr. (*see page 228*). In the summer of 1972 he welcomed to his home his grandson James Anderson and Mrs. Anderson, who moved to Covington to teach in the local public school system.[35]

James Roscoe Anderson is the son of Dr. Sams' only child, Clara Newton Sams (now Mrs. Lewis E. Thompson of Indianapolis), and Dr. Horace Anderson of Jacksonville. He received the AB degree from Florida State University and the MA from the University of Southwestern Louisiana. His wife is the former Martha K. Blue of Gulfport, Mississippi.[36]

Once again there is youth and laughter in the high-ceilinged rooms of *Dixie Manor*. Regal with the dignity of gracious old age, it looks down benignly upon the city which has grown up around it. One suspects that Thomas F. Jones, the Osborn Rogers', and "Miss Corrie" would be happy to know that the home they once treasured is still loved by its occupants and admired by those who view it across a rolling green lawn.

XIV
"WHITEHALL"

Covington's most monumentally imposing house is a Greek Revival mansion fronting upon Franklin Wright Park and located almost opposite the Episcopal Church of The Good Shepherd.

The property on which it is situated was once a part of the Henry County holdings of Mrs. Sarah Flanegan, who had received as a dowry from the estate of her husband, Joel Flanegan, extensive tracts of land in the Ninth District of Henry (later Newton) County.

Over a period of several years Mrs. Flanegan gradually disposed of her holdings, one of the first such transactions being the sale of nearly four acres to McCormick Neal in 1829. Eight years later, on 10 February 1837, she sold a sizeable tract to one David Dickson. He, in turn, sold much of this property on 18 January 1840 for a consideration of $800. His deed to John Harris describes the property as follows:

> a certain parcel of land ... on the road leading from Covington to Monticello a little south east of the dwelling house where Mrs. Bankston now lives thence running west along the line of a Small parcel of land Sandford Welburn purchased of Sarah Flanegan also along Conyers' line to the South west corner of the big field formerly owned by Mrs. Flanegan a little south west of where John Eubanks now lives thence north along the said field to Dr. H. J. Bates's line thence east along Bates's line to his corner to the said Monticello road and near where Thos. Davis now lives, thence along said road nearly south to the beginning corner, including the houses [sic] where Mrs. Bankston now lives containing twenty-four acres...[1]

At the time of this transaction "the road from Covington to Monticello" was what is known today as Church Street.

The present Monticello Street ended at what is now South Street, where the former Flanegan holdings began. Thus the Bankston and Bates houses mentioned in the deed were situated upon tracts whose frontage included all or most of the triangular block now graced at its extremities by the Methodist and Episcopal churches.[2]

The property purchased by John Harris had upon it, as noted, a house in which lived a Mrs. Bankston. Probably she continued to live in her little house, although it is possible that it was either incorporated into the large house which was soon built for Mr. Harris or that he occupied it while construction was underway. Considering the scale of the new structure, the probability given here seems reasonable.

John Harris, who had lived for some years two blocks north of his new property (see page 68), achieved prominence and wealth on a scale which few men have equalled in the century since his death.

He was born in Pennsylvania on 1 December 1803. A reconstruction of several unconnected pieces of information suggests that he was a son of Revolutionary Soldier John Harris (1763–1824) and that he was reared in Warren County.[3]

It is a matter of record that on 8 December 1832 twenty-nine year-old John Harris married fifteen-year-old Susan Ann Henderson. The bride was a daughter of Isaac Purnell Henderson and his first wife, the former Sarah Bridges of Oglethorpe County. Her father, who was born in Snow Hill, Maryland, on 11 March 1789, moved to Newton County as a young man and became one of its most influential citizens. In the session of 1837 he represented Newton County in the General Assembly. He rendered equally distinguished service as mayor of Covington before his death on 7 December 1864. By his second marriage, to Mrs. Ruth Shepherd Johnson, Isaac P. Henderson's children included Confederate General Robert J. Henderson and Georgia Commissioner of Agriculture John T. Henderson.[4]

John Harris was a public-spirited man who served his adopted town and county whenever asked to do so. He represented Newton County in the General Assembly from the session of 1835 through the session of 1839. In the last year of his two-year term as senator from the 27th District he served as president *pro tempore* at the extra session of that body. He was a member of the board of trustees of Southern Female College when it was chartered in 1851 and remained a trustee until his death. Long active in the Masonic Order, he became Grand Master of the Grand Lodge of Georgia in 1865. Somewhere along the way he acquired the title of "Judge," probably through service as a judge of the Inferior Court of Newton County.[5]

The house which was built for Mr. and Mrs. Harris was typical of the columned two-story frame houses erected during Georgia's Greek Revival period. It had Doric columns across the front and unusually large rooms within.[6]

Here the Harris children were born into the pleasant world of the privileged ante-bellum planter class. These were Susan, Sarah (later Mrs. J. A. B. Anderson), Aerie (later Mrs. Jacob A. Henry), Dora, Joseph, Isaac, William, Jack N., and John P. Harris, Jr.[7]

Several of Judge Harris' children preceded their father in death. His will refers to his deceased son William; to his daughters Aerie, Sallie, and Susan; and to his sons John P., Jack, and Isaac P. Harris. "For good and sufficient reasons, well known to all my children," this document states, "I bequeath no part of my estate to my son Isaac P. Harris. To his wife Susan P. Harris I give Five hundred dollars." [8]

John P. Harris, Jr. (*14 February 1836–25 October 1900*), whom the U.S. Census for 1860 identified as a twenty-five-year-old merchant, served in the Civil War as quartermaster sergeant with the "Newton Anderson Guards" (Company E., 53rd Regiment, Georgia Volunteer Infantry). Later he studied law and entered into a partnership with Ellijay F. Edwards. His home was located on Railroad (now Emory) Street.[9]

The younger Harris was much-married, his wives being (1) Susan E. Slack, whom he wed 4 June 1861; (2) Lucy Catharine Anderson* (*21 March 1842—26 October 1869*), whom he married 29 October 1865; (3) Elizabeth A. Groves (*1 August 1840—10 June 1885*), who became his wife 14 June 1871; and (4) Mrs. Louise F. Jones, whom he wed 15 December 1885. [10]

In his will John P. Harris, Jr., directed that he be buried beside his former wife Bettie A. Harris and that not one cent was to go to Louise F. Harris, the testator "having finally and forever separated from her." The will then provides that Harris' estate be used "for supporting, educating and raising a boy child born [4 September 1891] of one colored woman Lisor Morris, to be named William . . ." A codicil two years later makes the same provision for "one other boy born of said Lisor Morris named James [born] Feby. '93." [11]

In addition to his handsome house in Covington, Judge John Harris owned an extensive plantation at the intersection of the Madison and Sand Town (now Newborn) roads east of Covington. Here on 18 November 1864 Federal Troops led by Major General J. C. Davis, commander of the 14th Corps, encamped for the night. They were in the company of Major General W. T. Sherman, commander of the Military Division of Mississippi, who was en route to a rendezvous with the 20th Corps at Milledgeville and thence to Savannah. [12]

In his *Memoirs* General Sherman wrote:

> I walked up to a plantation-house close by, where were assembled many negroes, among them an old, gray-haired man, of as fine a head as I ever saw. I asked him if he understood about the war and its progress. He said he did; that he . . . supposed that slavery was the cause, and that our success was to be his freedom . . . I then explained to him that we wanted the slaves to remain where they were, and not to load us down with useless mouths, which would eat up the food needed for our fighting-men; but that, if they followed us in swarms of old and young, feeble and

*Lucy Catharine Anderson was a daughter of Joseph S. Anderson (*see page 186*).

helpless, it would simply load us down and cripple us in our great task. . . . It was at this very plantation that a soldier passed me with a ham on his musket, a jug of sorghum-molasses under his arm, and a big piece of honey in his hand, from which he was eating, and, catching my eye, he remarked *sotto voce* and carelessly to a comrade, "Forage liberally on the country," quoting from my general orders.* On this occasion, as on many others that fell under my personal observation, I reproved the man, explained that foraging must be limited to the regular parties properly detailed, and that all provisions thus obtained must be delivered to the regular commissaries, to be fairly distributed to the men who kept their ranks. . ." [13]

Brevet Major George Nichols, Sherman's aide-de-camp, later recalled:

> Near Covington there was a certain large plantation . . . A jollier set of negroes I never saw than these when the blue coats came along. Horrible stories of our cruelty to the negroes were told by their masters to frighten them, but the negroes never put faith in one word. I asked the head man: "Well, how do you like the Yankees?"
>
> "Like him? Bully! bully! bully! I'se wanted to see 'em long time . . . I tinks, and we'se all tinks, dat you'se down here in our interests."
>
> In other parts of the South the negroes I have seen seem to understand there is a man named Lincoln, who had the power to free them, and had exercised it. In this neighborhood there is a stratum of ignorance upon that subject. All knowledge of that

---

* Sherman's Special Field Order No. 120, issued at Kingston, Georgia, on 9 November had specified that

"The army will forage liberally on the country . . . [E]ach brigade commander will organize a good and sufficient foraging party, under the command of one or more discreet officers, who will gather, near the route traveled, corn or forage of any kind, meat of any kind, vegetables, cornmeal, or whatever is needed by the command, aiming at all times to keep in the wagons at least ten days' provisions for his command, and three days' forage. Soldiers must not enter the dwellings of the inhabitants, or commit any trespass; but, during a halt or camp, they may be permitted to gather turnips, potatoes, and other vegetables, and to drive in stock in sight of their camp . . .

"As for horses, mules, wagons, etc., belonging to the inhabitants, the cavalry and artillery may appropriate freely and without limit; discriminating, however, between the rich, who are usually hostile, and the poor and industrious, usually neutral or friendly. Foraging-parties may also take mules or horses, to replace the jaded animals of their trains, or to serve as pack-mules for the regiments or brigades. In all foraging, of whatever kind, the parties engaged will refrain from abusive or threatening language, and may . . . give written certificates of the facts . . . and they will endeavor to leave with each family a reasonable portion for their maintenance . . ." [14]

nature has not only been kept from the blacks, but only a few of the whites are well informed. The lieutenant commanding the escort of General Sherman was born and has always lived in Milledgeville, is [sic] an officer of the first Alabama cavalry regiment, and tells me that he never saw a copy of the *New York Tribune* until he joined our army ... His adherence to the Union grew out of his natural abhorrence of slavery, whose horrors he had witnessed since childhood. His name is Snelling — a young man of good education, of high intelligence, simple-hearted, and brave ...

Pointing to the Atlanta and Augusta Railroad, which had been destroyed, the question was asked, "It took a longer time to build this railroad than it does to destroy it?"

"I would think it did, massa; in dat ar woods over dar is buried ever so many black men who were killed, sar, yes, killed, a workin' on dat road — whipped to death. I seed 'em sar."

"Does the man live here who beat them?"

"Oh, no, sar, he's dun gone long time" ... [15]

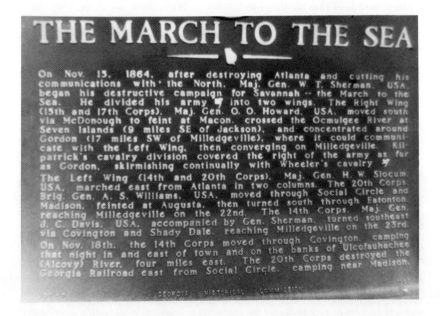

THE MARCH TO THE SEA

On Nov. 15, 1864, after destroying Atlanta and cutting his communications with the North, Maj. Gen. W. T. Sherman, USA, began his destructive campaign for Savannah -- the March to the Sea. He divided his army into two wings. The Right Wing (15th and 17th Corps), Maj. Gen. O. O. Howard, USA, moved south via McDonough to feint at Macon, crossed the Ocmulgee River at Seven Islands (9 miles SE of Jackson), and concentrated around Gordon (17 miles SW of Milledgeville), where it could communicate with the Left Wing, then converging on Milledgeville. Kilpatrick's cavalry division covered the right of the army as far as Gordon, skirmishing continually with Wheeler's cavalry.

The Left Wing (14th and 20th Corps), Maj. Gen. H. W. Slocum, USA, marched east from Atlanta in two columns. The 20th Corps, Brig. Gen. A. S. Williams, USA, moved through Social Circle and Madison, feinted at Augusta, then turned south through Eatonton, reaching Milledgeville on the 22nd. The 14th Corps, Maj. Gen. J. C. Davis, USA, accompanied by Gen. Sherman, turned southeast via Covington and Shady Dale, reaching Milledgeville on the 23rd.

On Nov. 18th, the 14th Corps moved through Covington, camping that night in and east of town and on the banks of Ulcofauhachee (Alcovy) River, four miles east. The 20th Corps destroyed the Georgia Railroad east from Social Circle, camping near Madison.

GEORGIA HISTORICAL COMMISSION

Another of General Sherman's staff officers, Assistant Adjutant General Major Henry Hitchcock, also recorded in his diary the stories related to him of the brutal treatment accorded the railroad workers. This additional entry is from his diary:

> Stopped for the day at the farm of Judge Harris ... He and family reside in the town: has only his "quarters" on the farm: is a "heavy man" [*i.e.*, one of influence] ... has quite a farm, and said to have sixty or more slaves. Number of log and frame buildings on farm — chief, a large double-log cabin with hall ... Plenty of forage, poultry, hogs, etc....
>
> Judge Harris is a prominent man hereabouts. Nichols had a long talk with his negro driver and came back full of indignation. The women say that their master, though an elderly man, and with a family, obliges them to submit to him, and straps them if they refuse... [16]

The termination of hostilities and the unequivocal defeat of the Confederacy brought an end to the horrors of slavery and also to the gracious way of life which it had made possible for a small segment of southerners. The aftermath of the Civil War was in some ways almost as harsh as had been the struggle itself. Free Negroes oftentimes refused to work, believing in their ignorance that President Lincoln or General Sherman would provide for them. In agrarian areas such as Newton County this meant that there were no "hands" to work the fields, which resulted in a continuation of a shortage of food supplies. All segments of society were affected, and families which formerly had been wealthy now found themselves in straitened circumstances.

Judge John Harris survived the great sectional conflict by twelve years, dying on 6 June 1878 at the age of seventy-four years. He was buried in the new Covington City Cemetery beside his wife (*8 May 1817–7 March 1866*).[17]

A few months later Judge Harris' town house was bought from his estate by Jack N. Harris and his sisters Aerie, Susan and Dora. On 3 January 1881 they sold it to William J.

Metcalf for $2950. A 250-acre portion of the more-than one thousand-acre plantation east of Covington was sold on 26 December 1884 to J. W. Sockwell (*see page 142*) for $2000. The latter, together with an adjoining 60 acres, had been purchased by Judge Harris in 1857 for $3000. The depreciated value thirty-one years later provides a telling insight into economic conditions prevailing at the time.[18]

Mr. Metcalf, the man who bought the Harris family home in Covington, is said to have come to Covington to marry Miss Frances Usher (*see page 126*) on 12 December 1876 and to have tarried year after year in a vain attempt to persuade her to go with him to a distant state.[19]

Mr. and Mrs. Metcalf undoubtedly brought renewed gaiety to their lovely home. And presumably they could live together happily — so long as they did not leave Covington. As evidence of Mr. Metcalf's devotion to his wife, an old deed records that on 17 February 1879 he purchased from his brother-in-law, Robert O. Usher, 273 acres of land in the 10th District of what had formerly been Henry County, and that on 10 August 1882 he deeded the property to his wife for $500 "and the natural love and affection which he has and bears to his said wife." [20]

The young husband appears to have recognized eventually that he would never dislodge his wife from her niche in her family and among her lifelong friends. Accordingly, on 23 September 1885, by which time he was living in Izard County, Arkansas, William J. Metcalf sold his Covington house to Franklin Wright. The price was only $1,000, and it procured for the purchaser not only the house itself but also thirteen acres surrounding it.[21]

Robert Franklin Wright was born in Putnam County on 12 December 1821 and was educated at Mercer University. He married, 21 December 1857, Salina Frances Robinson, who was born in Jasper County on 16 June 1831. The couple lived briefly in Newborn and many years in Oxford before taking up residence in their columned Covington house. Mr. Wright owned and operated a large plantation in the Leguinn District of Newton County.[22]

The Wrights maintained their home beautifully, as well as enhancing its appearance. Where formerly there had been only a half-moon carriage drive in front of the house, Mrs. Wright added a white sand walk from the front steps to the street and bordered it with boxwood. A beautiful boxwood-bordered rose garden was created at the rear of the house. The couple named the place *The Cedars* because of the large number of trees of that species which formed a bower for their home.[23]

Mr. Wright presented to the City of Covington the triangular plot of ground in front of his house which had been created

Courtesy of Miss Marjorie Weldon, Atlanta

THE CEDARS, home of Mr. and Mrs. Franklin Wright, *circa* 1900. The lady in white is Mrs. Frank Weldon of Atlanta, whose marriage was brilliantly solemnized here in 1894. Seated are her brothers Boykin Wright of Augusta and Robert F. Wright of Elberton.

some time earlier when Monticello Street was extended so as to merge with Church Street. The appreciative City Fathers named it Franklin Wright Park in honor of the donor.[24]

The Wrights were known far and wide for their lavish hospitality, and the house which they bought from the Harris heirs was the scene of numerous gala social affairs. Many prominent persons were entertained under its hospitable roof, especially during the annual commencement at Emory College.[25]

Two favorite and frequent guests were President Warren A. Candler of Emory and the noted evangelist Sam Jones. On one occasion the latter teasingly asked Mrs. Wright, who was noted for never saying anything unkind about anyone, what she had to say about the Devil. The gracious lady promptly replied, "Well, you must admit he is never idle." [26]

On 17 October 1894 the Wrights' home was the scene of a brilliant event which attracted state-wide interest. That was the wedding of Miss Jeannie Wright, younger daughter of the family, and Frank W. Weldon. The bridegroom, a native of Cecilton, Maryland, and a graduate of St. Johns' College, was night editor of *The Atlanta Constitution*.[27]

The ceremony was performed by Dr. Isaac Stiles Hopkins, president of Georgia School of Technology and a former president of Emory College. A contemporary newspaper account of the rites said in part:

> The marriage occurred . . . at the home of the bride's parents, "The Cedars" . . . a splendid, typical southern home, and the arrangement of the handsome rooms made the ceremony faultless in every detail. The parlor was beautifully arranged with flowers innumerable . . .
>
> When the bridal party was entering the parlor and about to advance to the proper place, ribbons were held by little Misses Madge Wright and Constantine Chesnut and Bessie Wood and Master Frank Wright. The ushers, Mr. Boykin Smith and [Mr.] Julian Harris, walked at the head of the bridal party and stood on either side of the bank of flowers where Dr. Hopkins stood to perform the ceremony . . .

Other attendants were Mr. Ransom Crawford, best man —
Miss Florence Childs; Miss Nellie Womack — Mr. Alfred Newell:
Miss Florence Henderson — Mr. Robert L. Adamson; Miss Kate
Bigham — Mr. W. H. Taylor.[28]

When the young couple returned from a wedding trip to
Chicago, Niagara Falls, New York, and Washington, they made
their home in Atlanta for the remainder of their lives. Mr.
Weldon became nationally known as a newspaperman and
numbered among his friends President Theodore Roosevelt,
actress Lily Langtry, writer Joel Chandler Harris, and poet
Frank L. Stanton.[29]

Mr. and Mrs. Franklin Wright's other children were Boykin
Robinson Wright, an attorney in Augusta who served in the
General Assembly (1905–'08) and as Attorney General of
Georgia (1902); James Columbus Wright, who died as a young
man; Margaret Adelaide Wright, who became the wife of J. C.
Benjamin Chestnut of Wilmington, North Carolina and Savan-
nah; and Robert Franklin Wright, Jr. The last-named son was
Assistant Commissioner of Agriculture for seventeen years and
was co-editor of *Georgia: Historial and Industrial* (1901). He
married Janie Martin Tate, and their son Tate Wright of
Athens married Virginia Cook, who was a granddaughter of
Covington's Civil War hero Major William D. Conyers, Jr., and
a great-granddaughter of prominent pioneer doctors H. J. Bates
and W. D. Conyers (*see page 137*).[30]

Mr. and Mrs. Franklin Wright both lived to enjoy a
venerable old age, she dying on 21 February 1905 at the age
of seventy-three and he surviving until 18 December 1919, six
days past his ninety-eighth birthday. They had spent their last
years in the homes of their sons and daughters, but both were
buried in Covington.[31]

The Harris-Metcalf-Wright house was sold on 12 August
1903 to N. S. Turner for $6500. The substantial increase over
the price which Mr. Wright had paid for it in 1885 was
due both to improved economic conditions and to the rich

ornamentation with which the Wrights had embellished the interior of the house.[32]

Nathaniel Snead Turner, the new owner, was born on a farm near Gaffney, South Carolina, on 10 September 1863. His rise from the modest circumstances of his youth in the grim years following the Civil War had been remarkable. After living in Milledgeville several years, he had come to Covington in 1894 and become a cotton broker. Around the turn of the century his expertise in this field attracted the attention of T. C. Swann, who was planning a new corporation to succeed and expand his partnership with O. S. Porter in a small textile mill. The result of the efforts of Mr. Swann and such other local capitalists as Mr. Porter, John F. Henderson, and W. C. Clark resulted in the incorporation of Covington Mills in 1900. Mr. Turner was given a small number of shares in the business as a part of his agreement with Mr. Swann.[33]

Mr. Swann died in 1906, shortly after announcing that the mills had expanded and that the number of workers had been increased to 250. He was succeeded as president by Mr. Turner, under whose leadership the enterprise continued to grow and flourish. By the time the corporation was sold in 1955 (and shortly thereafter closed), it had grown from the original 5,000 spindles to 30,000 and its employees had increased to 400.[34]

In his capacity as president of Covington Mills Mr. Turner was known for his generosity to practically every worthy cause in the community. At his death on 8 November 1931 he was eulogized as Covington's "richest and most influential citizen." His will contained only one bequest, leaving his entire estate to be divided equally among his widow and his four children.[35]

Mr. Turner married (1) Miss Louly Trippe of Milledgeville and (2) her sister Miss Julia Trippe. His children, all born of the first marriage, were Natalie (the late Mrs. E. B. Rogers), Florence (Mrs. Robert O. Arnold), Louly (Mrs. Robert R. Fowler. See page 88), and Nathaniel S. Turner, Jr.[36]

The marriage of Florence Turner to Robert O. Arnold of Athens, later of Covington, was a brilliant event at her father's home on 20 March 1930. *The Covington News'* rhapsodic account of the wedding said in part:

> Decorations of green and white were used down the long stairway ... [and] along the bannisters were fastened shepherd's crooks showered with flowers and tied with tulle. An isle [*sic*] was formed of small pedostals [*sic*] entwined with smilax from the stairway through the hall leading to an improvised altar of palms and easter lilies with candlebras [*sic*] placed on either side with long burning tapers ...

The bride was gowned in eggshell satin, wore a veil of imported lace attached with orange blossoms, and carried a bouquet of orchids and valley lilies. She was given in marriage by her brother, her sister Louly served as maid of honor, and best man was David Arnold of Hampton.

Bridesmaids were Miss Eugenia Arnold of Athens and Miss Ora Upshaw, Mrs. Thomas C. Swann, and Mrs. E. B. Rogers, all of Covington. They wore long pink chiffon dresses and

R.O. ARNOLD HOME
A relatively new house which captures the charm of Old Covington.

pink hats, and carried bouquets of pink roses showered with forget-me-nots. Ushers were Messrs. E. B. Rogers, Thomas C. Swann, Harry Arnold of Monroe, and M. L. Manne of Athens.[37]

During the twenty-eight years in which N. S. Turner lived in the former Harris-Metcalf-Wright house he transformed it from a lovely Greek Revival home into a monumentally imposing residence whose proportions dwarfed every other ante-bellum residence in Covington. He extended the Doric colonnade across the north side, added a balcony over the front door, raised the roof line to accommodate a third floor with dormer windows, and ornamented the crest of the roof with a captain's walk. Inside, he added a sun parlor, enlarged the already-imposing dining room by the addition of a bay window, and changed the bannisters and newel posts on the stairway between the first and second floors.[38]

While structural changes were made by Mr. Turner, it was his daughter-in-law, Mrs. N. S. Turner, Jr., who made the house a showcase for a choice collection of fine old furniture, oriental rugs, beautiful porcelains, and crystal chandeliers which she collected with the skill of a connoisseur.[39]

Mrs. Turner, the former Martha Burney of Waynesboro, moved into the house following the death of her husband's step-mother in 1950. The younger woman, a glamorous blue-eyed blonde, was educated at Shorter College. She served as president of the Garden Club of Georgia in 1959–1960. Her husband, who was educated at Georgia Tech and later worked for Covington Mills, served three terms as mayor of Covington (1960–'66). The Turner children are Sarah, Frank (who currently serves as city manager), and Nat S. Turner, 3rd, of Gainesville.[40]

In addition to their handsome town house, the Turners have a rustic cabin a couple of miles away where they spend weekends and a part of every summer. This sylvan retreat of 222 acres was acquired from Covington Mills on 1 November 1955 for "Ten Dollars and other valuable consideration." [41]

The present owners of Judge John Harris' former residence have changed the name from *The Cedars*, as it was called during the time it was owned by the Franklin Wrights, to *Whitehall*. Here the Turners have entertained frequently at small informal gatherings and at larger, more elegant parties.

One of the loveliest affairs held in the handsome home in recent years was the wedding of the Turners' only daughter, Sarah Burney Turner, to Lieutenant Leroy Hampton Simkins, Jr., of Augusta, on 28 July 1956. The young couple spoke their vows in the drawing room before an altar of six white pedestals in staggered heights entwined with smilax and holding seven-branch candelabra. The stairway which the bride descended was festooned with swags of smilax caught at intervals with arrangements of pink carnations. Outside, the boxwood-bordered front walk was lined with hurricane lamps holding white candles.[42]

WHITEHALL
Residence of Mr. and Mrs. N. S. Turner.

Today *Whitehall* holds memories of weddings, gala parties, distinguished guests and prominent owners who have enjoyed its dignity and spaciousness for one hundred and thirty years. It is an impressive reminder to Covingtonians of today of the rich heritage which they have in the city's many beautiful old houses which are preserved and still enjoyed.

XV

HOME OF "THE HONEST MAN"

One of the lovely ante-bellum houses for which Covington is noted is a classic Greek Revival structure on Church Street which faces Franklin Wright Park.

It was built, probably in the 1850s, for William C. Campbell, who may have been a son of Charles E. T. W. Campbell (*see page 111*). The original owner sold the property on 25 July 1857, the deed stating that for $2700 he transferred title to Lot Number 15 in Square C "with improvements," together with a lot to the south of that property and two hundred acres of farm land.[1]

The purchaser was Solomon DeWald, a rich Hebrew gentleman who had moved to Covington "from up North." In 1858 he purchased extensive tracts of land between the Covington-Monticello road and Dried Indian Creek and on what is now the north side of Georgia Highway 278 east of Pace Street. Almost nothing is known about Mr. DeWald or his family except that during the harsh days of Reconstruction he was the only resident who voluntarily sacrificed his home in an effort to raise money to pay his creditors. This selfless and unusual act caused him thereafter to be referred to as "The Honest Man." He is said to have lived in Atlanta after leaving Covington, but a local newspaper in 1889 recorded the death of his wife at Rutledge.[2]

On 11 January 1870 Solomon DeWald sold his home and two acres of land to Robert R. Wood for $2000.[3]

Robert Richardson Wood (*3 September 1834–1 May 1903*) was a son of Covington's first settler, Cary Wood (*see pages 3, 16*). He was born, reared and educated in the town; perhaps, like so many other youths, he also attended Emory

College. On 10 May 1855 he was united in marriage to Martha Jacqueline Bates (*26 September 1833–29 December 1898*), daughter of Dr. Horace J. Bates *(see pages 136-137).* Their children were Cary, 2nd, who lived and died in Bluffdale, Texas; Alice Irene, who died at the age of nineteen; and Robert R. Wood, Jr., who married Jane Elizabeth Boyd of Atlanta, in which city he spent most of his adult life.[4]

In the great sectional conflict which plunged a divided nation into chaos between 1861 and 1865, Robert R. Wood performed patriotic duty with the Confederate States Army. He was commissioned as acting quartermaster on 20 August 1862 and appointed major and quartermaster on 21 November 1862. In the wake of Federal forces marching through his home town, he was assigned to duty as quartermaster of Holtzclaw's Brigade on 1 December 1864.[5]

Major Wood's military service, however exemplary, would hardly attract more than passing attention were it not for an accident of fate which caused him to be at the right place at the right time, and thus to be a key figure in a memorable and pathetic drama.

On 5 May 1865 he was one of a large group of Confederate government officials and army officers who assembled in the quiet village of Washington in Wilkes County, Georgia. President Jefferson Davis, his family, and top officials of his government had fled from Richmond after it had fallen to Union forces, pausing in North Carolina until General Joseph E. Johnston surrendered to General William T. Sherman at Durham Station. They headed for Georgia by way of Abbeville, South Carolina, traveling from that city in a train of five wagons and three ambulances. Upon arriving at Washington they were met by a large group of commissioned officers. There, in the home town of Robert Toombs, the leading apostle of discontent and the most ardent advocate of war, the administration which had begun with such splendid pyrotechnics was ignominiously disbanded.[6]

The last act of the Confederate government was to dispose of the last $10,000 of gold bullion which remained in its treasury. This was done in a short order written hastily upon coarse yellow writing paper. By a curious coincidence the receipt appears at the top of the paper and the order at the bottom, indicating that it was all one transaction. Thus did Major Raphael J. Moses of the commissary department turn over to Major Robert R. Wood of the quartermaster department the last resources of a government which in four years had disbursed more than one billion dollars in the prosecution of a stupendous rebellion. The bullion concerned was, by order of Secretary of War Breckenridge, turned over to the quartermaster for distribution to troops returning home in defeat and to provide hospitals with rations and necessary medicines.[7]

The order and the receipt, transposed for sequentiality, read as follows:

Maj. R. J. Moses, C.S., will pay $10,000, the amount of bullion appropriated to Q. M. Dep. by Sec. War, to Maj. R. R. Wood. By order of Q. M. Gen.

W. F. ALEXANDER, Maj. and Ass. to Q. M. Gen.

5 May 1865, Washington

Washington, May 5, '65

Received from Maj. R. J. Moses three boxes estimated to contain $10,000 in bullion. This has not been weighed or counted, and is to be opened before two commissioned officers and a certificate of contents made, which certificate is to be forwarded to Maj. R. J. Moses, and by the amount certified to the undersigned is to be bound.

R. R. Wood, Maj. and Q. M.[8]

And so ended ingloriously the efforts of brave, sincere, and misguided men to disunite a nation dedicated to the proposition that all men are created equal in their right to life, liberty and the pursuit of happiness. The four years of war had cost Georgia alone $481,000,000 in money; $272,000,000 in value of slaves lost; 40,000 of its white population lost; 2,000 square miles of land stripped and ravaged; one fourth of her railroad tracks destroyed; and a public debt in excess of $18,000,000.[9]

The despondency induced by the military disasters of 1863 and 1864, and deepened by the March to the Sea and its aftermath, had given rise throughout Georgia to a weary readiness to concede defeat. There was a general willingness to return to the Union and an implicit belief that this would be accomplished at the price of the abandonment of slavery. When news of General Robert E. Lee's surrender at Appomattox reached a grieving southland, none who heard it with relief could have imagined that the horrors of war were to be exchanged for the restrictions, privations, indignities, and fears of Reconstruction.[10]

When the din of battle had ceased and the Confederacy's leaders had been imprisoned, Major Robert R. Wood returned to his family in Covington. He must have rejoiced to find his dear ones safe and relieved to find that the town had suffered but little in the way of destruction during the years of war. But life in the next year or two was not to be easy, for the most basic commodities were so scarce and so expensive that they were beyond the reach of all but a small handful of persons who had even a little money.

Nevertheless, Robert Wood plunged into the task of rebuilding his life and of attempting to recoup what had been a more-than adequate competence. Soon he and his brother-in-law, Osborn T. Rogers *(see pages 146-150),* were engaged in a general mercantile business under the firm name of Wood & Rogers. An advertisement in a Covington newspaper several years later listed their stock as including spring and summer goods, ladies' dress goods, gents' furnishings, ready made clothing, boots and shoes, hats and caps, family groceries, hardware, crockery, wood ware, "and plantation supplies generally." Immediately above this ad was a simlar one for

Washington, May 5/65.

Received from Maj. R. R. Moses. Three Bags estimated to contain Ten Thousand Dollars in Bullion they has not been weighed or counted, and is to be opened before two Commissioned Officers and a certificate of contents made which certificate is to be forwarded to Maj. R. R. Moses, and by the annual certificate to the undersigned is to be bound to.

R. R. Wood

Maj. & Q. M.

Maj. R. R. Moses C. S. will pay the [Ten thousand dollars] end of Bullion appropriated to Q. M. dept by Secy War & Maj. R. R. Wood

May 5/65 —

Washington —

By order of President

W. F. Alexander

Maj. & Asst to the Q. M. Gen.

the firm's chief competitor, C. D. Pace & Co.*, on the north side of the Public Square, which boasted of a more limited range of merchandise: dress goods, gents' furnishings, hardware, groceries, & etc.[11]

After a decade or more together the two men dissolved their partnership. By that time Robert R. Wood's mother (*see pages 18-19)* had died and his wife's father (*see page 140*) followed in a few years. The two older persons were probably the wealthiest surviving members of their generation at the time of their deaths, so Robert and Jacqueline (Bates) Wood were financially freed to enjoy a more leisurely life than they had known since the Civil War. The couple moved to Atlanta, where their sons Cary and Robert, Jr., were already living. They lived out their twilight years in that city, but upon death their bodies were returned to Covington for burial in the Wood family plot.[13]

In the years following the Woods' departure from Covington their house on Church Street was rented by the J. A. Stewart family. Mr. Stewart was a local merchant, being a partner in the firm of Swann, Stewart & Company. His partners were Thomas C. Swann, D. A. Thompson (*see page 117)* and J. A. B. Stewart. This firm had earlier been known as Swann, Stewart & Thompson; subsequently, as noted on page 22, it was known as Swann-Davis Company and as T. C. Swann Company.[14]

Joseph Alexander Stewart was born in Rockdale County on 17 October 1845, a son of John Lewis and Julia Ann (Hollingsworth) Stewart. He was married on 30 January 1873 to Caroline Julia Robinson (*19 February 1852—23 August 1927)* of Jasper County, who was a niece of Mrs. Franklin Wright of Covington (*see page 164*).[15]

---

*This business was also known variously as Pace, Carr & Cody; Pace, Carr & Cureton; and Carr & Cureton.[12] The other partners were George T. Carr (*see page 152*) and Alfred Cureton (*page 105*). For C. D. Pace see page 38.

The Stewarts were among Covington's leading families during their relatively brief residence in the city. The parents were prominent socially, as were their children Estelle (later Mrs. George K. Selden of Atlanta), Daisy (who became the wife of Water F. Roberts of Utica, New York), Eloise (later Mrs. James P. Champion of Albany), Frances (who was married to Dr. Hugh Inman Battey of Atlanta, and after his death lived in Albany), Anita (later Mrs. Armstrong of Atlanta), and Adger Stewart (who married Anna Briggs Carter and lived in Louisville, Kentucky). The daughters all were educated at Vassar, and the son at Georgia Institute of Technology.[16]

Following the untimely death of Joseph A. Stewart on 31 July 1890 and the subsequent removal of his widow and children to Atlanta, the Robert R. Wood house on Church Street was occupied for several years by Mr. and Mrs. Emmett Womack.[17]

Mr. Womack was a native of Schley County and a veteran of service in the Confederate States Army. After returning from the war he walked to Oxford to enroll in Emory College. While living in the home of Mr. and Mrs. Christopher C. Wright he fell in love with their daughter Eleanor Rebecca, whom he married on 11 September 1870. The bride was a niece of Dr. Frank B. Wright and Mrs. Felix Franklin and a grandniece of Franklin Wright, all of Covington.[18]

In 1889 Mr. Womack and his father-in-law purchased from Mrs. Robert R. Wood a small dwelling located at the rear of her house. Later, when the Wood residence became available, the Womack family moved into it. There the Womacks' daughter Nelle grew to young ladyhood. A gifted musician, she served as organist at the Methodist church for several years before becoming a music teacher at what is now Georgia College at Milledgeville. On 23 November 1898 she became the wife of Judge Edward Roberts Hines of that city. In later life Mrs. Hines authored a book, *A Treasury Album of Milledgeville and Baldwin County, Georgia*. Her parents moved to

Milledgeville and spent their last years in Georgia's former capital city.[19]

The next occupants of the Wood house were Raymond Roberts and his family. Mrs. Roberts, the former Mae Wright, was a cousin of Mrs. Womack and also of Mrs. Newton Z. Anderson, whose husband later bought the property.[20]

Dr. Anderson (*15 January 1871–25 July 1955*) was a prominent physician and a large owner of real estate who served as vice president of the Bank of Covington and as president of the First National Bank. He bought the Wood house as an investment. His own home was located to the north of it, on land which formerly had been owned by the Woods. The Anderson house is now the home of Dr. Anderson's son and daughter, Franklin and Annie Pauline Anderson.[21]

On 15 March 1916 Dr. Anderson executed a deed to J. L. Elliott for $7200, in return for which he transferred title to "all that tract ... whereon stands what is known as the Robert Wood residence, with frontage of Eighty feet, more or less, on Church Street . . ." The deed was recorded on 9 January 1917.[22]

Jackson Lattimore Elliott was born in the Salem community of Newton County on 11 August 1883. While still a young man he moved to Porterdale and opened a retail grocery store. Subsequently he organized Porterdale Mercantile Company with O. W. Porter as a silent partner, and engaged in a general retail business. In 1917 Mr. Elliott and his wife, the former Georgie Smith (*28 September 1883–17 July 1962*), whom he had married in 1905, moved to Covington. There the couple reared their children in the former Wood house. These were Emily (Mrs. Sidney Cox of Waynesboro), Elizabeth (Mrs. Joseph Heard of Covington), Ruth, Charles, and George.[23]

Mr. Elliott was a public-spirited man who served three terms as mayor of Covington, was president of the Kiwanis Club, and spent twenty-five years as Sunday School superintendent, trustee, and choir member at the First United Methodist Church. Upon his death on 10 November 1961 *The Covington News* said he "was an avid sportsman; a good business man; a loyal church member; devoted to his family; good friend and neighbor — a solid citizen . . ."[24]

Ruth, the last-named daughter of Mr. and Mrs. Elliott, was married at her parents' home on 24 February 1938 to Everett H. Pratt, a brother of P. W. Pratt *(see page 228)*. The bride was attired in a copper-colored dress with which she wore gold accessories. The house was decorated for the quiet ceremony with arrangements of early spring flowers.[25]

DEWALD - WOOD HOUSE
Later occupied by the Stewart, Womack, Roberts, Elliott and Pratt families.

Many years later, following the death of her parents, Mrs. Pratt and her husband moved back to her girlhood home. Mr. Pratt, a Covington merchant, purchased the house from the executors of Mr. Elliott's estate for "$10 and other valuable considerations" on 28 August 1962.[26]

Mr. and Mrs. Pratt are the parents of Sue (Mrs. Charles Lewis, of Columbus); Michael, of Rochester, New York; and Everett Pratt, Jr., a captain in the Air Force.[27]

Today the white-columned house which was built for "The Honest Man" is a well-kept Covington landmark. It has withstood the passage of many years with dignity and still presents a pleasing vista in its setting of fine old trees.

XVI
"POVERTY HILL" AND OTHERS

The most beautiful site for a house in all of Covington is a rolling tract on East Conyers Street which has been graced by two of Covington's most distinguished houses.

Long before the Civil War the property was a part of the princely holdings of the Reverend Charles Haynie Sanders (*see pages 37, 40*). Following the death of the minister, businessman, and Emory trustee, his real estate was subdivided and sold to a number of local residents.

One such purchaser was William P. Anderson, who acquired from the Reverend Mr. Sanders' executors on 2 December 1851 five parcels of land for the sum of $922. These were identified as numbers 60, 61, 65, 66 and 67, according to the Survey made by E. L. Thomas, and comprised a part of Land Lot 247 in what had originally been Henry County.[1]

The new owner was born 12 January 1821, a son of Joseph Stuart Anderson (*28 July 1793–20 April 1871*) and his first wife. The father had come to Georgia from Lancaster County, Pennsylvania and taken up land grants in Henry and Walton counties. After the creation of Newton County from parts of Henry and Walton, Joseph S. Anderson deeded a large tract of land as the site for the county seat. His first purchase of land in the new county was made on 13 May 1822 when he paid $202 for Lot No. 13 in Square B in the " Town of Newtonsboro." On 2 September of that year he acquired for $190 the site of the present Newton County Courthouse. Years later when the Georgia Railroad was being constructed from Augusta to Atlanta, he personally directed his slaves in laying the tracks across his property between the Alcovy and Yellow rivers.[2]

183

Lucy Hawkins Cunningham (*1800–1840*), first wife of Joseph S. Anderson, was born in Oglethorpe County, Georgia, and was married to Mr. Anderson on 6 June 1820. Her father was George Cunningham (*1771–1859*), a Revolutionary soldier from Pittsylvania County, Virginia, who received land grants in Georgia. He married Agnes Patrick (*1781–1820*), a native of Greene County, in Oglethorpe County on 6 March 1798. The couple later moved to Newton County, where Mr. Cunningham was one of the first county commissioners.[3]

Joseph Stuart Anderson was one of the prominent and wealthy pioneer citizens of Covington and Newton County. His home was a large frame structure on the north side of the Covington-Madison road (now Floyd Street), and the plantation which surrounded it extended to the Alcovy River. The drive leading to the house, the site of which is now occupied by the E. L. Ficquett School, was later named Anderson Avenue in his honor. The original plantation was enlarged on 2 December 1851 when Joseph S. Anderson bought from the estate of the Reverend Charles H. Sanders 110 acres between the Georgia Railroad tracks and the property of Judge A. B. Longstreet and Dr. Alexander Means, who were, respectively, the second and fourth presidents of Emory College.[4]

"Colonel" Anderson, as he was usually called, was a businessman as well as a successful planter. In his early days he was a maker of bridles, saddles, and harnesses. Later, after Emory College was chartered in 1836, he and Robert O. Usher (*see page 122*) built an hotel in the new village of Oxford to accommodate students at the college. When the boys started living in private homes, however, the partners had the structure dismantled and reassembled facing the Public Square in Covington (now the northwest corner of Clark and Hunter streets). There they engaged in a general mercantile business under the firm name of Usher & Anderson.[5]

Following Mr. Usher's death in 1859 he was succeeded as a partner by Nicholas P. Hunter, who had been employed by

ONE-TIME HOTEL

Long a Covington landmark, this building was originally erected in Oxford as a hotel for Emory students. Moved to its present site on the Square at Clark and Hunter streets prior to the Civil War, it escaped destruction in a disastrous fire which destroyed all other buildings on the north side of the Square on 31 December 1883 only because of its gravel roof and the valiant efforts of firefighters.[6]

the firm since 1847. A native of North Carolina, where he was born on 18 September 1818, he had come to Covington in 1836 and worked for several years as a tailor. Brimful of energy and self-reliance, young Mr. Hunter devoted himself untiringly to business and to the acquiring of valuable parcels of real estate.[7]

When Joseph S. Anderson retired from an active role in the business, he was succeeded by his son William P. Anderson. The firm of Hunter & Anderson continued to supply the community with everything from piece goods and groceries to caskets and plows until the partnership was dissolved by Mr. Hunter's death on 29 January 1885. Subsequently the ground floor space which it had occupied was taken over by a similar business owned successively by Thomas Shepherd and his son William B. Shepherd *(see pages 45-46).* The dignified old building which had housed these pioneer businesses was acquired early in this century by N. S. Turner *(see page 168)* when he foreclosed a mortgage given by the financially-strapped Shepherd family. Since that time a bank and various professional offices have occupied the space behind the columned veranda from which Covingtonians stoically watched Sherman's forces enter the town in 1864.[8]

Joseph and Lucy (Cunningham) Anderson were the parents of William Patrick, George Thomas, Jane (Mrs. Carter), and Elizabeth Margaret Parks Anderson (Mrs. Henry T. Henry).[9]

Joseph S. Anderson and his second wife, a school teacher from Vermont named Catherine G. Ryan, whom he married in Newton County on 26 January 1841, were the parents of Lucy, who became the first wife of John P. Harris (see page 160), and Mary Frances Anderson. By his third wife, née Bliss, Colonel Anderson was the father of James L. B. Anderson.[10]

George Thomas Anderson, younger son of Joseph S. Anderson's first marriage, became one of Covington's most illustrious sons. Born on 3 February 1824, he left his studies at Emory College to serve as a lieutenant of Georgia Cavalry in the Mexican War. He was commissioned in the United States Army in 1855, but resigned three years later while serving as a captain of the 1st Cavalry Division.[11]

When the first call for volunteers was issued at the beginning of the Civil War, "Tige" Anderson organized an infantry company in Walton County. With the formation shortly thereafter of the 11th Georgia Infantry Regiment, he was elected colonel in command. On 1 November 1862 he was appointed brigadier general, and thereafter he led his command in battles at Fredericksburg, Gettysburg, Chicamauga, Knoxville, and throughout the Virginia campaign of 1864. He was present at General Robert E. Lee's surrender of the Confederate States Army at Appomattox. On 25 August 1865 he took the oath of allegiance to the United States of America, and on 13 November 1866 he received a full pardon from President Andrew Johnson.[12]

Following the war General Anderson served for a time as agent for the Georgia Railroad in Atlanta and later as chief of police in that city. Subsequently he served in the latter capacity and as tax collector at Anniston, Alabama, where he died on 4 April 1901. He married (1) Elizabeth Bush Ramey of Walton County, in 1848, and (2) Miss Spillers of Eufaula, Alabama.[13]

More legends, half-truths, and misinformation have grown up around "Tige" Anderson than surround the name of any other man in the history of Newton County. One story has been repeated so often that it has become almost an Article of Faith, yet it is totally lacking in accuracy. This account states that when General Sherman passed through Covington on his infamous March to the Sea, he spared the town because it was the home of his West Point roommate "Tige" Anderson. The truth of the matter is that General Anderson did not attend West Point, and that what Sherman actually said was that he had been at the military academy with one *Sam* Anderson, whose *sister* invited him to dinner while he was in Covington. An examination of rosters of students during William T. Sherman's four years at West Point reveals that the only man by that name who was there at the same time was Samuel Smith Anderson, a Virginian who was graduated in 1841. Thus we must assume that Sherman referred to a Virginia-born Covington matron when he wrote in his *Memoirs*:

> I remember, when riding around by a by-street in Covington, to avoid the crowd that followed the marching column, that some one brought me an invitation to dine with the sister of Sam. Anderson, who was a cadet at West Point with me; but the messenger reached me after we had passed the main part of the town. I asked to be excused, and rode on . . .[14]

Despite the General's failure to accept her invitation, the kind lady's dinner was not wasted. As Sherman's assistant adjutant general, Major Henry Hitchcock, wrote in his diary:

> [T]he good people of Covington got up a deputation of citizens to meet their distinguished visitor ("brute Sherman") and to offer

him all sorts of supplies, etc. ... One lady, I hear, had a fine
dinner ready for him, which he did not hear of [in time]– but
Captain Cole (signal officer) did and went there and kindly
partook . . .[15]

William Patrick Anderson, "Tige's" older brother, was born
on 12 January 1821 in that part of Walton County which
later in the year formed a portion of newly-created Newton
County. Early in life he entered the mercantile firm of which
his father was a partner, and by 1870 he had acquired a
comfortable fortune and retired from active business. He was a
trustee of Southern Female College and of its successor,
Southern Masonic Female College (*see pages 112-118*) almost continuously between 1855 and 1882. Prominent throughout the
state as a Mason, he served as master of the Golden Fleece
Lodge No. 6 of Covington longer than any other man in the
early history of that fraternity.[16]

On 11 February 1847 William P. Anderson married Miss
Sarah Frances Camp, daughter of Mr. and Mrs. Gerard Camp
(*see page 217*) of Covington. Their first home was a cottage
at the northeast corner of Floyd and Elm streets. A few years
later this property was acquired by the family of George B.
Daniel (*see page 224*), and since 1909 it has been the site of
the First Baptist Church.[17]

As previously noted, William P. Anderson purchased in 1851
five parcels of land from the estate of the Reverend Charles
H. Sanders. Almost immediately he had the property swarming
with workmen, and soon the framework of a large house
could be seen. When completed the beautiful columned structure rose majestically over the surrounding countryside. It was
situated beyond the town limits of Covington, south of an
extensive forest and north of the farm lands of Mrs. Sarah A.
Sanders (*see pages 40-41*).

The Anderson estate extended along the south side of the
present Conyers Street between what is now Legion Drive and
Dearing Street. To the east of it stretched acre after acre of

cotton fields which were a part of the vast Dearing Plantation. The latter property was owned by Dr. John Jackson Dearing (*16 February 1823–30 January 1905*), a native of Virginia who had acquired an enormous tract of land which stretched from the original Sanders holdings eastward to the Alcovy River. Dr. Dearing and his wife, Indie (*27 June 1826–22 February 1906*) lived in a charming frame house at the Covington end of the plantation. This cottage facing upon the Covington-Madison road (present southwest corner of Floyd and Dearing streets) passed by inheritance to the Dearings' daughter Eugenia and thence to her nephew Perino Dearing. The latter was reared across Floyd Street in the home of his parents, John M. Dearing (*9 January 1858–23 July 1920*) and the former Mattie Calloway (*25 November 1857–6 November 1929*). Perino Dearing's wife is the former Hortense Braswell of Loganville.[18]

DEARING HOME

When Mr. and Mrs. William P. Anderson moved into their new house in 1852 its rooms immediately resounded with the happy noises of a growing family. The Anderson children were Susan; Lucy, who died in infancy; William Hunter, who married Elizabeth Horton of Peconic, Long Island, in which city they lived the latter years of their lives; Mary Virginia, who became the wife of (1) Edgar D. Martin and of (2) Frank Crowley, both of Crawford, Georgia; Joseph Patrick, who married Minnie Buice and lived successively in Atlanta and San Francisco; Inez Luween, whose husband was Thomas J. Shields of Covington; Miriam, who became the wife of Francis Justin Vonderau of Atlanta; and Fannie Jane Anderson.[19]

The last-named daughter of Mr. and Mrs. Anderson incurred their displeasure by marrying on 31 May 1874 Samuel Carleen Rheburgh, the family's Swedish-born coachman. After an estrangement of several years, during which time the younger woman's health began to fail, Mr. Anderson built for the Rheburghs a cottage in the middle of the block opposite his estate. On 6 December 1884 title to the property was transferred by Mr. Anderson to his son-in-law for a token consideration of $300. Mrs. Rheburgh died in 1890 at the age of thirty-six, leaving five children: Carl William, Francis Albert, John Leslie and the Misses Rose and Christine Rheburgh.[20]

On 24 December 1895 S. C. Rheburgh married as his second wife Miss Olga Borg, who like himself was a native of Sweden. A romantic legend holds that she had been his childhood sweetheart, that she came to the United States to attend the World's Columbian Exposition in Chicago in 1893 and, hearing that her old friend was a widower, that she traveled to Atlanta and renewed their acquaintance. As Miss Borg was born only three years before Mr. Rheburgh's first marriage, however, this pleasant tale is patently untrue. Children born of the second marriage were: Mildred and Richard, who died early in life; Otto Reed, who now lives in Baltimore; Emil Sigurd, who married Mrs. George Raybun, née Marcelle Robinson of

RHEBURGH-HARDMAN HOUSE

Erected by William P. Anderson as a home for his daughter Fannie (Mrs. S. C.) Rheburgh. Subsequently occupied by the Hennessey, Sockwell and Hardman families.

Covington; Stephen Candler, now a retired Air Force colonel; Olga, who became the wife of James Morgan of Covington; and Elsie, who is the widow of John F. Meacham of Atlanta.[21]

Soon after his second marriage Mr. Rheburgh had his house turned to face Floyd Street instead of Conyers Street. The cottage with its gingerbread trim was still situated in the middle of the block, and a long drive lined with silver poplars led to it from Floyd Street. A year before his second wife's death in 1914, Mr. Rheburgh sold the property and moved into a house on the opposite side of the street. The earlier house subsequently was owned successively by a Mr. Hennessey; Charles S. Thompson (who moved it closer to Floyd Street when he developed the "Eastern Heights" subdivision); and J. W. Sockwell and his children, Charles A. Sockwell (*see page 142*), Miss Sallie Mae Sockwell, and Mrs. R. M. Mobley. The last two persons occupied it until it was sold in 1964 to the present owners. Today, beautifully remodeled into a Williamsburg-style cottage and furnished with a choice collection of antiques, it is the home of S. Lanier Hardman, a local pharmacist, and his attractive wife Martha.[22]

As a result of the Civil War and its aftermath, William P. Anderson lost his considerable fortune. During the harsh years of Reconstruction life became such a marginal existence for him and his family that he dubbed his home *Poverty Hill.* Title to the house and sixteen acres immediately surrounding it had been transferred to his business partner Nicholas P. Hunter some years earlier to satisfy loans made to Mr. Anderson by the latter. Upon Mr. Hunter's death in 1885, his will directed that his friend James M. Pace (*see page 39*) was to receive his watch and "a Sum of money . . . Sufficient to buy him a fine horse and a fine buggy and harness." The remainder of the bachelor Mr. Hunter's estate was left to his long-time associate and friend, William P. Anderson. Thus Mr. Anderson, who had continued to live in his columned mansion even after transferring title to it, became once again the nominal owner of the property.[23]

On 10 September 1886, however, James M. Pace, executor of the Hunter estate, sold the house and eighty acres of land to Amory W. Sibley of Augusta for $3000. Five days later Mr. Sibley transferred title to Josiah Sibley for the same consideration. These men, both prominent in their native Augusta, apparently never lived in the Anderson house. On 1 November 1888 Josiah Sibley sold the property to William B. Lee of Covington for $6800, thus more than doubling his money in a period of two years.[24]

Mr. and Mrs. William P. Anderson spent their last years with their daughter Mrs. Vondereau in Atlanta. Upon the occasion of the former's death on 21 [?] October 1895, *The Covington Star* said of him:

> He was honest and square in all his dealings; and when, through the misfortunes of business, he failed, as an honest man, he gave up everything, even his home and household goods, to his creditors, leaving himself and family absolutely penniless.

When his seventy-three year-old widow passed from life three years later the same newspaper commented:

She was a woman remarkable for her gentle and sweet disposition ... Misfortunes seemed to fall heavily upon her during the latter years of her life ... [but] she never mourned or complained ...[25]

This noble pair exemplified in their lives the finest qualities of the ante-bellum aristocracy of the Old South. Sadly, in death the record of their earthly sojourn is regarded with a mixture of awe and disbelief by a generation to which the term *noblesse oblige* is only a foreign phrase. Mr. and Mrs. Anderson, their daughter Fannie, and members of the Rheburgh family rest in the plot dominated by a handsome monument to Nichold P. Hunter in Covington City Cemetery.[26]

William B. Lee, already noted as purchaser of the former Anderson estate, was a member of a pioneer Newton County

Courtesy of Mr. and Mrs. S.A. Ginn

POVERTY HILL, the beautiful ante-bellum home of Mr. and Mrs. William P. Anderson. The name was lightly given to his estate by Mr. Anderson in recognition of the disastrous affect the Civil War and its aftermath had upon his fortunes. (Burned.)

family. His grandfathers were James Lee, who came to Georgia from Virginia *circa* 1790, and the Reverend John Webb, a Methodist preacher who was elected judge of the Inferior Court of Newton County in 1850. The latter, losing everything he possessed in the Civil War, was a merchant at Newborn for four years before his death in 1870. The Reverend Mr. Webb's daughter Mary (*19 March 1817–9 October 1879*) became the wife of William Sheffield Lee (*2 May 1815–1 May 1885*), son of James Lee. Children of this marriage were Margaret Ann (Mrs. Sams); Mary Frances (Mrs. Belfield); John Webb (*1841–1928*), a prominent and beloved Covington physician; Augustus James (*1843–1865*), a Confederate officer who died of battle wounds; Julia Jane Josephine (Mrs. R. W. Clark. *See page 212*); William Bell; Walter Elbert; Sarah Louisa; and Eugene Orson Lee (*see pages 230–231*).[27]

William Bell Lee was born in Newton County on 21 November 1847 and died at Quitman, Georgia on 16 August 1928. At the age of sixteen he served with the State Militia in the Civil War. On 10 November 1869 he married Miss Laura Butler, daughter of the Reverend Joseph Bell Butler of Durhamville, Tennessee, originally of Elbert County, Georgia. Mrs. Lee died at Louisville, Georgia on 15 June 1904. The couple's first home was a stone house situated on a part of Lot 2 in Square B, which is the middle portion of the block on the west side of the Public Square. Here was born their son Ernest Eugene Lee (*26 September 1876–21 December 1962*), who married Miss Ava Bomar (*31 August 1877–17 June 1950*), daughter of Captain and Mrs. A. R. Bomar of Covington (*see page 208*). The latter couple lived many years in Dallas, Texas before returning to Covington following his retirement. Widowed and childless, Ernest Lee bequeathed his Floyd Street residence to his wife's niece-in-law Mrs. William B. Travis (now Mrs. William W. Aiken. *See page 211*), whom an in-law had termed "a wonderful woman of sterling character."[28]

On 2 June 1894 William B. Lee sold to the Middle Georgia

& Atlantic Railway Company a strip of land from the eastern portion of the former Anderson estate, "the width to be what is necessary for . . . a right of way." Thus was what is now the Central of Georgia Railway enabled to enter Covington, primarily for the purpose of providing service to and from the textile mills in the city and in Porterdale. The railroad's tracks still cross such major streets as East Conyers, Floyd, Elm, Pace, Emory, and the extension of Clark Street. On 30 December 1895 Mr. Lee sold to George D. Butler for $500 a parcel of 25 acres between the railroad's right-of-way and the Dearing plantation.[29]

William B. Lee became greatly upset by the deep cut which the railroad made in the property adjacent to his home preparatory to laying its tracks. His resentment of what he considered needless mutilation of the earth was coupled with one of his favorite dislikes to result in a development which provided the town with vast amusement. One of Mr. Lee's real estate holdings was a two-story frame building at the southeast corner of Church and College streets. Part of it was devoted to an undertaking establishment owned by Mr. Lee and operated for him by a manager; the remainder was devoted to the studio of an excellent photographer named W. R. Perkins. Mr. Lee, a man of violent likes and dislikes, entertained an especial dislike for the hapless Mr. Perkins. He expressed this cogently in a newspaper advertisement pertaining to a sale of soap at his general store on the Square. The soap, so claimed the advertisement, would "remove anything except railroad cuts and photographers." [30]

W. B. Lee's general store was the grandest emporium in town. Situated in the middle of the block on the south side of the Square, its front was ornamented by a deep porch with high roof supported by long fluted wooden columns. Beneath this protection against sun and rain was a tantalizing assortment of Georgia Rattlesnake watermelons which had been grown on the Lee farm, as well as bicycles, plows, and other hardware.[31]

After living in the old Anderson house ten years, William B. Lee sold it on 12 February 1898 for $4000. The purchaser was one O. C. Pope of Hancock County, who transferred title to Clark Banking Co. on 14 January 1901 for a consideration of $2175. The next owner of the house and the surrounding forty-eight acres of land was George D. Butler, who bought it for $4000 on 28 December 1911. As some or all of Mr. Butler's children are known to have been born in the house, it is likely that he had rented it between the time of Mr. Pope's purchase and the date on which ownership passed to him.[32]

George Dallis Butler was born at Peter's Point in Elbert County on 3 April 1858. At Troup, Texas, on 2 January 1884 he married Mary Lucy Henry, daughter of Dr. and Mrs. Henry Thompson Henry of that city. The Henry family had formerly lived in Covington, where a cottage was built for them on Floyd Street in 1858. It occupied a portion of a seven-acre tract which Dr. Henry had purchased from his brother-in-law William P. Anderson on 15 August 1863 for $2200. This house is now owned and occupied by Miss Sarah Mobley, daughter of the late Mr. and Mrs. R. M. Mobley (*see page 191*). Dr. Henry (*2 March 1823–16 January 1892*) was a dentist who had attended Emory College before serving as captain of a company in the 6th Regiment of the First Brigade, 1st Division, Georgia State Troops, in the Civil War. His father, William R. Henry, who moved to Newton County from North Carolina, was said to be a first cousin of Revolutionary patriot Patrick Henry.[33]

Dr. Henry's wife was the former Elizabeth Margaret Parks Anderson (*17 March 1833–4 August 1918*), a daughter of Covington pioneer Joseph S. Anderson (*see page 186*). Their children were: Gertrude, who married Coleman McKay, of Troup, Texas; Clara, who became the wife of James Ayres of Troup and later moved to Bowie, Texas; Hugh, who married Elsie Lurkin of El Paso, in which city they lived; Eleanor; and Mary Lucy Henry.[34]

HOME OF DR. HENRY T. HENRY
Now the residence of Miss Sarah Mobley.

The last-named daughter of the Henrys returned to Coving-
ton after her marriage to George Dallis Butler. When she later
moved into the handsome columned house on Conyers Street
which her husband bought from William B. Lee, she became
mistress of the home which had been built for her uncle
William P. Anderson. There her daughters Eleanor (now Mrs.
Fulton B. DeVane of Quitman) and Katharine (later Mrs.
Hurst of Pelham) and her sons David and George Dallis Butler,
Jr. spent their childhood. Another daughter, eight-year old
Belle, had died before the family moved to *Poverty Hill*. David
Butler married Laura Gaither, a great-granddaughter of Coving-
ton pioneer Cary Wood (*see pages 3, 16*), and their daughter
Mary Lucy became the wife of Lamar Callaway, now post-
master at Covington.[35]

The Butlers' beautiful old house was destroyed by fire only
a few years after they acquired it. Mr. Butler immediately

decided to rebuild; meanwhile, he settled his family in a small cottage near the front gate of the property which had originally been the home of the estate's overseer. Somehow he never got around to putting up another house on the site of the original mansion. When the Depression of the late 1920s arrived he borrowed money on the property before moving to Pelham, where he died on 17 April 1937. On 2 January 1928 he had transferred title to three of his children for one dollar and the assumption of the loans. Nine days later they gave the Bank of Newton County a note for $4320, with the property as collateral. On 29 December 1931 Thomas C. Swann *(see page 26)*, and his sister Mrs. James H. Porter *(see pages 24, 235)*, acting individually as representatives of the still-unsettled estate of their late father, paid off the note and thereby aquired ownership of the property.[36]

On 30 March 1936 Mr. Swann and his sister sold to Mrs. S. A. Ginn for $4700 that "tract of land commencing at a rock well . . . on Conyers Street . . . [and continuing] East 1475 feet . . . to the Central of Georgia Railway Company line . . . containing fifty-five acres . . . excepting one acre . . . off the southeast corner . . . "[37]

The new owner, the former Lois Spears of Mansfield, had attended Wesleyan College prior to her marriage to Stephen Alexander Ginn on 18 August 1927. Mr. Ginn, a native of Royston, had come to Covington to enter the automobile business with his brother Rucker Ginn *(see pages 65-66)*. Following the latter's death he became sole owner of the business, which he continues today with the assistance of his nephew Rucker Ginn, Jr., and his son-in-law William D. Fortson, Jr.[38]

Mr. Ginn has been one of Covington's most prominent and influential citizens. In addition to membership in the Kiwanis Club and other organizations, he has served as mayor of Covington and as chairman of the board of trustees of the Newton County Hospital Authority.[39]

In 1941 Mr. and Mrs. Ginn and their family moved from their former home on Church Street (*see page 36*) into the beautiful two-story brick house which had been erected for them on the site once occupied by William P. Anderson's home. The new structure has six square brick pillars which make the facade remind some persons of the fictional *Tara* in the filmed version of Margaret Mitchell's epic *Gone With The Wind*.[40]

Here the Ginns reared their daughters Elizabeth (who became the wife of Kelly Alford, Jr., of Lawrenceville), Frances (now Mrs. John Stark of Atlanta), and Stephanie, as well as their niece and nephew Mary Ellen and Rucker Ginn (*see page 66*).[41]

The grounds of the Ginn residence were the scene of a beautiful reception following the wedding at the Baptist church of Stephanie Ginn to Lieutenant William Deadwyler Fortson, Jr., on 18 June 1966. The terrace was lighted for the

RESIDENCE OF MR. AND MRS. S. A. GINN
Sometimes called the *Tara* of Covington, this beautiful house occupies the site of the ante-bellum home of Mr. and Mrs. William P. Anderson.

occasion by patio lamps holding garlands of white summer flowers flecked with gardenias. The bride, wearing an ivory *peau de soie* gown trimmed with Brussels lace and carrying a bouquet of Eucharist lilies outlined with green and white caladium leaves, received with the bridegroom and their parents. After Lieutenant Fortson completed his tour of duty with the Air Force, he and his lovely young wife returned to Covington for residence.[42]

The Ginn house is situated atop of knoll from which is visible a breathtaking view of pastures and gardens. A long, straight drive lined with beautiful old trees leads from East Conyers Street to the house, and around the front of the property the original stone wall built for William P. Anderson adds a note of picturesque antiquity. By any standard the Ginn house is one of the showplaces of Covington.

XVII

"THE COTTAGE"

One of Covington's most distinctive old houses is a raised cottage of a type which is seen more frequently in coastal Alabama and Mississippi than in inland Georgia.

This beautiful edifice has been the subject of more inaccurate stories concerning its early history than any other structure in town. The favorite tale has been quoted so often in conversation and has appeared so frequently in print that it is now accepted as a matter of fact. According to it, the house was built by Judge John J. Floyd (*see pages 89-97*) as a wedding gift to his daughter when she married in 1859. This romantic account usually includes a remark to the effect that the Judge's own house a block and a half nearer town seems to keep a watchful eye upon the honeymoon cottage. Not surprisingly, and equally inaccurately, the little house has often been referred to as the *Floyd*-Neal-Patterson residence.[1]

The truth of the matter is that the house was built by McCormick Neal about a year after his marriage to Frances Ann Floyd on 26 April 1853. On 16 December of the year in which he was wed young Mr. Neal purchased from Lemuel D. Thompson for $620 "all that tract or parcel of land situate, lying and being in the County of Newton bounded as follows[:] on the West by the avenue leading to Jos. S. Anderson's residence, on the North by said Anderson's land[, on the] East by John Floyd's [lands, and on the] South by the road leading from Covington to Madison containing four acres more or less . . . " This description of the property leaves no doubt that it originally extended northward from the northeast corner of the present Floyd Street and Anderson Avenue to the intersection of Anderson Avenue and Hicks Avenue, eastward to the western boundary of what is now referred to as the Cook-Adams-Williams property (*see page 215*), from which point it extended southward to the present Floyd Street and thence westward to Anderson Avenue.[2]

The tract to the east of the land purchased by Mr. Neal probably is the heart of the persistent story that Judge Floyd presented his daughter a beautiful new house as a wedding gift. On 26 May 1859 John J. Floyd deeded to McCormick Neal "in consideration of the love and affection I have and bear unto my daughter Frances A. Neal, wife of the said McCormick Neal," a parcel of land "beginning at the southeast corner of the lot purchased by the said McCormick Neal of and from Lemuel E. [*sic*] Thompson where the said lot comes to the street leading towards the Alcovy river and running East along the said Street across the branch to a rock corner near a persimmon tree thence [north] to another rock corner on the lane which separates the lot of said Neal from Col. Anderson's land, thence a little south of West along the south side of said lane to another rock corner on the East side of the avenue leading from the street to Col. Anderson's house, thence south along the east side of the said avenue to the northwest corner of the said lot the said Neal purchased of the said Thompson as aforesaid, thence East along the line of said lot to the north east corner thereof, then south to the beginning corner forming an L ... containing five acres more or less ... together with all ... appertenances ... " This, unquestionably, refers to the property upon which the Cook-Adams-Williams house now stands and to a meadow bisected by a stream which is located to the east of it. The description of the lane at the north of the property, running "a little south of West," fits perfectly the present Hicks Avenue, a dead-end street of approximately one block in length running a little north of east from Anderson Avenue.[3]

Judge Floyd, who owned an extensive tract of land on the north side of the street which now bears his name, gave a portion of it to his son-in-law because in those days married women could not own property in their own names.[4]

McCormick Neal was well able to afford to build a fine house for his bride. His father, pioneer citizen McCormick Neal the elder (*see pages 33-37*), had left a substantial estate upon his death in 1834. The younger man's mother subsequently married the Reverend Charles H. Sanders, and after his death Mrs. Sarah Ann (Batts) Sanders was the largest landowner in Covington and the richest woman in the county (*see page 41*). Upon her death in 1866, her son McCormick Neal became executor of her large estate, the value of which had been drastically reduced by the loss of slaves and Confederate money and bonds at the end of the Civil War.[5]

Born 28 April 1832, only two years before his father's death, McCormick Neal had grown to maturity in his parents' beautiful Church Street residence (*see pages 33-34, 41*). We can imagine that his marriage to Fannie Floyd, uniting as it did two prominent and well-to-do families, must have been an important social event in the little city. As his own mother had numerous children living at home, the young couple probably lived with Judge and Mrs. Floyd until their own home was completed.

The house into which Mr. and Mrs. Neal moved *circa* 1855 was beautifully proportioned and well-suited both for entertaining and for the rearing of children. Its high-ceilinged rooms, many windows, and spacious piazza made it delightfully cool during even the hottest summer days. The detail of the woodwork, mantels, and moldings was handsome but relatively simple. Careful attention was given to the selection of hardware, resulting in doorknobs of silverplate and keyholes with flaps. The furnishings of the house were among the handsomest in Covington, and later they were augmented by several choice items from the beautiful home of Mr. Neal's mother.[6]

For the few years allotted them before the Civil War destroyed their fortunes and brought bleakness and despair into the lives of nearly everyone in town, Fannie and "Mac" Neal lived happy, privileged lives. Their home was the scene of many gay social affairs which attracted friends from Covington and Oxford, as well as from Madison, Monroe, Social Circle and the Brick Store community.[7]

The advent of the Civil War caused an abrupt change in this pleasant pattern. The Neals' friends joined local military units and soon were jubilantly on their way to meet the enemy. Fannie's brother John Floyd and McCormick's half-brother Charles Sanders both joined Lieutenant Colonel Jefferson Lamar's "Lamar Infantry," as did their friends William D. Conyers, Jr., Richard Simms, Jr., and other young men from Covington's finest families. Colonel Lamar, brother of the later-famous L. Q. C. Lamar, died while leading a charge at Crampton's Gap, Maryland, in 1862; Lieutenant Simms was killed in an engagement at South Mountain, Maryland, a few days earlier; and Major Conyers died upon the field at Spotsylvania Court House, Virginia, in 1864.[8]

As the horror of war brought grief and hardship close to home, Mrs. McCormick Neal joined other local women in sewing and knitting for the men of the Confederate States Army. She spent many hours with the Women's Sewing Society, of which her mother was president. As conditions worsened the women began making banadages and, after the establishment of military hospitals in Covington and Oxford, they rendered devoted service as volunteer nurses. They changed the name of their volunteer group to the Hospital Aid Society.[9]

McCormick Neal's activities during the years of the great sectional conflict are not known in detail. Presumably the twenty-nine year-old husband and father joined the State Militia or one of the local home defense units. Major (later

RESIDENCE OF MR. AND MRS. McCORMICK NEAL
This view, *circa* 1930, shows some of the superb exterior ornamentation.

General) James P. Simms mentioned in a letter to his mother (*see page 59*) in late 1862 that "Mr. Neal has gone home," so we may assume that the writer referred to McCormick Neal and that he had gone to Virginia to see his younger half-brother "Charley" Sanders.[10]

The 1860 United States Census lists Mr. Neal as Farmer/Guardian, shows his real estate holdings to have been $8,000 and his personal estate valued at $7,000, and reveals that in addition to his wife and children he had under his roof four teen-age orphans. Ten years later, even though his mother had died in 1866 and left him a portion of her considerable estate, his Reconstruction-era realty was valued at only $3,000 and his personal estate at $2,500. The same record lists him as "Clerk in Dry Goods Store," which poignantly attests to the severe financial reverses suffered by most Georgians in the fifteen years immediately following the end of the war in 1865.[11]

McCormick Neal subsequently must have been elected to a judgeship — probably of the Inferior Court of Newton County — for on several occasions local newspapers referred to him as "Judge." One story stated that he had been staying in Atlanta for some time and that he had a few days earlier completed a visit to the Covington home of his son and his family. "He is looking like one of fifty; is in fine health. . . . With his regular uniform habits which he has ever observed," the item continued, "we don't see why he should not live to be ninety and possibly one hundred . . . "[12]

In the hard years of Reconstruction, Fannie Neal devoted herself to her family and continued to participate in the drastically curtailed social life of the community. The war-time Hospital Aid Society became in 1866 the Memorial Association* and devoted its energies and funds to caring for the graves of soldiers and to ministering to those who had been widowed or orphaned by the war. Mrs. Neal was elected first president of the Memorial Association, a position which she held for the remainder of her life.[13]

Fannie and McCormick Neal were the parents of three children: Mary, who was married to William A. Spencer of Covington; Nellie, who became the wife of Theodore Maybank of Charleston, South Carolina, and lived in Anniston, Alabama; and McCormick, Jr., who married Clara Perry of Covington.[15]

Double sorrow came to the Neal family when both Mrs.

*Subsequently the Memorial Association became the Daughters of the Confederacy and, ultimately, a chapter of a national organization known as the United Daughters of the Confederacy.[14]

Neal and her daughter Mrs. Spencer died in 1891. They were buried on the plot of Mrs. Neal's parents, Judge and Mrs. John J. Floyd, in the city cemetery.[16]

Mrs. Spencer left three small children: Neal W. Spencer, who married Cleo Stewart of Covington after serving in the Spanish-American War, and lived thereafter in Atlanta; Helen, later Mrs. Searcy of Eufaula, Oklahoma; and Clara Belle ("Rosebud"), who became Mrs. Pickett of Calahan, Florida.[17]

The father of these children worked in Atlanta for a while, commuting daily via the Georgia Railroad, but subsequently he became bookkeeper for Clark Banking Co. In 1906 William A. Spencer and his second wife, Elizabeth, a former Covington school teacher, and his younger daughter, Rosebud, moved to Nassau County, Florida.[18]

The Spencer daughters were popular members of the younger social contingents during their years in Covington. In 1899 one local newspaper devoted portions of three columns on its front page to record a gala birthday party for Rosebud and a similarly festive affair in honor of Helen's eighteenth birthday. Both parties were held at *Ferncrest*, their home on Floyd Street. Invited to the former were the Misses Lillian Clarke, Leonora Owsley, Clara Carr, Hyda Heard, and Catherine Butler, and Tom Swann, Lester Lee, Walton Clark, Will White Clark, Simms Heard, John Callaway, Emmett Wright, Dudley Guinn, and Clifford Henderson. The guest list for the second party included Misses Olive Swann, Flora Carr, Ethel Belcher, Fannie Henderson, the honoree's aunt Mrs. May-bank, and Messrs. Davis, Simms, Carr, Heard, Henderson, J. R. and Ed Stephenson, Hays, and Smith.[19]

McCormick Neal outlived his wife by twenty-six years, most of which he spent in Atlanta. Although removed from the familiar and beloved scenes of "home," he had congenial friends in the city, as well as numerous relatives to whom he was devoted. In the latter category were his son of the same name, his grandson Neal W. Spencer, and his half-sister Mrs. William A. Hemphill (*see page 39*).[20]

With McCormick Neal's death on 28 June 1915, Covington lost a distinguished native son who in his life had exemplified the finest qualities of the town's leading pioneer settlers. There then remained in Covington no descendant of the original McCormick Neal and his wife, nor even of the latter and her second husband, the Reverend Charles H. Sanders.[21]

McCormick Neal, Jr., the third person to bear the name, was a disappointment to his family and friends. Like Ashley Wilkes in *Gone With The Wind*, he was unable to cope with the harsh existence which supplanted the privileged life for which he had been reared. Apparently never ambitious or steady in his habits, he had become little more than a by-the-hour handy man before he left Covington for Atlanta. There he found employment as a foreman with a construction company, but within a few years he was working as a carpenter.[22]

Clara (Perry) Neal finally took her son Jack back to Covington, where they lived with her sister and brother-in-law, Mr. and Mrs. James E. Philips. Following Mrs. Neal's death in 1916, the boy was reared by the Philipses. Gifted as a singer and attractive in person and manner, he left Covington as a young man and is said to have risen to a responsible position with a major New York bank.[23]

When the last of the family left the lovely Neal house on Floyd Street, most of the beautiful furnishings were sold at auction. Many of the choice items were purchased by Dr. W. D. Travis and N. S. Turner, who used them to advantage in their own attractive homes.[24]

The house itself was rented for several years by Captain and Mrs. A. R. Bomar, who left their handsome columned house at Chapel Hill, in Douglas County, and came to Covington so their daughters could attend Southern Masonic Female College. During their years in town Captain and Mrs. Bomar were attractive additions to the social life of the community.[25]

One of the daughters of the household, Frances Maud Bomar (*5 August 1875—26 August 1951*), was married to Dr.

William Darracott Travis in a ceremony at her parents' Covington residence on 24 November 1897. "After the ceremony was over," a newspaper account stated, "an elegant lunch was served in the parlors, and the happy couple left immediately for Jacksonville . . ." Upon their return they took up residence across Floyd Street in the home of Dr. Travis' mother.[26]

The Travis residence had been built for the elder Mrs. Travis' parents, Mr. and Mrs. Robert Bass Livingston, after the columned mansion on the west part of their property had burned *circa* 1868. Mr. Livingston (*30 December 1813–11 May 1888*) had moved to Newton County with his parents, Joseph and Elizabeth (Bass) Livingston, from his native Jefferson County in 1822, at which time the father purchased a plantation which had been drawn in a land lottery by his wife's grandfather, Revolutionary soldier John H. Bass. The Livingstons were cousins of Leonidas Felix Livingston, who represented the Fifth District in Congress from 1890 to 1910 and who is regarded as the father of rural free delivery of U.S. mail.[27]

Joseph Livingston's will, which was probated in 1838, bequeathed to his son Robert B. "that lot whereon I now reside," indicating that his wife had preceded him in death. The couple had at least one other child, Mary, who married William B. Foreman of Washington, Georgia.[28]

Robert Bass Livingston and his wife, the former Eliza Pharr McLaughlin (*25 August 1815–3 March 1892*) of Newton County, built near the site of their original columned house on Alcova (later Floyd) Street an attractive one-story cottage. Upon their death it passed to their daughter Allie Margaret (*17 June 1845–15 April 1918*), who by then was the widow of Dr. Amos Campbell Whitfield Travis (*18 December 1835–2 April 1890*). The latter, who had served as assistant surgeon of the 8th Georgia Infantry Regiment, CSA, had been a practicing physician in — and mayor of — Conyers before his retirement to Covington shortly before his death.[29]

Dr. and Mrs. A. C. W. Travis were the parents of John Livingston Travis, an honor graduate in Emory's Class of 1887, who practiced law in Savannah in partnership with his youngest brother; William D. Travis, of whom more later; and Robert Jesse Travis, who graduated with first honor in Emory's class of 1897, practiced law in Savannah, and served as an Army colonel in World War I and as a major general* in World War II.[30]

In 1893 the Travis residence was so severely damaged by fire that the entire front portion had to be rebuilt. In 1921, three years after the death of his mother, Dr. William Darracott Travis remodeled his ancestral home so successfully that in the half-century since then it has remained one of the most attractive houses in Covington.[31]

Dr. Travis (*21 November 1870–6 December 1948*), a graduate of Emory College (1890), the University of Maryland, and New York Polyclinic, was for many years a prominent Covington physician. Upon coming home on a visit in 1897 he found the town suffering from a raging epidemic of diptheria. He wired for a supply of a recently-developed antitoxin and soon had the epidemic under control. He was the first physician to use the new vaccine outside of the laboratory.[32]

Dr. and Mrs. Travis always occupied a leading position in Covington's social life and they both were widely admired. Their children were William Bomar and Allie Louise Travis. The latter married Dr. William White Aiken of Covington and Lyons, who after her death married her brother's widow, the former Parepa Moore. Mrs. Aiken returned to Covington from her native Lyons shortly after the death of her second husband in 1971. She makes her home in the house which she inherited from Ernest E. Lee (*see page 194*), which is next door to the home in which she lived with her first husband.[33]

* Travis Field, the Savannah municipal airport, was named in honor of General Travis. The memory of his son, Brigadier General Robert Falligant Travis (USMA '28) is perpetuated in Travis Air Force Base, California.

TRAVIS RESIDENCE

The Travis house is now owned by William Darracott Travis, 3rd, sone of Mrs. Aiken and the late William Bomar Travis (*24 October 1912—6 October 1960*). A graduate of Georgia Military College, he attended Mercer University and the University of Georgia. Mr. Travis, who is with the U.S. Government in Atlanta, has freshened the house both inside and out and has enhanced its setting by the use of boxwood and other evergreens. His wife is the former Paula Sherlock of Methuin, Massachusetts, and their daughter is little Miss Julia Travis.[34]

Across the street, the beautiful house in which William Travis' grandparents were married (*see page 209*) seems to keep a watchful eye upon Floyd Street. After Captain and Mrs. Bomar returned to their home near Douglasville, owner McCormick Neal rented it to the Clarke family. Finally, on 3 January 1909, he transferred title to Love A. Clarke for a mere $1800. A few years earlier, on 23 June 1903, he had sold to Mr. Clarke for $625 three acres adjoining the house, the property being a portion of the tract which had been transferred to Mr. Neal by his father-in-law in 1859. The house itself could not be sold at that time because Mr. Neal

had given mortgages to one Ike W. Brown and Clark Banking
Co. in 1896 and 1898, respectively.[35]

Although L. A. Clarke purchased the house, his parents, Mr.
and Mrs. R. W. Clarke, actually lived in it. Robert W. Clarke
(*1845–1917*) had served in Company B, 53rd Georgia Regiment, in the Civil War and was for many years city marshal of
Covington. On 5 January 1869 her married Julia Jane Josephine Lee (*1845–1915*), daughter of Judge William S. and
Mary (Webb) Lee of Newton County (*see page 194*). She was
a sister of three prominent Covington men: Eugene O. Lee
(*see page 230*), Dr. John W. Lee and William Bell Lee (*see
page 194*).[36]

Mr. and Mrs. Clarke's children were Lillian; Maggie, who
married (1) E. Stoney Steadman, Covington-area newspaper
editor, and (2) Walter Childs, a prominent widower of Newborn (*see page 65*); Mary, who married Ernest G. Merck of
Spalding County; Love A., whose widow, Florence, married (2)
a Mr. Jarrard; William L., of Covington; and John P. Clarke of
Fulton County.[37]

On 1 December 1915 Mrs. Julia Clarke's heirs sold to Mrs.
Anna E. Milner for $2000 "a six-room dwelling known as the
Clark home place, formerly the McCormick Neal Place . . . " [38]

Mrs. Milner and her family did not move into the house
immediately, but waited until her husband, Colonel R. W.
Milner, had sold his long-time residence farther out Floyd
Street. From that time until they left Covington around 1920,
the family occupied the former Neal house.[39]

Robert Wells Milner (*21 July 1861–8 February 1930*) was
for many years a prominent Covington attorney. Early in this
century he served as County Administrator and as a director
of the Bank of Covington. By his first wife, the former Cora
Bolton, who died in 1910, he had several children, none of
whom lived in Covington as adults. His second wife, the
former Anna Mitchell of Lawrenceville, was the widow of
Thomas B. Bush, a Tennessee-born railroad construction

engineer. He died *circa* 1905, leaving four young sons, including Tandy E. Bush who married Eugenia Guinn of Covington (*see page 121*).[40]

Upon leaving Covington the Milners lived for a while in Lithonia, in Tennessee, and in Lawrenceville. It was in the latter town that Colonel Milner died in 1930. He was buried beside his first wife in the city cemetery in Covington.[41]

For several years after the Milners moved away the former Neal house was rented to John T. Swann. Known locally as "Jack," he was a man who went from riches to poverty to riches with the regularity of a metronome. He was a brother of Dr. W. K. Swann, who later moved next door to the Floyd Street home of their capitalist cousin, Thomas C. Swann. Later Jack Swann, his wife and their sons Coy and James moved to Atlanta, where he eventually made another fortune through the operation of a series of parking garages.[42]

While Jack Swann and his family were living at *The Cottage*, Mayor A. S. Hopkins decided that the great trees which arched over the streets leading from the Square must be cut down. This aroused such a clamor of protest and indignation from the people of Covington that His Honor's proposal was defeated. But Mayor Hopkins, who was also head of the local "Klavern" of the Ku Klux Klan as well as being a practicing dentist, was not to be routed by public opinion. On successive nights he and some forty members of the hooded order moved purposefully from block to block, systematically cutting down every tree they encountered. As they moved out Floyd Street to Anderson Avenue, they saw Jack Swann sitting on the front steps of his house with a loaded shotgun on his knees.

"All right, boys," he said, "you've cut down your last tree."

"Aw, Jack," the Mayor retorted, "we're your friends! You wouldn't shoot *us*!"

"That's what *you* think, Dr. Hopkins," Mr. Swann said. "Now tell your men to go home and forget about destroying any more trees."

And so the brave men in their bed sheets turned their footsteps homeward and, thanks to Jack Swann, many great old trees were spared their free-swinging axes.[43]

Next tenants of the old Neal house were Mr. and Mrs. James B. Downs and their children. Several years later, on 15 April 1930, Mrs. Milner sold it to Mr. Downs. He, in turn, sold it on 4 February 1936 to R. H. Patterson for $3000. The decline in price was due more to the Great Depression than to a sudden deterioration of the property. The years had taken their toll, to be sure, but the house remained structurally sound. It was to regain its former beauty under the patient and skillful direction of Mr. Patterson and his energetic wife.[44]

Mrs. Patterson, long a local school teacher, is a native and life-long resident of Covington. The former Sarah Clyde Hutchins, she moved while still a child into the former Cook-Adams house near her present home on Floyd Street. Her grandfather, William F. Williams, had purchased the property so that his adored granddaughter could have "advantages." Young Miss Hutchins grew up in the commodious old house and left it only when she went away to attend Lucy Cobb Institute in Athens. On 23 November 1935 she was married to Rufus Henry Patterson, a native of Shadydale, who was for many years a local insurnace agent. The couple has a daughter, Sarah Margaret Patterson of Atlanta, and a son, R. H. Patterson, Jr., a pharmacist in Hartwell.[45]

For nearly forty years Mr. and Mrs. Patterson have worked long and hard to restore the old Neal house to its original state. The transformation wrought by their painstaking efforts is marvelous to behold. Both within and without the "cottage" reflects the care, devotion and money which have been lavished upon it. With its beautiful old wood gleaming and its brass and silver fixtures shining, the house is a show-case for the handsome furnishings which Mrs. Patterson has collected with discrimination over a period of many years. The attractive brick wall at the rear of the property encloses an old-fashioned garden which complements the charming and distinctive house.[46]

COOK-ADAMS-WILLIAMS HOUSE

Erected in 1904 for Mrs. C. J. Cook. The site of the house once belonged to Judge John J. Floyd (*see pages 89—97*), who on 26 May 1859 deeded it to his son-in-law McCormick Neal (*see page 202*). The latter sold it to Mrs. Cook on 13 January 1904 for $500.

After living in the house only eleven years, Mrs. Cook sold it to L. D. Adams (*see page 85*) on 19 June 1911 for $3400. Mr. Adams and his wife lived there until they built a house on the opposite side of Floyd Street and half a block nearer the Square (*see page 85*). On 9 March 1920 Mrs. Mamie F. Adams sold the property to W. F. Williams for $11,000.

William Franklin Williams (*10 October 1855—15 October 1925*), a native of Greene County, was a railroad locomotive engineer and a farmer.

He and his wife, née Sarah Ellender Campbell (*18 October 1855—7 January 1934*), were the parents of Margaret Williams (*3 July 1875—3 June 1960*), who became the wife of James Edward Hutchins (*25 May 1873—8 January 1958*), a grocer in Covington and Atlanta.

The house passed by inheritance from Mr. and Mrs. Williams to their daughter Mrs. Hutchins and thence to the latter's daughter Mrs. R. H. Patterson. Although she now lives in the beautifully restored McCormick Neal house nearby, Mrs. Patterson still owns her ancestral home.[47]

THE COTTAGE (Clark)

Contemporary view of the lovely Neal - Patterson house.

Whether referred to as the Neal-Patterson house or, as Mrs. Patterson prefers, *The Cottage*, the former home of McCormick Neal the younger is today one of Covington's architectural treasures. The Library of Congress long ago indicated its importance by recording measured drawings and a photograph for the edification of future generations. Happily for Covingtonians of today, the house itself stands as a pristine relic of a by-gone era.[48]

This is the home Mama visited

When she was a young lady.

XVIII
DR. ARCHIBALD CAMP'S HOUSE

An attractive ante-bellum cottage set far back from Conyers Street was originally the home of a member of one of Covington's prominent pioneer families.

The property upon which it was built once formed a part of the vast holdings of Charles H. Sanders, who probably was the wealthiest man in ante-bellum Covington (*see page 40*). Twelve acres of the east part of Lot Number 65, located on the south side of what later became Conyers Street and extending approximately from the present railroad tracks to what is now Dearing Street, were sold subsequent to a survey made of the Sanders lands in November 1851.[1]

The buyer was Dr. Archibald Lacy Camp, a prominent local physician and merchant. His father, Gerard Camp (*5 December 1794–5 December 1861*) was one of the earliest settlers of Covington. His mother was the former Martha Lacy of Warren County (*7 October 1796–8 July 1879*). The elder Camps' other children included Charles, Septimus G., John Randolph, William J., Germaine T., Hannah, Martha (Mrs. Dorsett), and Sarah Frances (Mrs. William P. Anderson).[2]

Dr. Archibald Camp probably began construction upon his house at about the time he married his second wife, Marietta H. Sayers, on 28 September 1858. There his children, Avah, Archie, Eulah, and Charley, spent their earliest years. Before the youngest was born, however, the dark clouds of an impending crisis loomed over the Camps and their fellow citizens.[3]

Relations between North and South, which had been worsening for some time over the twin issues of economics and slavery, became so strained in 1860 that war appeared to be inevitable. Dr. Camp and his brother Charles declared adamently that they would not fight. They were proud of their heritage as American citizens, and held in high esteem the memory of their grandfather Samual Camp (*1753–1802*), who as a Revolutionary soldier had helped to forge the new nation which southern hotheads now sought to rent asunder.[4]

Years later a descendant of Dr. Camp wrote that he was a delegate to a convention held in Macon at which the question of secession was voted upon. A majority of the delegates had been instructed to vote that Georgia remain in the union, but the eloquence of such firebrands of Robert Toombs swayed many of them. Dr. Camp remained steadfast, however, and voted against so desperate an act as secession. (While it is a matter of historical record that the Secession Convention convened at *Milledgeville* on 16 January 1861 and that Newton County's representatives to it were *Alexander Means, W. S. Montgomery*, and *Purmedus Reynolds*, this anecdote is useful in presenting a picture of Dr. Camp in the context of the times.)[5]

The ordinance of secession was passed on January 19 and signed by the Governor two days later. Dr. Camp immediately converted into United States currency everything he owned except his home, his general mercantile store at Clark and Monticello streets, and his slaves. The latter were left in custody of his sister and brother-in-law, Mr. and Mrs. William P. Anderson, whose property adjoined the Camps' on the west (*see page 188*). Then, with the help of his youngest brother, nineteen year-old Septimus, Dr. Camp and his family made their way north. Arrested almost immediately as a political prisoner, he was freed as a result of personal intervention by Secretary of War Edwin M. Stanton. It is believed that the latter was prompted to act by Secretary of State William H. Seward, who likely had known some of Dr. Camp's family during his brief tenure as a Putnam County schoolmaster in 1819.[6]

Meanwhile, Dr. Camp's brother Charles had been arrested for refusing to report to the local conscripting officer of the Confederate States Army. A handsome, well-dressed man, he owned a large plantation and operated a bag and twine factory near Covington. Despite his renowned prowess with the rifle which was his constant companion, he firmly refused to fight in a war of which he strongly disapproved. He was sent to a prison camp in Virginia, where he complained that he was unable to bathe for an entire year.[7]

Two of the Camp brothers served in the Confederate army, and both were captured and imprisoned. When finally they were relased these two made their way to Cutchogue, Long Island, where they joined their brother Archibald and his family. When at last the South capitulated, Dr. Camp ended his long exile and sailed from New York for Savannah. In the latter city the family saw for the first time the devastation left in the wake of the war.[8]

Upon reaching Covington Dr. Camp found a less shocking spectacle, but nonetheless a sad state of affairs. As he wrote later, he returned to find "my big house ruined. Poor folks moved in with the hogs, all the furniture stolen, no crops, just weeds. Negro quarters in ruins, medical practice gone . . ." His store on the Square had been burned, along with many others, after the Yankees had first looted it.[9]

His brother Charley reached home emaciated, ragged, and barefoot. He was so debilitated from his long confinement that he was scarcely able to stand for many weeks. When he told his former slaves that they were free and could leave or stay, as they chose, they loudly declined to depart, saying "We love you, Marse Cholly." [10]

The Yankees had bivouaced at Charles Camp's plantation and had taken his carriage, two blooded horses, most of the cattle and mules, and killed all of the pigs. The owner's superb store of liquid refreshment had been spared, together with a large quantity of food and ten mules and two wagons, because of the cleverness of a huge Negro man named Smokey. Having been saved from the chain gang by "Marse Cholly," Smokey forever after rendered unhesitating and devoted service to his benefactor. It was he who had hidden many valuables and necessities in abandoned cabins deep in the woods and thus kept a few precious items safe from the invading Yankees.[11]

Gradually recovering from his ordeal, Charles Camp* was married on 23 November 1865 to Julia McCracken, daughter of a local cabinetmaker. In less than two years, the bridegroom died as a result of his wartime imprisonment. A few weeks later his widow was delivered of a beautiful daughter who was christened Charles Josephine. On 10 February 1870 Mrs. Camp became the wife of Oliver S. Porter, a Yankee-born widower who had rebuilt her husband's war-damaged factory, as well as Dr. Archibald's grinding mill. From then until her death in 1953, Charles Camp's daughter was known by the name of her step-father, who built upon the nucleus of the Camp factory the huge Porterdale Mills which still are an important factor in the economic life of the Covington area.[12]

Meanwhile, Dr. Archibald Camp lost no time in trying to pick up the fragments of his pre-war life. The house was repaired and gradually refurnished, and after a time a new store building was erected opposite the courthouse. The children were growing into attractive young adults, and Dr. Camp confidently looked to a happy and secure future.[13]

Alas, it was not to be — at least not in Covington. The old friends and neighbors who once had been Dr. Camp's patients now sought professional services elsewhere. Even worse, he and his family were cooly excluded from the social life of the community. Families which had arrived upon the scene many years after his own, and whose blood was less blue and whose

* Charles Camp (11 February 1830–5 July 1867) was a colorful character whose exploits are delightfully preserved in Uncle Charley and His Rifle, by his grandnephew Archel L. Camp (Boulder, Colorado: 1960).

PORTERDALE

This attractive house in Porterdale is believed to have been built for Charles Camp. For many years it was the home of his widow and her second husband, Oliver S. Porter. In recent decades it has been the residence of the superintendent of the Bibb Company's mill, which was the foundation upon which the Porter fortune was built.

money — if such there were — was all new, now presumed to make a pariah of a man whose conscience had not permitted him to engage in fratricidal warfare.[14]

One can imagine with what mixed emotions — disappointment, contempt, regret, hope — Dr. Camp finally determined to leave his home town and seek a new life elsewhere. In 1872 he and his family moved to Colorado, where he acquired large tracts of farm land near a colony peopled by men who were building irrigation canals from the Coche la Poudre River. Some of his descendants a hundred years later still lived in the vicinity of Boulder.[15]

The move to Colorado brought anguish to at least one member of the Camp family. Two years later Dr. Archibald wrote to his sister-in-law Julia Porter to say that young Archie had set out with thirty cents in his pockets to walk the 1,760 miles back to Georgia. The youth arrived three months later, hungry, ragged, and anxious to see his beautiful cousin Carrie Carroll. His Anderson relatives gave him some money and a suit of clothes, and then he set out to win the shy Carrie. She capitulated, and they were married on 26 May 1875. Dr. Camp sent the bridegroom $1,700 with which to open a grocery store, but Archie extended credit to so many friends and relatives that he soon went broke. With Carrie and their new baby,* he regretfully returned to Colorado.[16]

It is probable that Dr. Camp's house in Covington was rented during the first years after his departure. On 4 January 1878 the owner transferred title to the house and twelve acres to his daughter Mrs. Eulah Stillwell of Rockdale County. One week later she sold it to the Reverend J. M. Brittain for $5000. A father's love undoubtedly accounted for the much lower price of $1500 which Mrs. Stillwell had paid for the property.[17]

Jabez Marshall Brittain, the new owner of Dr. Camp's former home, was born in Oglethorpe County on 4 May 1842. His grandfather, George Brittain, had moved there from Virginia in 1797, and his father, Henry Brittain, was ordinary of the county for many years.[18]

Young Mr. Brittain had attended Mison Academy in Lexington, Georgia, and had been graduated from Franklin College (now the University of Georgia) in 1861. On 29 September of that year he was mustered into the Confederate States Army, in which he served until August 1864. Having been baptized into the Baptist Church at Antioch in 1857 and subsequently licensed to preach by the church at Lexington, he was appointed chaplain of the 38th Georgia Regiment in 1863. Almost simultaneously, and while still in uniform, he was ordained to preach by the Lexington church.[19]

*Archibald L. ("Archel") Camp (1876–1968). In his old age he authored the delightful collection of family stories entitled *Uncle Charlie and His Rifle* which is the source for some of the data in these pages.

In January 1865 the young preacher married Miss Ida Calla-way, granddaughter of the noted Reverend Enoch Callaway. Five children were born of this union.[20]

The Reverend Mr. Brittain moved to Covington to become principal of the local Male Academy. He held the additional positions of pastor of the Baptist churches in Conyers and Salem, and of the First Baptist Church in Covington.[21]

It is said that one of the factors influencing his decision to move to the seat of Newton County was the proximity of Emory College, where his sons would be afforded an oppor-tunity to receive a sound classical education. One son, Marion Luther Brittain, received the A.B. degree from Emory in 1886. He went on to a distinguished career as Superintendent of Fulton County Schools, State School Commissioner and State Superintendent of Education. The climax to his career came in 1922 when he was installed as president of Georgia School (now Institute) of Technology, in which capacity he served until his retirement in 1944. It must have afforded him partic-ular pleasure to become president of an institution which was the natural outgrowth of technological experiments conducted at Emory College under the auspicies of Isaac S. Hopkins, who left the presidency of Emory to become Tech's first president. In his own history of Georgia Tech* Dr. M. L. Brittain mentioned with appreciation the contributions made to that institution by Oliver S. Porter of Newton County, an original member of the governing board and a long-time Tech trustee. (Mr. Porter, it will be remembered, had married Dr. Archibald Camp's widowed sister-in-law.)[22]

Dr. J. M. Brittain apparently left Covington in November 1889, for *The Covington Star* recorded the marriage on 2 October of his daugher Lillian to Mr. H. D. Arnold of Washington "at the home of her parents" and the marriage on 20 December of his son Luther to Miss Lettie McDonald

* M. L. Brittain, *The Story of Georgia Tech* (Chapel Hill: 1948)

FIRST BAPTIST CHURCH

Construction was begun in 1909 upon this handsome structure at the northeast corner of Floyd and Elm streets. The site had previously been occupied by the cottage which was owned before the Civil War by Mr. and Mrs. William P. Anderson and Mr. and Mrs. George B. Daniel. Subsequent owners included Mr. and Mrs. Eugene O. Lee and Mr. and Mrs. N. S. Turner (*see pages 188, 231*).

The dedicatory sermon was preached on 24 December 1911 by the Reverend Dr. J. M. Brittain of Atlanta only a few weeks before his death. The beloved clergyman had been pastor of the church for several years in the 1880s.

As noted on page 6, this is the fourth edifice to be occupied by the local Baptist denomination. It was extensively remodeled in the 1960s.[23]

of Atlanta, at which one of the officiating ministers was "Dr. J. M. Brittain of Augusta." Upon his death in Atlanta on 11 February 1912, a few weeks after he had preached the dedicatory sermon for the new First Baptist Church in Covington, it was said that, "His sweet, gentle, Christ-like spirit was demonstrated in everything he did and said, and all who knew him loved him . . . " [24]

For thirty years the Camp-Brittain house was occupied by a succession of families. For a ten-year period beginning in 1908 it was rented by Millard E. Parker (*1856–1923*), who moved to Covington from Notasulga, Alabama. With him came his second wife, née Lizzie Peddy (*1865–1957*), and their children Ruth, Iola (later Mrs. Harry Dietz), and Julius (who subsequently moved to Columbus). Also included in the family group were six children born of Mr. Parker's first marriage: Alma, Ethel (later Mrs. Hugh Murray of Atlanta), Mabel (who became the wife of P. T. Austin of Covington), Rena (later Mrs. Sinclair of Roland, North Carolina), Robert and Grady. The two sons, together with their brother Earnest who had preceded the family to Covington, later moved to Atlanta. Two married daughters, Fannie and Ruby, remained in Alabama. [25]

Mr. Parker opened a grocery store in a building on the north side of Floyd Street, near the Pace Street intersection. His wife, later assisted by his daugher Alma, soon acquired a reputation among Covington's prominent matrons as a seamstress of uncommon ability. [26]

After the Parkers moved out the former Camp home was occupied briefly by Mr. and Mrs. Harmon King. Eventually it passed into the possession of J. D. Gardner and H. W. King, who sold it on 28 August 1919 to J. W. Wright for $4000. Mr. Wright in turn sold it to A. S. McGarity on 9 November 1922 for $5000. Less than three months later, on 20 February 1923, the property changed hands again when Howard Piper acquired it for $4000. The last transaction excluded a lot extending fifty feet along Conyers Street which Mr. McGarity had sold to Mrs. A. B. Loyal.[27]

Howard Piper, a carpenter and building contractor, was born in Newton County on 28 February 1878 and died in an Atlanta hospital on 10 June 1958. He and his wife, Ida, had four sons and two daughters, two of whom — Mrs. Cleo Butler and Virgil Piper — were long-time residents of Covington.[28]

The Piper family occupied the Camp-Brittain home only two years, selling it on 16 February 1925 to Mrs. Frances Godfrey Candler for a consideration of $5500. Not included in the sale was a small portion of the property which Mr. Piper had sold to Edward H. Lewis.[29]

Mrs. Candler was the former Frances Godfrey, daughter of Mr. and Mrs. P. W. Godfrey (see page 227) of Covington. Her husband, Charles Candler, was born and reared in Oxford, where his father, the Reverend (later Bishop) Warren A. Candler, served as president of Emory College for ten years beginning in 1888. The senior Candler was a brother of Coca-Cola tycoon Asa G. Candler, whose munificent benefactions materially aided Emory in its latter years at Oxford and which made possible its removal in 1919 to the rolling Druid Hills campus in Atlanta.[30]

Mr. and Mrs. Charles Candler restored the Camp-Brittain house and grounds to what must have been a modern approximation of their original beauty. The rooms were furnished handsomely, and there the Candler daughters Caroline (now Mrs. Lowry Hunt of Madison) and Frances spent their girlhood. During these years the house was the scene of many social affairs and of gatherings for the Oxford academic community of which the family remained an integral part. The Candlers' annual oyster roasts were memorable events on the local social calendar.[31]

When the Candlers moved to Madison following the death of Mr. Godfrey, their Conyers Street home was sold to T. C. Meadors on 18 August 1941 for $7000.[32]

GODFREY-GREER HOUSE

This house at the southeast corner of Conyers and Davis streets was erected early in the present century for Mr. and Mrs. Peter Walton Godfrey. The columns across the front of the house had origionally adorned the facade of the old Pitts Hotel on the east side of the Square, which had been erected as a dormitory for students at Southern Female College (*see pages 112-118*).

Mrs. Godfrey was one of Covington's social leaders, renowned for her elaborate luncheons, teas and dinners. Her home was staffed with numerous servants and she presided over it with grace and charm. Mrs. Godfrey founded Christian Science churches in Covington and Madison, and was once president of the local chapter of the United Daughters of the Confederacy.

Mr. Godfrey was in business with his son-in-law under the name of Godfrey & Candler, Wholesale Grocers. The first manager of the local telephone exchange, he was a director of the Bank of Covington.

After many years in their adopted city the Godfreys returned to his native Madison and restored a handsome ante-bellum house. Subsequently Mr. and Mrs. Charles Candler sold their Covington home and moved into it.

The former Godfrey residence in Covington is now owned and occupied by Mr. and Mrs. W. Thomas Greer.[33]

Thomas Clarence Meadors was a native of the Leguinn community of Newton County, where he was born 20 July 1891. He was a popular middle-aged bachelor at the time of his marriage to Lily Mae Webb, a local school teacher who hailed from Loganville. Long employed by Heard-White Mercantile Co., he had started Meadors Freight Line when the store went out of business in 1930. Mr. Meadors had served as a second lieutenant in the Quartermaster Corps in World War I. At various times he was a Mason and a Shriner, a member of the Kiwanis Club, treasurer of the Methodist church, first adjutant of the local American Legion post, and a member of city council. He died 18 April 1955.[34]

For several years after the loss of her husband Mrs. Meadors conducted a kindergarten. Then, on 17 December 1958, she was married to Parks Winfield Pratt in a quiet ceremony at her home. The bride was attired for the occasion in a powder blue satin dress with which she wore a corsage of pink carnations. The bridegroom, a widower, was a self-made man who had attained success as a saw mill operator and as part owner of a building supplies business. He died 21 May 1963 at the age of sixty-seven.[35]

In the last decade the lovely cottage built for Dr. Archibald Camp has evidenced increasingly the thought and effort which Mrs. Pratt has expended upon it over a period of many years. The spacious, high-ceilinged rooms are an appropriate setting for the attractive furnishings which she has collected carefully and arranged tastefully. There Mrs. Pratt presides with the regal dignity of a queen. Although she never had children of her own, she welcomes the children and grandchildren of her contemporaries and is in every way a gracious hostess to friends of all ages.

HOUSE BUILT FOR DR. A. L. CAMP

This attractive ante-bellum cottage, erected *circa* 1859, was the boyhood home of the late Dr. M. L. Brittain, one-time president of Georgia Tech. It is now the residence of Mrs. P. W. Pratt, Sr.

XIX

THE LEE-ROGERS HOUSE

One of Covington's handsomest residences was built at the northwest corner of Monticello and Pennington streets in 1899. The site, like others in the immediate vicinity, had once been a part of the holdings of Mrs. Sarah Flanegan. It was bounded on the north by the home of Franklin Wright (*see pages 164–167*) and to the south of it, separated by Pennington Street, was the former Osborn T. Rogers mansion (*see pages 146–147*).[1]

The tract of nearly twelve acres was purchased by E. O. Lee on 7 January 1897 from W. B. Shepherd (*see pages 45–46*), executor of Mrs. S. B. Mixon. The property had earlier been the site of the home of Mr. Shepherd's parents, Mr. and Mrs. T. J. Shepherd. When it burned late in the 1890s that house was occupied by Mrs. Mixon, who may have been a sister of the younger Shepherd.[2]

Immediately after purchasing the property from Mr. Shepherd, E. O. Lee became engrossed in plans for the house which he intended to build, and soon construction was underway. When completed the two-story brick structure with white columns flanking the front entrance was a house of classic elegance. In the ensuing years it was to be home to the Lees' growing family and the scene of many brilliant social affairs.[3]

Eugene Orson Lee was born on 11 April 1859, the youngest child of William Sheffield and Mary (Webb) Lee (*see page 194*). On 8 April 1884 he married Miss Tommie Anderson (*1 July 1865–16 October 1928*), a daughter of Dr. J. C. Anderson and the former Amanda Belcher of Starrsville. Mrs. Lee was a sister of Dr. N. Z. Anderson (*see page 180*) of Covington, and their grandfather, Colonel Newton Anderson (*11 May*

1813–2 July 1886), was a long-time sheriff of Newton County.[4]

Eugene O. Lee owned and operated a general store on the west side of the Square. His business was flanked by his competitors: on the south the business operated by Dr. J. J. Dearing (*see page 189*) and his sons J. M. and A. E. Dearing, and on the north by the firm of [Edward] Heard, [Charles] White & [D. A.] Thompson.[5]

Mr. Lee was a successful businessman and a public-spirited citizen. He was a director of the First National Bank and in 1898 he was elected mayor of Covington. Through ability and hard work he amassed a comfortable fortune, but in the grim Depression which began in 1929 he was virtually wiped out. Less than a year later *The Covington News* reported: "Mr. Eugene O. Lee, one of Covington's most prominent citizens,

HOME OF MR. AND MRS. E. O. LEE
Subsequently the residence of the late Mr. and Mrs. E.B. Rogers.

... passed away at his mansion on Monticello Street ... He was connected directly and by marriage ... with many prominent County families ..."[6]

Mr. and Mrs. Lee were the parents of Lester (*see page 240*), Berto, Gladys (who became the wife of H. Barron Kelly of Monticello and later lived in Hendersonville, North Carolina), Lillian, Dorothy, Doctors Carlton and Jack, and Eugene O. Lee, Jr.[7]

The beautiful Lee residence passed from the family on 12 February 1931 when N. S. Turner (*see pages 167–8*) foreclosed on a mortgage which he held on the property. Years earlier Mr. Turner and his family had hospitably been taken into the Lee home when they were new in Covington. Subsequently he had purchased the Lee's former home at the northeast corner of Floyd and Elm streets, site of the present Baptist church.[8]

Next occupants of the Lee home on Monticello Street were Mr. Turner's daughter and son-in-law, Mr. and Mrs. Emmett Butler Rogers. Mr. Rogers (*1892–1969*), who was known to his friends as "G. W.," was a Covington native who had left town for a year or two as a young man. Upon his return in 1904 *The Georgia Enterprise* informed its readers that "Mr. Butler Rogers ... has rented a house on Corley hill and will be found behind the counter for Swann-Davis Co." On 7 June 1928 he married Miss Natalie Rogers (*1898–1969*), an alumna of Shorter College, and soon thereafter her father made a place for him at Covington Mills, of which Mr. Turner was then president.[9]

On 17 August 1950 the Rogers' only child, Julia, was married to Robert William Hamilton, Jr., in an afternoon ceremony at her parents' home. The bride wore for the occasion a ballerina-length gown and fingertip veil, and carried a bouquet of asters and chrysanthemums.[10]

Later a small house was erected for the newlyweds on the south side of the Rogers home. Upon the deaths of both of her parents in 1969 Mrs. Hamilton inherited her girlhood home; however, she elected to remain in the house where she had reared her daughters Jane and Emma.[11]

Today the Lee-Rogers house is occupied by young Miss Jane Hamilton. Most of the furnishings remain as they were during her grandparents' lifetimes, but they have been augmented by some of the furnishings from the noted Burge-Bolton house (*see pages 93, 129*), which her mother purchased in 1969 and sold shortly thereafter.[12]

The stately old house is graced by the beauty and youth of its chatelaine. Only a few doors to the north Miss Dorothy Lee lives in a small apartment, close enough to permit her to be reminded of happier days when she, too, was young and enjoying the beautiful home in which she grew to young ladyhood.

XX
THE PORTER-ROGERS-TUCK HOUSE

Floyd Street has been called one of the most beautiful streets of ante-bellum houses to be found anywhere in the South. The first three blocks of this avenue are, in truth, notable for the grace and dignity of the columned houses which nestle under a canopy of towering oaks, elms, and pecan trees. Cheek-by-jowl with these handsome reminders of another era are unpretentious structures which serve only to emphasize the beauty of the Greek Revival houses.

The first house one sees on Floyd Street after leaving the Square is, curiously enough, not one of its oldest. It is, however, a columned structure of imposing proportions which serves as an introduction to its neighbors.

The site of the house was identified in the plan of Newtonsboro as Lot 13 in Square D. It was sold by the town's commissioners to Amos Welborn of Morgan County and John Loyall, and on 10 December 1822 the latter purchased the former's interest for $80.50. Subsequently acquired by Cary Wood, whose beautiful columned house occupied the next lot to the east, it was sold after his widow's death to James T. Corley (see pages 72, 106). The small cottage on the property may have been built as an early home for one of the Wood sons or daughters. Soon after Mr. Corley purchased it on 6 February 1877 for $750, he sold a portion of the College Street frontage to the Baptist church as the site for a new house of worship (see page 6). Next owner of the cottage was A. B. Simms (see pages 57, 61–64), who in 1889 sold it to Wilkins Willingham for $1000. Mr. Willingham and his wife, née Emma Wright, lived in the house until the turn of the century, when the property was acquired by James H. Porter.[1]

Mr. Porter had the cottage demolished and a new house erected in 1903 for his bride, the former Olive Swann (*see page 24*), whose parents then lived in the former Cary Wood residence next door. The fathers of the couple, Oliver S. Porter (*see page 220*) and Thomas C. Swann (*see page 23*), had formerly been business associates and close friends. A disagreement over a personnel situation at Covington Mills, of which the two men were founders, caused a bitter and permanent estrangement. Mr. Swann emphatically forbade his daughter to see James Porter, but by then the young people were deeply in love. They eloped on 18 December 1902.[2]

The bride, who was born on 3 February 1876, had finished her education at fashionable Lucy Cobb Institute in Athens, graduating in the class of 1893. The bridegroom, born on 24 January 1873, was educated at Emory College, after which he went to work in his family's textile mills.[3]

Mr. and Mrs. Porter occupied their columned Floyd Street house only a few years. In 1907, nine years after the Porterdale mills were sold to Bibb Manufacturing Company, Mr. Porter was asked to go into the company's general offices in Macon. He was made treasurer in 1909, vice president in 1910, and vice chairman of the board in 1936. Following Mr. and Mrs. Porter's removal to Macon they maintained a stately town house on College Street and a Normandy-style country home, *Porterfield*, on an estate south of the city. The trial rose gardens at the latter were termed the most extensive in the South.[4]

Mrs. Porter became a leading social figure in Macon and in time her husband was recognized as that city's most outstanding philanthropist. His benefactions included the donation of Porter Field, Porter Hall, and Mary Erin Porter Dormitory to Mercer University, and of the Porter Family Auditorium to Wesleyan College. After the death of his wife Mr. Porter presented many of their handsomest furnishings, paintings and *objects d'art* to the Olive Swann Porter Rooms at Wesleyan;

he also endowed the Olive Swann Porter book fund at Washington Memorial Library in Macon and gave her magnificent silver tea service to the Savannah headquarters of the Georgia Society of the Colonial Dames of America. Covington and Porterdale also benefitted from James. H. Porter's generosity, chiefly through the donation of a large sum of money to the Julia A. Porter Memorial Methodist Church which he had built as a memorial to his mother in the latter place, and the establishment of various trust funds which made substantial contributions toward the construction of the present Newton County Hospital and other worthy community projects. Although they lived in Macon most of their adult lives, both Mr. and Mrs. Porter always retained a great affection for the scenes of their youth, and upon Mrs. Porter's death on 3 August 1939 and Mr. Porter's death on 13 June 1949 their remains were entombed in their mausoleum in Covington City Cemetery. The couple was childless.[5]

When the Porters moved to Macon their Floyd Street house was sold to James Franklin Rogers for $4225 on 1 April 1913. "Colonel" Rogers, a prominent attorney in Covington, was born in Walton County on 12 December 1856, a son of Perry S. Rogers and his first wife, née Martha Ivy. He was a student at the University of Georgia for one year beginning in 1875, after which he enrolled in Emory College, from which he was graduated in 1878. After studying law under future governor Henry D. McDaniel of Monroe, he was admitted to the bar in 1879. He practiced his profession at Social Circle before moving to Covington in 1885.[6]

During his more than thirty years as an attorney and leading citizen of Covington, Colonel Rogers served variously as city attorney, solicitor of the Court of Newton County, and as attorney for the Central of Georgia Railroad and the Covington Mills. On many occasions before his death in 1922 he was honored for his outstanding qualities as a leading member of the bar and as a public-spirited citizen.[7]

PORTER-ROGERS-TUCK HOUSE
Erected for the late Mr. and Mrs. James H. Porter

Colonel Rogers married (1) Emma Celestia Ray of Walton County, 10 April 1879, and, several years after her death in 1887, (2) Mrs. Belle Wadsworth Knox of Alabama, in December 1894. His only child, Emery Ray Rogers, was born of the first marriage. The second Mrs. Rogers had a son, James Knox, who was for a while his step-father's law partner.[8]

During her years in Covington Mrs. Belle Rogers devoted much time to beautifying the little garden at the rear of her home. She was active in affairs pertaining to the Presbyterian church and the United Daughters of the Confederacy, and served for a time as president of the local chapter of the latter. One of her activities was to sell bowls of soup for five cents each to pupils from the public school in the block back of her white-columned home. Many a grown man of today remembers running to "Miss Belle's" back porch at lunch time with a nickel clasped tightly in one hand.[9]

On 6 November 1923 E. R. Rogers, as administrator of his father's estate, sold the Floyd Street house to Mrs. Louise

Gheesling Tuck, wife of Covington attorney Reuben Tuck, for $7250.[10]

Reuben McDaniel Tuck was a native of Walton County, where he was born on his father's plantation on 31 October 1887. After attending the public schools in Monroe he matriculated at the University of Georgia, from which he was graduated in 1912 with the Bachelor of Laws degree. He began the practice of his profession at Winder, served in 1913 and 1914 as secretary to Congressman Samuel J. Tribble, and upon returning from Washington entered into a law partnership in Monroe. After serving overseas in World War I he moved to Covington, where he was for many years associated with Colonel James F. Rogers, whose house eventually became his own home.[11]

"Colonel" Tuck, as he was called in the old-fashioned manner of addressing distinguished members of the bar, was for many years an active force for civic betterment in his adopted home town. He was the first city recorder, president of the Newton County Bar Association, and for many years he was city attorney. A courtly gentleman of the old school, he steadfastly refused to buy an automobile, and his erect figure was a familiar sight as he strode briskly around Covington.[12]

Colonel Tuck was married on 21 October 1920 to Miss Louise Gheesling of Greensboro, Georgia. They became the parents of two sons, Dr. Goodwin Gheesling Tuck, who now practices medicine in Covington, and Reuben Tuck, Jr., of Marietta.[13]

Following Mrs. Tuck's death in 1965 at the age of seventy-one, Reuben M. Tuck continued to live in their Floyd Street home until his own death on 20 May 1969. On the latter occasion *The Covington News'* tribute to him said in part:

> Col. Tuck's innate integrity and dedication to the principles of his profession and his religious convictions were legendary; and won the respect and esteem of his fellowmen in the community he loved and served. . .[14]

After years of neglect, during which Colonel Tuck had virtually camped out in a portion of his home, the structure was bought on 13 July 1970 by Mr. and Mrs. J. C. Ward. Although the new owners had a home on Monticello Street and had recently converted the former First Baptist-Christian Science church at the rear of the Porter-Rogers-Tuck house into apartments, they set about enthusiastically to restore their latest acquisition. Now repaired and freshly painted, it is once again a credit to the historic street upon which it fronts.[15]

XXI

THE LEE-PORTER HOUSE

One of Covington's most imposing Greek Revival houses was erected on East Conyers Street for Lester Lee, son of Mr. and Mrs. Eugene O. Lee (*see page 231*).

The property upon which it is situated was, in Covington's early days, included in the holdings of the Reverend Charles H. Sanders (*see pages 37, 40*). The entire block, designated as Lot 24 in Square D, subsequently was owned by Charles Camp, James T. Corley, and Henry Anderson ("Person of Color"). On 5 January 1912 the eastern half of the block was sold by Mrs. C. W. Anderson to Lester Lee for $1000.[1]

Mr. Lee soon erected upon the site a beautiful two-story house with magnificent Corinthian columns. There he and his attractive wife, née Mary Carithers of Monroe, delighted in entertaining. They were gracious hosts and their home became a favored gathering place for congenial groups of friends from Covington and other parts of Georgia.[2]

Lester Lee owned and operated a drugstore on the east side of the Square. Modern, spacious and attractive, it had a large soda fountain which was popular with businessmen, young matrons, and members of the high school set. Mr. Lee may have over-extended himself in building and furnishing a fine home and in equipping his place of business so handsomely, for soon he was bankrupt. On the first Tuesday in August 1914 Charles C. King and others, as Trustees in Bankruptcy, sold the Lee residence at public outcry. It was bought by Mrs. Lee's mother, Mrs. Sudie Carithers, for $4,500.[3]

The Lee family continued to live in their beautiful home, and there Lester and Mary (Carithers) Lee reared their children: Caroline, James Robert, Eugene O. 3rd, and Lester

Lee, Jr. Some years later the family moved to Elberton, where Mr. Lee operated a drugstore which was continued after his death by his son and namesake.[4]

On 31 July 1924 Mrs. May C. Lee, as sole heir of her then-deceased mother, sold her home to O. W. Porter. The transaction involved "a certain sum of money and the exchange of house and lot on corner of Emory and Clark Street where O. W. Porter resides . . ."[5]

The purchaser was Oliver William Porter, a genial man who was known to his legion of friends as "Wick." A son of Oliver S. and Julia (McCracken) Porter (*see page 220*), he was born on 31 March 1875 and was reared in his family's home in nearby Porterdale (*see page 221*). For some years a partner in the Porterdale Mercantile Co. (*see page 181*), he became in later life an owner of the Nixon-Porter-Turner Ginning Company. Mr. Porter was an active and prominent supporter of many of Covington's most worthwhile enterprises. He was a Kiwanian, a Mason, a Shriner, and a member and deacon of the Presbyterian church. Elected to the Covington Board of Education in 1934, he became chairman four years later. He served as a member of City Council and in his last years was deputy clerk of Newton Superior Court. At the time of his death on 20 March 1947 it was said that, "Throughout his entire life Mr. Porter took an active interest in the business, civic, and religious welfare of the community . . . Hundreds of friends paid final tribute to [him] . . ."[6]

Soon after purchasing the Lester Lee residence Mr. Porter moved his family into the house on East Conyers Street. There he and his wife, the former Elizabeth Jane Todd (*1 October 1889–4 April 1960*) of Due West, South Carolina, reared their three children. On 1 October 1930 Mr. Porter transferred ownership of his house to his wife.[7]

During their years in the beautiful Greek Revival structure the Porters and their friends made it a center of social life for young and old alike. Mrs. Porter furnished it with handsome antiques, two of which excited considerable comment when the house was opened for the first public tour of Covington homes in 1948. One of these was an English clock whose face bore, instead of numerals, the name of its original owner, Oliver Porter, great-grandfather of "Wick" Porter. The other item of interest was a magnificent four-poster bed with canopy in which General George Washington was said to have slept. It had formerly belonged to the late Mrs. James H. Porter of Macon, née Olive Swann of Covington (*see pages 24, 235*), who had acquired it from the estate of her friend Mrs. Mary Washington Bellamy of Macon, who was a descendant of one of the First President's half-brothers.[8]

Mr. and Mrs. Porter's daughters Julia and Harriett were attractive girls who enjoyed great social popularity during their young ladyhood. In August 1942 they were married to Doctors John and Ralph Scurry, brothers who practiced together in Greenwood, South Carolina. Their beautiful double wedding took place in Julia Porter Memorial Methodist Church in Porterdale, which their uncle James H. Porter of Macon (*see pages 235-236*) had given to the community as a memorial to his mother. The brides, wearing coronets adorned with lace brought from Europe by Mrs. James H. Porter, were given in marriage by the latter's husband and by their father. Later the brides' parents gave a lovely reception at their handsome home.[9]

An unexpected development prior to the wedding necessitated a substitution among the groomsmen and undoubtedly caused Mr. and Mrs. Porter much anxiety. This came about when their only son, Oliver William Porter, Jr., disappeared only one day before the ceremony. When he could not be located, his close friend Thomas Swann, 3rd was pressed into service as substitute groomsman. It later developed that shy young "Billy" Porter had fled the scene of wedding preparations to enlist in the Marine Corps. Less than three years later he lost his life in a savage battle on the Pacific island of Iwo

LEE-PORTER MANSION
During the years when it was the home of the Eugene O. Lees and the
O.W. Porters, this impressive structure was the scene of many gala social affairs.

Jima. When his body was returned home for interment following the end of World War II, it was Corporal Porter's
friend "Tom" Swann who handed his grieving mother the
American flag which had covered her son's casket.[10]

On 13 January 1959 Mrs. Elizabeth T. Porter transferred
ownership of her home to her daughters "for $10 and in
consideration of the love and affection which she bears said
children." Three years later Mrs. Porter died while visiting her
daughters in Greenwood. She was buried beside her husband
and son in Covington, in which city she had long been a
prominent figure. She was a member of the Covington Presbyterian Church, where she had taught the Young Matrons' Class
and later the Adult Class for a number of years. On the
national level Mrs. Porter had served as president of Women of
the Church at two different times. She had been active in the

Covington Garden Club, the Woman's Club, and the Sergeant Newton Chapter, DAR.[11]

On 21 April 1962 the Mesdames Scurry, née Porter, sold their parents' home to J. A. Crimmins of Lamar County for "$10 and other valuable considerations." Two years later, on 26 June 1964, Mr. Crimmins sold the property to Mrs. Drew W. Ashworth on the same terms. Mrs. Ashworth, a beautician, and her husband, a plumber, occupied the house until they returned to Atlanta in 1972. The property was then put on the market.[12]

EPILOGUE

And thus we conclude our journey into the past.

It is hoped that the reader feels now that he knows the men and women who peopled the houses which he has visited vicariously. Their course is run; their place in the annals of Covington is secure.

The beautiful houses which inspired this look backward remind us of times which are no more. Their soaring columns and graceful dignity provide an aura which, hopefully, will increasingly be a source of pride to present and future residents of Covington and of Georgia. These great houses are a rich legacy from the past which should be cherished and passed on as the heritage of generations yet unborn. Their ultimate fate rests, to a great extent, with the people of the community.

> A thing of beauty is a joy forever;
> Its loveliness increases; it will never
> Pass into nothingness
> — Keats, *Endymion*

A SUGGESTED DRIVE
PAST COVINGTON'S OLD HOUSES

(These are private homes and not open to the public.)

From the Public Square drive east on Floyd Street. In the second block is:

1. First Baptist Church. Across from it is:

2. The Porter-Rogers-Tuck House (No. 1146). Across from it is:

3. Ginn Apts. (No. 1155). Across the street is:

4. *Swanscombe* (No. 1164). Next to it is:

5. *The Floyd House* (No. 1184). Across the street is:

6. *Usher House* (No. 1187). On opposite side in next block is:

7. Wood Apts. (No. 2130). Two doors east is:

8. The Travis residence (No. 2154). On opposite corner is:

9. *The Cottage* (No. 2149). Two doors east is:

10. Cook-Allen-Williams House (No. 2173). Two blocks east, on right side of Floyd Street at Mill Street, is:

11. The Henry-Mobley House (No. 3166). One-half block east is:

12. Rheburgh-Sockwell-Hardman House (No. 3190). Less than two blocks away, on the right-hand corner of Dearing Street, is:

13. The Dearing home (No. 1022). One block east on left side is:

14. Bethany Assembly (facade of Neal-Sanders house). Drive to first street on right (Adams); turn right and go one block; turn right and go back into Floyd Street; continue one block to Dearing; turn left and go one block to East Conyers Street; turn right. In middle of block on left side is:

15. The Camp-Pratt house (4158 E. Conyers). Cross tracks. On left is:

16. Home of Mr. and Mrs. S. A. Ginn. Two blocks west on left side is:

17. The Lee-Porter House (No. 2146). Two doors west is:

18. The Godfrey-Greer House (No. 2126). Turn right onto Davis Street. Second house on right is:

19. *The President's House* (No. 1123). At next corner turn left onto College Street. First structure on right side is:

20. Former carriage house at *Swanscombe.* Next to it is:

21. Former Baptist-Christian Science Church (No. 1143). Across from it is:

22. The Callaway home (No. 1144). At corner turn left;

Woman's Club will then be on right. Go two blocks to Conyers Street and turn right. Property on right was formerly the site of the Neal-Sanders house, while the Batts-Camp house formerly occupied the block on the left. At traffic light turn left onto Church Street. First United Methodist Church will be on right, and at the other end of the block behind it will be The Church of The Good Shepherd (Episcopal). Across from the latter is:

23. The DeWald-Wood-Pratt house (No. 2171). Straight ahead is:

24. *Dixie Manor* (607 Pennington Street). Across from it is:

25. The Lee-Rogers-Hamilton house (2204 Monticello Street). At triangular park in front of this house turn right onto Monticello Street and head north. On left is:

26. *Whitehall* (No. 2176). In middle of next block, on left, is:

27. The Bates-Terrell-Borella house (No. 2108). At next corner is:

28. *Edwards House* (No. 1184). On opposite corner is:

29. Post Office, which occupies the former site of the Conyers-Pickett residence. Proceed north on Monticello to next traffic light and turn left onto Reynolds Street. At next corner, on left side of street, is:

30. Brown-Anderson-Allen House. Turn right onto Hendricks Street and go to second traffic light; turn left onto Clark Street. On left is:

31. Presbyterian church. Continue approximately six blocks to traffic light at Clark and West streets. Turn right. On left behind trees is:

32. *Clark's Grove.* At next street on right, turn into Corley Street. In middle of block on left is:

33. The Carr-Cody-Corley House, now sadly deteriorated. Proceed to corner and turn left. At Stone Mountain Street, turn left and go one block to West Street; turn right and go some four blocks to:

34. *Lawnwood* (No. 5155 N. West Street). Go two blocks to Emory Street and stop. Turn right to return to Covington. Turn left to Oxford's old houses and the campus of Oxford College of Emory University.

35. *Mt. Pleasant* is located about six miles east of Covington, via Highway 278. Head toward Madison and turn down unpaved Cedar Lane. House is on left.

36. Morehouse residence at *Burge Plantation* is about ten miles east of Covington on the Eatonton road. Leave town on Highway 278 and follow signs toward Eatonton. House is on left side of road less than a mile after a four-way highway stop. Across the road is:

37. The original Burge home, which formerly occupied the site of the Morehouse residence.

SOURCE NOTES

I: THE SETTING

1. Allen D. Candler and Clement A. Evans, eds., *Cyclopedia of Georgia* (Atlanta: 1906), II: 337–338.
2. *Ibid.*, 362–363, 712; Mary Givens Bryan, comp., *Georgia Official & Statistical Register 1957–1958* (Hapeville: 1958), p. 705; The Rev. George White, *Historical Collections of Georgia* (New York: 1854; reprint Danielsville, Ga.: 1968), p. 574.
3. George Gilman Smith, D.D., *The Story of Georgia and The Georgia People* (Macon: 1900), pp. 360–361; "History of Brick Store Community," n.d., of which Mrs. Walter C. Emmel appears to be the author, *circa* 1964; speech delivered by Mrs. Annie Laura (Robinson) Dodson of Oxford before the Madison Town Committee of The Colonial Dames of America in 1950, examined through the courtesy of the author.
4. Mary Sessions Mallard, "History Corner," *The Covington News*, 3 June 1971; letter from William A. Parker of Atlanta to the Newton County Historical Society accompanying his gift for the restoration of Brick Store, 1971. Charles Malvin Jordan, donor of Brick Store, died 14 November 1972 at the age of 79, and his obituary appeared in *The Covington News* on 16 November 1972.
5. Warren Grice, *The Georgia Bench and Bar* (Macon: 1931), pp. 112, 113, 114, 153, 254, 356; Smith, *The Story of Georgia and the Georgia People, idem.*; Sergeant Newton Chapter, DAR, Historical Marker in front of Brick Store.
6. Donald Stephenson in a conversation with the author on 26 October 1972.
7. Georgia Historical Commission Marker 11 C 8 in Social Circle; Speech by Mrs. Dodson, *idem.*
8. *Code of Georgia Annotated* (Atlanta: 1966), p. 163; William C. Dawson, *Compilation of The Laws of The State of Georgia Passed By The General Assembly, Since The Year 1819 To The Year 1829, Inclusive* (Milledgeville: 1831), p. 441; George White, *Statistics of the State of Georgia* (Savannah: 1849), p. 451; letter to the author from the Office of Information Services, Department of the Army, Washington, D.C., 11 March 1972.
9. The Rev. Adiel Sherwood, *A Gazetteer of Georgia* (Macon, Griffin and Atlanta: 1860; reprint Atlanta: 1970), p. 103; White, *Historical Collections, op. cit.*, p. 575. Quotations are from the former.
10. Lucian Lamar Knight, *Georgia's Landmarks, Memorials and Legends* (Atlanta: 1913, 1914), II: 910; unidentified newspaper clipping owned by Miss Sarah Mobley; Donald Stephenson in a conversation with the author on 7 Nov. 1970.
11. Copy of *Act* (1822) in possession of Miss Sarah Mobley; Deed Record I ("eye"): 406.
12. Candler and Evans, *Cyclopedia of Georgia, op. cit.*, III: 352–353.
13. Mrs. Thaddeus Horton, "Ante-Bellum Homes of Covington Splendid Illustration of Beautiful Unrivaled Architecture of the Old South," *The Atlanta Constitution*, 21 September 1913.
14. *Idem.*
15. Franklin M. Garrett, *Atlanta and Environs* (New York: 1954), I: 150, 191,

218—219; G. C. Adams, "Chronicles of Newton," *The Covington News*, 21 Oct. 1927; "History of First Baptist Church of Covington, Georgia," *The Covington News*, 13 Aug. 1926; Deed Record S: 555; Georgia Historical Commission Marker on Highway 278 in Covington commemorating Garrard's raid; cornerstone of present First Baptist Church; Miss Lois Gray, Historian of First Baptist Church, in conversations with the author on 20 Dec. 1971 and 17 Nov. 1972; Mrs. Charles S. Thompson and her sister Mrs. Ralph L. Turner of Atlanta (née Sarah and Bonner Simms, respectively, of Covington) in a conversation with the author on 27 Jan. 1971; tombstone in the Colley Family Cemetery on Alcovy Road.

16. *The Covington Star*, 5 Mar. 1889. The writer signed himself "Donohoo."

17. L. Wilson Jarman, "A Walk Around the Square [in 1889]," *The Covington News*, 14, 21 May 1953.

18. Donald Stephenson in a conversation with the author on 11 July 1971.

19. A. D. Meador, "The History of Covington," *The Covington News*, 20 Oct. 1915.

II: THE BROWN-ANDERSON HOUSE

1. Mrs. George Allen in a conversation with the author on 4 August 1972.

2. Deed Records A: 264, O: 302; Mrs. W. S. Cook, Sr., in a conversation with the author on 3 Nov. 1971. Although Deed Record O: 302 states that Coleman Brown "lived and died" on the property obtained from Mr. Reynolds, the letter quoted on page 59 of the present work proves that he was killed on the battlefield in 1862.

3. James I. Robertson, Jr., ed., *The Diary of Dolly Lunt Burge* (Athens: 1962), p. 82; Marriage Records 1850—59: 169, 1860—1865: 259; Will Record 3: 20; letter from James P. Simms quoted on page 59 of the present work.

4. Deed Record O: 302.

5. *The Covington News*, 31 Jan. 1912; *The Covington Star*, 2 April 1901; United States Census 1870—Georgia—Newton County, p. 89.

6. *The Covington Star*, 2 April 1901; *The Georgia Enterprise*, 2 April 1901; Deed Record L: 423—424; Will Record 3: 131—132; Hawkins' tombstone in Covington City Cemetery.

7. *The Covington News*, 31 January 1912.

8. Will Record 4: 185—187.

9. Deed Record 20: 184; Mrs. Allen, *idem.*; tombstones in Covington City Cemetery.

10. *The Covington News*, 3 Dec. 1926; Will Record 4: 410—416; tombstone in Covington City Cemetery.

11. Deed Record 21: 141; Mrs. Cook, *idem.*

12. Deed Record 38: 198; Marriage Record 1: 163; Mrs. Cook, *idem.*

13. Deed Record, *ibid.*; Mrs. Allen, 10 Oct. 1972.

14. Mrs. Allen, *idem.*

III: SWANSCOMBE

1. Lucian Lamar Knight, *Georgia's Bi-Centennial Memoirs and Memories* (Atlanta: 1932), II: 386—387, and *Georgia's Landmarks, Memorials and Legends* (Atlanta: 1913, 1914), II: 911.

2. Deed Record S: 362; Will Record 4: 202; Family Record of Louise Haygood (Mrs. Hugh H.) Trotti of Decatur; Index card at State Department of Archives and History, in Atlanta, citing *Military Record 1779–1839*, p. 185.

3. Family Record, *ibid.* For Dyer-Robinson see *The Covington Star*, 2 Feb. 1897; Deed Record 7: 392; Will Record 4: 10–11.

4. Henry Morton Bullock, *A History of Emory University* (Nashville: 1936; reprint Atlanta: 1972), pp. 56–57, citing *Minutes* of the Georgia Conference of the Methodist Church, 16 Dec. 1836; William C. Dawson, *Compilation of The Laws of The State of Georgia Passed By The General Assembly, Since The Year 1819 To The Year 1829, Inclusive* (Milledgeville: 1831), p. 441; Knight, *Landmarks, idem.*; Abstracts From Minutes of the Inferior Court, 5 August 1822, p. 9; Deed Records B: 255, E: 503–504; Inferior Court Records 1824, p. 20.

5. Deed Record B: 123.

6. Knight, *Landmarks*, II: 912; Frederick Doveton Nichols and Frances Benjamin Johnston, *The Early Architecture of Georgia* (Chapel Hill: 1957), pp. 118–119, 125, 131, 139, 281–282; personal examination of *Swanscombe's* structure by the author.

7. Knight, *Landmarks, idem.*; Petition of Joseph Mitchell against Cary Wood, with itemized Attachments, 1839 (filed in metal drawer in Office of Clerk of Newton County Superior Court).

8. Family Record, *idem.*; Mrs. David Butler of Covington and Robert R. Wood of Atlanta, great-grandchildren of Cary Wood, in conversations with the author on 9 Mar. 1970 and 8 Aug. 1971, respectively; tombstones, Covington City Cemetery.

9. *Idem.*

10. Superior Court Minutes 1858–1863: 362–364; Will Record 8: 249–250.

11. Lillian Henderson, *Roster of the Confederate Soldiers of Georgia 1861–1865* (Hapeville: 1960), IV: 509; *Memoirs of General William T. Sherman* (New York: 1875), II: 180; the late Thomas C. Swann [Jr.], as quoted by his widow (now Mrs. William B. Williford) on 30 Apr. 1971, concerning the encampment of Union troops across from the Wood house; Robert R. Wood, *idem.*

12. Deed Record S: 260–261, 520; Mrs. Butler, *idem.*

13. Mary Givens Bryan, comp., *Georgia Official & Statistical Register 1957–1958* (Hapeville: 1958), p. 1188; Lodowick Johnson Hill, *The Hills of Wilkes County, Georgia, and Allied Families* (Atlanta: 1922), p. 197; A. L. Hull, *A Historical Sketch of the University of Georgia* (Atlanta:1894), "Alumni, 1843," Lucian Lamer Knight, *A Standard History of Georgia and Georgians* (Chicago/New York: 1917), VI: 2787,2853; United States Census 1860 – Georgia – Newton County, p. 77.

14. Gen. Clement A. Evans, ed., *Confederate Military History* (Atlanta: 1899), VI: 381; Henderson, *Roster of Confederate Soldiers, ibid.*, IV: 508; *Southern Confederacy*, a newspaper published in Atlanta for five years beginning in 1859, issue of 22 Mar. 1862. Curiously, General Henderson is not listed in Ezra J. Warner, *Generals in Gray. Lives of the Confederate Commanders* (Baton Rouge: 1959) nor in Bell Irwin Wiley and Hirst D. Milhollen, *Embattled Confederates* (New York: 1964), although his service as a brigadier general, CSA, is established beyond doubt in the works cited by Evans, Henderson and Hull.

15. Knight, *A Standard History, idem.*, and Georgia's *Landmarks, ibid.*, II: 912; Family Record, *idem.*; Mrs. Butler, *idem.*; tombstones of General and Mrs. Henderson in Covington City Cemetery, the dates upon which conflict with the dates cited in Knight's *A Standard History.*

16. *The Covington Star*, 21 May 1901; Deed Record 13: 190—192.

17. Allen D. Candler and Clement A. Evans, eds., *Cyclopedia of Georgia* (Atlanta: 1906), IV: 290—291; Deed Records T: 687—688, W: 205—206, 13: 192. On 5 Jan. 1916 *The Covington News* carried a story headlined "T. C. Swann Company Quits After 37 Years."

18. Candler and Evans, *Cyclopedia of Georgia, idem.*; Knight, *Landmarks*, I: 680; *Memoirs of Georgia Historial and Biographical* (Atlanta: 1895), II: 652—653; Deed Records W: 205—206, X: 500, Z: 55—56; record in Swann Family Bible, now owned by Mrs. William B. Williford, who is Mr. Swann's daughter-in-law, and conversation with her on 1 August 1969; tombstone, Covington City Cemetery.

19. Candler and Evans, *Cyclopedia of Georgia, idem.*; Walter G. Cooper, *The Story of Georgia* (New York: 1938), IV: 79; Knight, *A Standard History*, VI: 2853; *Memoirs of Georgia, idem.*; *The Covington Star*, 20 Dec. 1898; *The Georgia Enterprise,* 22 Dec. 1899, 9 Feb. 1906; *The Weekly Enterprise*, 9, 16, 30 Mar. 1906; Deed Record Z: 52—53.

20. Candler and Evans, *Cyclopedia of Georgia, idem.*; Cooper, *The Story of Georgia, idem.; Georgia: Historical and Industrial* (Atlanta: 1901), p. 778; Knight, *A Standard History, idem.*; *Memoirs of Georgia, idem.*; *The Covington News*, 10 Nov. 1955 and 12, 19 Dec. 1963; *The Covington Star*, 18 Feb. 1896, 20 Dec. 1898, 14 Apr. 1900; *The Macon Telegraph*, 4 Aug. 1939; Record of Charters, I: 23—25, filed in office of Clerk of Newton County Superior Court; letter from Preston W. Carroll of Mansfield to Mrs. Frank Miller, 17 January 1964, which was examined through the courtesy of the recipient (now Mrs. William B. Williford).

Covington Mills was sold in 1955 by the last heir of the Swann family, who owned forty-nine per cent of the outstanding shares of the corporation, and the heirs of Founder T. C. Swann's associates. The accounts of the transaction which appeared in *The Atlanta Constitution*, 7 Nov. 1955, and *The Covington News*, 10 November 1955, do not *begin* to tell the complete story of this amazing "deal," which ultimately resulted in vast unemployment when, as reported in *The Atlanta Journal*, 11 Dec. 1963, and *The Covington News*, 12, 19 Dec. 1963, the new owners ceased operations. See also *Moody's Industrial Manual*, July 1958, p. 1450, and 1960 edition, p. 1145.

21. Candler and Evans, *Cyclopedia of Georgia, idem.*; tombstone in Covington City Cemetery. Mr. Swann's obituary appeared with a picture on page 1 of *The Georgia Enterprise*, 16 Mar. 1906, and the same newspaper carried a tribute to him on 30 Mar. 1906.

22. Candler and Evans, *Cyclopedia of Georgia, idem.*; *The Covington News*, 26 January 1922; entry in Swann Family Bible, now owned by Mrs. William B. Williford; tombstone, Covington City Cemetery. The quotation is from the *News.*

23. Medora Field Perkerson, *White Columns in Georgia* (New York/Toronto: 1952), p. 28; *Garden Gateways*, publication of The Garden Club of Georgia, Jan.–Feb. 1969, pp. 41, 43; Program for Commencement Exercises at Lucy Cobb Institute, 14 June 1893, now in possession of the author; Mrs. William B. Williford, sister-in-law of the former Olive Swann, in various conversations with the author between 1969 and 1972.

24. *Who's Who In Commerce and Industry* (New York: 1936), p. 925; *The Covington News*, 29 March 1945, which had a banner headline story and picture on page 1; Honorable Discharge of Thomas C. Swann [Jr.] for service in the United States Army from 9 Aug. 1917 to 13 Jan. 1919, now in possession of the author; David Butler and Mrs. William B. Williford in conversations with the author on 9 Mar. 1970 and 1 Aug. 1969, respectively. Mr. Swann's widow and son later gave two hand-carved pulpit chairs to the First [United] Methodist Church in his memory, as noted in Methodist Homecoming Bulletin, 13 June 1954, p. 4, a copy of which was made available to the author by Miss Martha Ramsey.

Sources for cutline beneath picture of Thomas Swann in his 1912 National automobile: letter to the author from Charlene M. Ellis of the Indianapolis Motor Speedway Corporation, 22 June 1971, and conversation with Mr. Swann's widow (now Mrs. William B. Williford) on 1 May 1971.

25. Perkerson, *White Columns, idem.*; Katherine Pierce, "Hostesses in Hoop Skirts at Covington's Tour of Homes," *The Atlanta Journal Magazine*, 24 Apr. 1949; Wylly Folk St. John, "Old South Tour of Covington," *The Atlanta Journal Magazine*, 19 Apr. 1948; "Old Homes of Covington," a booklet prepared by the Covington Garden Club (1969), p. 1; Mrs. William B. Williford in a conversation with the author on 1 Aug. 1969.

26. *Directory of the Phi Delta Theta Fraternity* (Oxford, Ohio: 1958), p. 259; *The Covington News*, 19 May 1949, which had a banner headline story and picture on page 1; Certificate of Graduation for Thomas Chalmers Swann from Darlington School, 2 June 1941, and Honorable Discharge of Thomas C. Swann III, private first class, for service in the Army of the United States from 10 July 1943 to 12 October 1945, both of which were examined through the courtesy of his mother. For accounts of various social affairs at which Mr. and Mrs. Swann were hosts see *The Covington News*, 10 Jan. 1930; 13 Sept., 18 Oct., 29 Nov. 1935; 7 Feb. 1936; 27 Aug. 1942, *etc.*

27. *The Covington News*, banner headline stories and pictures on page 1 in issues of 29 Mar. 1945 and 19 May 1949; Program for Dedication of Memorial Chapel at Darlington School, 7 December 1958, on which occasion young Mr. Swann's mother unveiled a window which she had given in memory of him. Other gifts by her to perpetuate his memory are the magnificent stained glass windows in The Church of The Good Shepherd (Episcopal), in Covington, and the Thomas Chalmers Swann 3rd Scholarship at Oxford College of Emory University. The author has in his possession a letter to the then-Mrs. Frank M. Miller from S. Walter Martin, president of Emory University, dated 21 Dec. 1959, in which he expresses appreciation for her generosity in establishing the scholarship fund.

28. Mrs. William B. Williford in a conversation with the author on 15 May 1971.

29. *Idem.*; undated clipping from *The Atlanta Constitution*, October 1951, and Certificate of Marriage, 12 October 1951, at Kenilworth, Illinois, examined through the courtesy of the former Mrs. Miller.

30. *The Covington News*, 28 June 1962; conversation with Mrs. William B. Williford on 8 May 1971. The former is a full-page advertisement for Parsons-Hutchins and Minnesota Paints, Inc., which features interior and exterior photographs of *Swanscombe* and an exterior photograph of the residence of Mr. and Mrs. N. S. Turner with this caption above the latter: "Blinds Painted with Resistol Swanscomb Green."

31. *The Atlanta Constitution*, 5 April 1963; *The Covington News*, 11 April 1963. Mr. Miller's widow (now Mrs. William B. Williford) has given to her stepson Edward F. Miller a copy of a letter which his father wrote to the Zone Finance Officer in Washington on 19 Mar. 1919 stating that he had served on active duty in the Aviation Section of the Signal Corps between 12 Dec. 1917 and 11 Dec. 1918 and that he was appointed second lieutenant on 8 May 1918. A native of Cairo, Illinois, where he was born on 17 Nov. 1897 and near where he is buried in Mounds Cemetery, Frank M. Miller was a graduate of Northwestern University and a retired executive with U.S. Gypsum Corp.

32. *The Montgomery Advertiser*, 25 June 1969; Certificate of Marriage, 23 June 1969, now in possession of the bridegroom. William B. Williford was reared in Americus, Georgia, and is an alumnus of the University of Georgia. A major in the Air Force of the United States (Ret.), he served on active duty in World War II (12 Sept. 1942–31 Jan. 1946) and during the Korean Conflict (10 Aug. 1950–9 May 1952). For more extensive data, see *Dictionary of International Biography* (London: 1972), Vol. IX, p. 1349.

33. *The Covington News*, 18 Oct. 1935, 7 Feb. 1936, 27 Aug. and 3 Sept. 1942; "Year Book/Sergeant Newton Chapter/Daughters of the American Revolution/1895–1970," pp. 2–3, 28; various conversations with Mrs. Williford between 1969 and 1972.

34. Wylly Folk St. John, "Old South Tour of Covington," *The Atlanta Journal Magazine,* 18 Apr. 1948. In addition to the published sources cited in these Notes for *Swanscombe*, see Celestine Sibley, "Covington's All Set: 'Home Tour' Saturday," *The Atlanta Constitution*, 23 Apr. 1948. (The four-color picture of the house which was used on page 1 of this issue is said to have been the first color photo ever used by an Atlanta newspaper.)

IV: THE NEAL-SANDERS HOUSE

1. Deed Records A: 617, B: 540–541, K: 617; Index card at State Department of Archives and History, in Atlanta, citing *Military Records 1808–29*, p. 44; tombstone in old Methodist portion of Covington City Cemetery.

2. Deeds, *idem.* and R: 251.

3. Miss Geniveve Scully of Atlanta has in her home beautiful silver and furniture which belonged to her great-grandmother, the former Mrs. McCormick Neal.

4. Mary Givens Bryan, comp., *Georgia Official & Statistical Register, 1957–1958* (Hapeville: 1958), pp. 999, 1188; Deed Record B: 301.

5. Deed Record K: 563; Mrs. Asa G. DeLoach of Atlanta, who in the course of a telephone conversation with the author on 28 Oct. 1972 stated that her late sister Lillian (Bigby) Jordan's first husband was McAllen Batts Marsh, son of E. W. Marsh and his first wife; E. Marsh Adair, of Trenton, Missouri, a grandson of the latter couple, wrote the author on 15 Nov. 1972 that his grandmother was the former Adelaide Batts; his cousin Miss Addie Augusta Wert of LaFayette, Georgia, wrote the author on 18 Nov. 1972 that

not only was E. W. Marsh's first wife from Covington—he himself had lived there briefly early in life with his father, Spencer Marsh "who, after coming from North Carolina in Indian times first stopped in Covington, then moved here . . ."

6. *The Covington News*, 21 Oct. 1927, 9 Mar. 1928; Deed Records K: 563, 30: 38; Marriage Record 1850—59; 161; O. Grant Gooden of Springfield, Pennsylvania, a great-grandson of Dr. Archibald Camp (*see pages 217—221*), who stated in a letter to the author dated 8 Oct. 1972 that Randolph Camp was a son of Gerard Camp; tombstones in old (Methodist) portion of Covington City Cemetery.

7. Edward Mayes, *Lucius Q. C. Lamar: His Life, Times, and Speeches, 1825—1893* (Nashville: 1896), pp. 56—58; Marriage Records 1843—48: 106, 1850—59: 101, C: 106; Mrs. D. Leon Wilson of Macon, Georgia, letter to the author dated 15 Dec. 1970; Miss Geniveve Scully of Atlanta, a great-granddaughter of the former Mrs. McCormick Neal, in conversations with the author on 14 Oct. and 18 Nov. 1970; tombstones in the old portion of Covington City Cemetery.

8. Deed Record E: 282; Marriage Record B: 174; Miss Scully, *idem.*

9. Mary Givens Bryan, comp., *Georgia Official & Statistical Register 1957—1958*, p. 1190; Dr. Charles C. Jarrell, *Oxford Echoes* (Oxford, Ga.: 1967), p. 12; Marriage Record 1849—1855: 8; Index card on Captain Lorenzo F. Luckie at State Department of Archives and History, in Atlanta; tombstone in old portion of Covington City Cemetery.

10. Marriage Record 1860—65: 99.

11. Bryan, *Georgia Official & Statistical Register*, pp. 999, 1188; Franklin M. Garrett, *Atlanta and Environs* (New York: 1954), I: 381—382; Will Records 1: 81—82, 1850—1871: 69, 335—336; Newton County Ordinary Donald Stephenson in a conversation with the author on 17 Oct. 1970; tombstones in old portion of Covington City Cemetery.

12. *The Atlanta Constitution*, 19 Sept. 1946, 22 June and 28 Oct. 1947.

13. *Idem.* The story of "Lady Haw-Haw" is told in outline form and with apparently some inaccuracies in Isabel Chrisler, "Demorest In The Piedmont," n.d., n.p., a booklet presumably published at Demorest, pp. 25—27.

14. Bryan, *Georgia Official & Statistical Register*, p. 1188; Marriage Records 1822—35: 240 and 1865—69: 309; Mrs. Ivy Smith of Jacksonville, Florida (née Caroline Wooten, great-granddaughter of Judge Pace, of Covington), in a conversation with the author at her summer home at Highlands, North Carolina, on 28 July 1971; tombstones in old portion of Covington City Cemetery.

15. *Bryan, Georgia Official & Statistical Register, idem.*; Garrett, *Atlanta and Environs*, I: 393; A. L. Hull, *A Historical Sketch of the University of Georgia* (Atlanta: 1894), "Alumni" listing in back of book; Lucian Lamar Knight, *Georgia's Landmarks, Memorials and Legends* (Atlanta: 1913, 1914), II: 923; *The Covington News*, 11 Sept. 1912; Deed Record K: 357; Marriage Record 1860—65: 37; tombstones in old portion of Covington City Cemetery.

16. Garrett, *Atlanta and Environs*, II: 103; W. E. Hopkins in *The Atlanta Journal*, 5 May 1939; *The Covington Star*, 29 Apr. 1885.

17. Marriage Record 1860—1865: 99; Tombstone in old portion of Covington City Cemetery. *Author's Note: The fairly extensive information concerning the Luckie and*

Pace families is given in this chapter because, of all the prominent pioneer Covington families, they are—almost without exception—the only ones whose histories cannot be told in the accounts of the city's extant columned mansions.

18. Garrett, *Atlanta and Environs*, II: 61, 176; Augustus Longstreet Hull, *Annals of Athens, Georgia 1801—1901* (Athens: 1906), p. 487; Hal Gulliver in *The Atlanta Constitution*, 6, 7 Apr. 1970; *The Atlanta Journal*, 18 Aug. 1902; *The Covington Star*, 20 Mar. 1888; Marriage Record 1867—74: 90; invitation to the Luckie-Hemphill wedding, owned by the couple's granddaughter Miss Geniveve Scully of Atlanta, who also provided various data on her antecedents in conversations with the author on 14 Oct. and 18 Nov. 1970.

19. Jarrell, *Oxford Echoes*, pp. 20—24; The Rev. George White, M.A., *Historical Collections of Georgia* (New York: 1854; reprint Danielsville, Ga.: 1968), pp. 575—579; George White, *Statistics of The State of Georgia* (Savannah: 1849), p. 451;

20. Deed Record K: 623 reveals that one of the Rev. Mr. Sanders' earliest purchases was made on 4 Dec. 1824 when he paid Thomas Swindle of Morgan County $200 for a tract of land in the tenth district of what had originally been Henry County.

21. Will Record I: 231—236.

22. *Georgia Laws, 1866*, p. 146.

23. Deed Record N: 326.

24. Deed Record O: 221.

25. I. W. Avery, *The History of the State of Georgia From 1850 to 1881* (New York: 1881), p. 464; Robert Preston Brooks, *The University of Georgia Under Sixteen Administrations 1785—1955* (Athens: 1956), p. 201; Clark Howell, *History of Georgia* (Chicago: 1926), IV: 613; *Masonic Messenger*, a publication of the Grand Lodge of Georgia, issue of June 1938; "In Crackerland With Ralph Smith," *The Atlanta Journal*, 29 Mar. 1933; obituaries of Dr. Shelton V. Sanford in the same newspaper, 15 Sept. 1945, and in *The Atlanta Constitution*, 16 Sept. 1945; "Some Early History of Newton County," by Mrs. R. M. Mobley, *The Covington News*, 21 Oct. 1927; *The Georgia Enterprise*, 5 Aug. 1904; Marriage Record 1867—74: 30; tombstone in Covington City Cemetery.

26. Deed Record O: 277.

27. Avery, *The History of the State of Georgia*, pp. 17, 53, 73, 348; Bryan, *Georgia Official & Statistical Register*, pp. 999, 1188; Lucian Lamar Knight, *Reminiscences of Famous Georgians* (Atlanta: 1902), II: 272; United States Census 1860—Georgia—Newton County, p. 40.

28. Garrett, Atlanta and Environs, I: 323, 327(69) and II: 818; *The Covington Star*, 14 Feb. 1888, 7 Feb. and 18 July 1893, 21 Jan. 1896; Marriage Records 1860—65: 35, 1874—84: 201, 496; Will Record III: 20; tombstones in old portion of Covington City Cemetery.

29. Mrs. William B. Williford in a conversation with the author on 11 Jan. 1971; tombstones in Covington City Cemetery.

30. Bryan, *Georgia Official & Statistical Register*, pp. 1000, 1189; Miss Sarah White Callaway in conversations with the author on 28 Oct. 1970 and 26 June and 20 Oct. 1972: tombstones, Covington City Cemetery.

31. Deed Record R: 251.
32. Tombstone, Covington City Cemetery.
33. *The Georgia Enterprise*, 9 Oct. 1903; Chrisler, "Demorest In The Piedmont," pp. 14—15; United States Census 1870—Georgia—Newton County, p. 90; Deed Record 5: 417—418; Marriage Record 1874—84: 60, 268.
34. L. Wilson Jarman, "A Walk Around The Square [In 1889]," *The Covington News*, 14 May 1953; Mrs. Charles S. Thompson and Mrs. Ralph L. Turner of Atlanta (née Sarah and Bonner Simms, respectively, of Covington) in a conversation with the author on 27 Jan. 1971; tombstone, Covington City Cemetery.
35. Deed Record 26: 130.
36. *Idem.* and p. 152.
37. *The Covington News*, 28 Jan. 1971; *The Covington Star*, 7, 15 June 1887; Deed Records U: 184—185, X: 72, 8: 38, 9: 154, 10: 225—226, 20: 215; Newton County Tax Digest 1971: 3; Leon Cohen in a conversation with the author on 3 Oct. 1972. Mr. Cohen stated that his uncle Abe Cohen, first of the family in Covington, died in Arizona in 1971 at the age of 100.
38. Deed Record 26:371.
39. Miss Martha Ramsey, daughter of C. D. Ramsey, in conversations with the author on 4 Nov. 1971 and 11 Nov. 1972; tombstones, Covington City Cemetery.

V: THE GRAHAM - SIMMS HOUSE

1. Henry Morton Bullock, *A History of Emory University* (Nashville: 1936; reprint Atlanta: 1972), pp. 31, 55—56, citing *Acts of the General Assembly of Georgia, 1834*: 150—151 and *1836*: 99—101 and "Emory College Trustees' Minutes," 6 Feb. 1837. Dr. Graham signed a deed of sale on 28 July 1842 (Deed Record I: 357), and the Inferior Court of Newton County granted his widow permission to sell some of his property in Nov. 1847 (Deed Record I: 543).
2. Deed Record I: 543, 544; Will Record I: 35—39.
3. Mrs. John B. Reeves (née Sarah, daughter of Henry and Henrietta Graves) in a conversation with the author at her home in Brevard, N.C. on 27 July 1971.
4. *Idem.*; tombstone of Solomon Graves in the cemetery at *Mt. Pleasant*, examined by the author on 31 Oct. 1970 through the courtesy of King Cleveland, who then owned the property.
5. John D. Wade, *Augustus Baldwin Longstreet* (Athens: 1969), p. 91; Elizabeth G. Neal, "Jingle Written by Judge Longstreet," *The Atlanta Journal* [*Magazine*], 27 Sept. 1925; Marriage Record A: 283; Mrs. Reeves, *idem.*
6. "History of Brick Store Community," n.p., n.d., of which Mrs. Walter C. Emmel presumably is the author, *circa* 1964; Mrs. Reeves, *idem.*
7. Deed Records 96: 518; 99: 1—4; 115: 604.
8. *The Covington News*, 21 September 1972.
9. Mrs. Reeves, *idem.*; Mrs. Charles S. Thompson of Atlanta (née Sarah Simms of Covington) in conversations with the author on 9 Dec. 1970 and 26 Jan., 14 Nov. 1971.

10. Dr. Goodrich C. White, "Old Oxford," *Bulletin of Emory University*, 15 Feb. 1948, pp. 3–13 (speech delivered before the Georgia Society of Historical Research, 9 Oct. 1947); Marriage Record C: 133; Mrs. Reeves, *idem.*

11. Mary Givens Bryan, comp., *Georgia Official & Statistical Register 1957–1958* (Hapeville: 1958), p. 118; Edward Mayes, *Lucius Q. C. Lamar: His Life, Times, and Speeches 1825–1893* (Nashville: 1896), 28–37, 45, 46, 56, 57–60, 72, 80, 89, 94, 103, 114, 120, 124, 128–129, 178, 265, 312, 316, 318, 446, 472, 528, 538; Deed Record I: 406; Mrs. Reeves, *idem.* (she is a granddaughter of Mrs. Graham's brother Iverson L. Graves). For a sensitive appraisal of L. Q. C. Lamar's notable and courageous political career, see John F. Kennedy, *Profiles In Courage* (New York: 1961), pp. 152–177.

12. Inferior Court Minutes, 1838–51: 224; Mrs. Reeves, *idem.*; tombstones at *Mt. Pleasant.*

13. Deed Record K: 405; tombstone at *Mt. Pleasant.*

14. Bryan, *Georgia Official & Statistical Register*, p. 1100; Philip Van Doren Stern, *Robert E. Lee: The Man and The Soldier* (New York: 1963), pp. 22–23; Mrs. Thompson, *idem.*

15. Bryan, *Georgia Official & Statistical Register*, p. 118; Mrs. Thompson, *idem.*

16. William C. Dawson, *Compilation of The Laws of The State of Georgia Passed By The General Assembly, Since The Year 1819, Inclusive* (Milledgeville: 1831), p. 441; Dr. Charles C. Jarrell, *Oxford Echoes* (Oxford: 1967); Mrs. Thompson, *idem.*

17. Deed Record G: 412.

18. Deed Record K: 405; *Masonic Messenger*, a publication of the Grand Lodge of Georgia, Sept. 1938; Mrs. Thompson, *op. cit.*, 26 Jan. 1971.

19. Resolution adopted by Golden Fleece Lodge No. 6 on "July 11, 5850," the original of which is owned by Judge Simms' granddaughter Mrs. Charles S. Thompson of Atlanta; tombstones in Oxford Cemetery.

20. Mrs. Willie Conyers Cook, "Clement Bates, Englishman . . .," *The Sunday American* [Sunday issue of *The Atlanta Georgian*], 11 Sept. 1932; Will Records II: 71–72 (RLS), III: 169–177 (HJB); Mrs. Thompson, *op. cit.*, 11 Jan. 1971.

21. Mrs. John B. Davis, "History of Covington U. D. C.," a copy of which was made available to the author through the courtesy of Miss Sarah Mobley.

22. Ezra J. Warner, *Generals in Gray* (Baton Rouge: 1959), pp. 277–278; Allen D. Candler and Clement A. Evans, eds., *Cyclopedia of Georgia* (Atlanta: 1906), III: 294; Record of "Newton Anderson Guards" (Co. E., 53rd Rgt. Ga. Vol. Inf.), at State Department of Archives and History, in Atlanta; "Muster Roll of Captain Henry T. Henry's Company," 31 January 1862, the original of which is owned by Captain Henry's grandson David Butler, through whose courtesy a copy was made available to the author on 9 Mar. 1970; Marriage Record 1860–65: 87.

23. Records at State Department of Archives and History; Mrs. Thompson, *Idem.*

24. *Idem.*

25. Davis, "History of Covington U. D. C."

26. The original of this letter is owned by Major Simms' niece Mrs. Charles S. Thompson of Atlanta, who graciously permitted the author to copy it on 9 Nov. 1971.

27. The original of this letter is owned by Major Simms' niece Mrs. Charles S. Thompson of Atlanta, whose own niece and namesake, Mrs. Fred Fletcher of Atlanta, kindly made a copy for the author of 30 Nov. 1971. The date and place of Lieutenant Simms' death are a matter of record at the State Department of Archives and History.

28. Index card at State Department of Archives and History: United States Census 1860—Georgia—Newton County, p. 16.

29. Index card at State Department of Archives and History. Charles H. Sanders [Jr.] is mentioned in the will of his mother, Mrs. Sarah Ann Sanders, in Will Record 1850—1871: 279—281.

30. John F. Kennedy, *Profiles In Courage* (New York: 1961), p. 160; Lucian Lamar Knight, *Georgia's Landmarks, Memorials and Legends* (Atlanta: 1913, 1914), II: 366, 945; Mayes, *Lucius Q. C. Lamar*, p. 24.

31. Douglas Southall Freeman, *Lee's Lieutenants* (New York: 1950), III: 634, 704n, 705, 773.

32. James I. Robertson, Jr., ed., *The Diary of Dolly Lunt Burge* (Athens: 1962), p. 91 (No. 79); Mrs. W. C. Clark, "Covington During The Sixties," *The Covington News*, 21 Oct. 1927.

33. Letter from A. B. Simms to his siter Lucy Simms, written from Fishers Hill, Va., 18 Oct. 1864, which is now owned by his daughter Mrs. Charles S. Thompson.

34. Mms. Thompson and Turner, *idem.*, 11 Jan. 1971.

35. The late Thomas C. Swann [Jr.] as quoted by his widow (now Mrs. William B. Williford) on 17 Dec. 1971.

36. *The Covington Star*, 1 Dec. 1886 and 31 May, 14 June 1887; Marriage Record 1860—65: 79.

37. Vessie Thrasher Rainer, *Henry County Georgia / The Mother of Counties* (Mc-Donough: 1971), pp. 192—193; *The Covington Star*, 14 June 1887; *The Georgia Enterprise*, 6 Feb. 1903; Mrs. Thompson, *idem.*, 11 Jan. 1971.

38. *The Covington Star,* 31 May 1887; *Masonic Messenger*, Aug. 1938; Will Record III: 261—263, 264—266.

39. *The Covington Star*, 31 May and 7, 14 June 1887.

40. Mrs. Thompson, *idem.*, 11 Jan. 1971.

41. Miss Leila Perry of Atlanta in a conversation with the author on 12 Nov. 1970. Miss Perry is a grandniece of Edward Heard (*see pages 97—98*). Her grandfather, Josiah Patterson of Dixie, was a cousin of the famous Baltimore beauty Betsey Patterson, first wife of Jerome Bonaparte, nephew of the Emperor Napoleon. Josiah Perry probably was a brother of Temperance (Perry) Williamson (*see pages 80, 110*).

42. *The Covington Star*, 14 June 1887.

43. *The Georgia Enterprise*, 31 Aug. 1900; Mrs. Thompson, *idem.*, in a conversation on 11 Jan. 1971 and in a letter dated 7 May 1972.

44. *The Atlanta Journal*, 23 June 1910; Marriage Record 1904—1913: 412; Mrs. Thompson, *idem.*, in a letter to the author dated 8 Nov. 1972.

45. Deed Record 20: 172.

46. *The Covington Star*, 4 Dec.1888,20 Dec. 1898; *The Georgia Enterprise*, 10 Apr.

1903; Will Record 4: 38–40, 226; Mrs. William B. Williford in a conversation with the author on 12 Dec. 1971; tombstones in Covington City Cemetery. For Walter Childs' first marriage (to Mattie Gay of Newborn) see Marriage Record 1874–84: 320.

47. Deed Record 20: 120; Mrs. Williford, *idem.*, 5 June 1971.

48. Deed Record 20: 462.

49. *History of Peach County, Georgia*, compiled by Governor Treutlen Chapter, DAR (Atlanta: 1972), p. 272; Mrs. Williford, *idem.*, and Rucker Ginn [Jr.] in conversation with the author on 19 Nov. 1971.

50. Last two of previous citations.

51. *Idem.*

VI: *EDWARDS HOUSE*

1. Deed Record D: 184.

2. Deed Record L: 150. This deed actually refers to Lot 16 in Square *E*, but as there was no such designation in the 1832 map of Covington it seems clear that the deed was for Lot 16 in Square *C*.

3. "Georgia D. A. R. Genealogical Library: Newton County, Georgia, Bible Records and Family Histories, Etc.," available on microfilm at Washington Memorial Library in Macon. Data provided Sergeant Newton Chapter, DAR, by L. L. Cody in 1915.

4. *Idem.*

5. *Idem.*; Deed Records L: 150, R: 300–301. *See comment at end of Note 2.*

6. L. L. Cody, "Reminiscences," *The Covington News*, undated clipping; "Georgia Genealogical Library," *idem.*

7. "Georgia Genealogical Library," *idem.*

8. Major General Robert J. Travis, *The Travis (Travers) Family and Its Allies* ... (Savannah: 1954), pp. 95–96; memorial tablet on East wall of First United Methodist Church.

9. *The Covington News*, 24 Apr. 1947; "Old Homes of Covington," a booklet prepared by the Covington Garden Club (1969), p. 5; Homecoming Program of First Methodist Church, 13 June 1954, a copy of which was kindly given to the author by Miss Martha Ramsey.

10. Catherine Marshall, *A Man Called Peter* (New York: 1951), pp. 43–45; *The Atlanta Constitution*, 25 Sept. 1954.

11. Lucian Lamar Knight, *Georgia and Georgians* (New York: 1917), III: 1753; Homecoming Program of First Methodist Church, *idem.*

12. Deed Records M: 601, O: 221. In the former the property is correctly identified as being in Square C, but the latter repeats the previously-cited error of designating it as being in Square *E*.

13. *Idem.*; tombstone, Covington City Cemetery.

14. Deed Record R: 279; Will Record 1850–1871: 279–281. See also Deed Record O: 321–323 re other property sold upon Osgood Sanders' attaining the age of twenty-one. *Comment at end of Note 12 applies here.*

15. Deed Record U: 416–417.

16. Deed Record W: 89.

17. *The Covington Star*, 27 June 1893; United States Census 1860—Georgia-Newton County, p. 25; tombstone, Covington City Cemetery.
18. *The Georgia Enterprise*, 30 May 1902; United States Census 1870—Georgia—Newton County, p. 238; Marriage Records 1865—69; 49 and 1869—74; 73.
19. Mary Givens Bryan, comp., *Georgia Official & Statistical Register 1957—1958* (Hapeville: 1958), p. 999; *The Covington News*, 26 April 1929, citing D. A. Thompson's history of Newton County as read before a meeting of the Kiwanis Club; *The Georgia Enterprise*, 30 May 1902; Deed Record S: 270.
20. *The Covington News*, 14 Oct. 1920; *The Covington Star*, 14 July 1896, 21 Sept. 1897, 19 Apr. and 8 Mar. 1898; *The Georgia Enterprise*, 13 Oct. 1899, *30 May 1902*; Marriage Record 1894—1904: 89.
21. *The Covington News*, 3 Jan. 1936; *The Georgia Enterprise*, 30 May 1902; tombstones, Covington City Cemetery.
22. Deed Record 26: 172.
23. Deed Record 24: 529.
24. *The Covington News*, 4 Oct. 1935, 22 Aug. 1957, 25 Mar. 1965; Deed Record 26: 172; tombstones, Covington City Cemetery.
25. Deed Record 27: 324.

VII: *CLARK'S GROVE*

1. Henry Morton Bullock, *A History of Emory University* (Nashville: 1936; reprint Atlanta: 1972), pp. 31, 35.
2. *Ibid.*, pp. 35, 39, 40.
3. E. Merton Coulter, "The Ante-Bellum Academy Movement in Georgia," *The Georgia Historical Quarterly*, Vol. V, No. 4, December 1921, p. 24, citing *American Annals of Education*, VI: 1836.
4. Edward Mayes, *Lucius Q. C. Lamar: His Life, Times, and Speeches 1825—1893* (Nashville: 1896), p. 29.
5. Bullock, *History of Emory, op. cit.*, pp. 29—31, 42, 52—55, 57, 75; Dorothy Orr, *A History of Education In Georgia* (Chapel Hill: 1950), pp. 142—145; Deed Record E: 503—504.
6. William Bailey Williford, Sketch of the author in reprint edition of Augustus Baldwin Longstreet, *Georgia Scenes* (Atlanta: 1971), pp. 1—3.
7. Bullock, *History of Emory*, pp. 17—18, 21; *The Georgia Enterprise*, 9 April 1869; Deed Records G: 4, L: 241.
8. Deed Record L: 241.
9. I. W. Avery, *The History of Georgia From 1850 to 1881* (New York: 1881), p. 222; Mary Givens Bryan, comp., *Georgia Official & Official Register, 1957—1958* (Hapeville: 1958), p. 1188; Franklin M. Garrett, *Atlanta and Environs* (New York: 1954), I: 926; Warren Grice, *The Georgia Bench and Bar* (Macon: 1931), p. 145; *Masonic Messenger*, a publication of the Grand Lodge of Georgia, June and August 1938.
10. Deed Records I ("eye"): 322, M: 437; Will Record I (One): 5—6.
11. John B. Harris, ed., *A History of the Supreme Court of Georgia* (Macon: 1948),

p. 15; Roe Herring Hendrick, *Lineage and Tradition of the Herring, Conyers, Hendrick, Boddie, Perry, Crudup, Denson and Hilliard Families* (Published Privately: 1916), p. 27; Lucian Lamar Knight, *Reminiscences of Famous Georgians* (Atlanta: 1907, 1908), I: 361–364; Deed Record A: 264; Marriage Record C: 108; U. D. C. record on Major William D. Conyers, Jr., a copy of which is owned by Miss Sarah Mobley.

12. Lucian Lamar Knight, *Georgia's Landmarks, Memorials and Legends* (Atlanta: 1913, 1914), I: 919; Minutes of Inferior Court 1822–1838; tombstones in Williamson-Conyers Family Cemetery in North Covington. Dr. Conyers' tombstone gives his middle name as *Dennison*, but Hendrick, *Lineage and Tradition, op. cit.*, p. 114, and Mrs. Willie Conyers Cook, "Clement Bates, Englishman, Emigrated to New England With Family in 1635," *The Sunday American*, Atlanta, 11 September 1932, both give it as *Denson*. The latter is used here inasmuch as Hendrick, *Lineage and Tradition*, p. 113, states that his mother was Betsey, daughter of *William Denson*.

13. Hendrick, *Lineage and Tradition, idem.*, pp. 112–113, 114; Sarah Blackwell Gober Temple, *The First Hundred Years. A Short History of Cobb County in Georgia* (Atlanta: 1935), p. 599; Will Record 3: 354–357. Sources for footnote data on Captain Kolb: Bryan, *Georgia Official & Statistical Register, op. cit.*, p. 1188; Hendrick, *Lineage and Tradition*, p. 115.

14. Hendrick, *Lineage and Tradition*, pp. 11, 14, 27, 28–29; Will Record 2: 300–303. Sources for footnote data on Henderson: Hendrick, *Lineage and Tradition*, p. 28; Lodowick Johnson Hill, *The Hills of Wilkes County, Georgia, and Allied Families* (Atlanta: 1922), p. 197. Sources for footnote data on Herring family: Hendrick, *Lineage and Tradition*, p. 11; William Bailey Williford, *Peachtree Street, Atlanta* (Athens: 1962), pp. 14, 22, 114.

15. Bullock, *History of Emory, op. cit.*, pp. 65, 66, 85; John and Donald Wade, *Augustus Baldwin Longstreet: A Study of the Development of Culture in the South* (Athens: 1969), p. 260. The existence of columns and a veranda on the house at *Clark's Grove* was mentioned to the author by Mrs. Charles S. Thompson of Atlanta (née Sarah Simms of Covington), Mrs. William B. Williford, N. S. Turner and others. A picture showing these appendages appeared in *The Covington News* on 28 October 1965.

16. Kate Cumming [Richard Barksdale Harwell, ed.], *Kate: The Journal of A Confederate Nurse* (Baton Rouge: 1959), p. 223; Dolly Sumner Lunt (Mrs. Thomas Burge), *A Woman's Wartime Journal* (New York: 1918), p. 8; Mrs. W. C. Clark, "Covington During the Sixties," *The Covington News*, 21 October 1927.

17. Walter A. Clark, *Under the Stars and Bars, or the Memories of Four Years Service* (Augusta, Georgia: 1900), as cited in A. A. Hoehling, *Last Train from Atlanta* (New York: 1958), pp. 107, 108, 139–130.

18. Lee G. Alexander and James. G. Bogle, "George Hewitt Daniel (1817–1864)," *The Atlanta Historical Bulletin*, September 1968, Vol. XIII, No. 3., pp. 21–22. In the same publication, Spring-Summer 1972, pp. 31–38, the authors give additional information about the Daniel and Colley families. Included is a picture of Daniel's tombstone in the Colley Family Cemetery on Alcovy Road which shows that he was born in 1816 instead of in 1817 as the title of the first installment indicated. *For*

other references to Daniel's father-in-law, Elder Joel Colley, in the present work, see pages 6, 151n.

19. *Official Records of the War of the Rebellion* (Washington: 1891), Series 1, Vol. 38, Part II, p. 809.

20. The changes in the appearance of the Clark residence are apparent from an examination of a picture in Lucian Lamar Knight, *Georgia's Landmarks, Memorials and Legends* (Atlanta: 1913, 1914), II: opposite p. 912 (which is reproduced in the present work) and a picture which appeared in *The Covington News*, 28 October 1965. Numerous Covington residents have said that they remember the structure in its last years as shown in the latter. Information concerning the Clarks' hospitality was obtained by the author in a conversation with Mrs. Charles S. Thompson of Atlanta (née Sarah Simms of Covington) on 14 November 1971.

21. *The Georgia Enterprise*, 10, 17 August 1883. All but the last sentence is from the former.

22. *The Georgia Enterprise*, 8 August 1902; Will Record 3: 180—183; tombstones, Covington City Cemetery.

23. *The Georgia Enterprise*, 30 January 1885, 23 April 1906; Marriage Record 1884—1894: 2; "William White Clark's Family Bible Records," copied in 1935 by Mrs. A. L. Loyd for the Sergeant Newton Chapter DAR, and made available to the author on 2 October 1972 by Mrs. Harry Dietz from a copy filed in the Newton County ordinary's office.; Mrs. Henry Odum, Sr., present owner of the W. C. Clarks' Victorian house in North Covington, in a conversation with the author on 4 October 1970.

24. *The Covington Star*, 10 June 1885; Deed Records I: 406, S: 362; Marriage Record 1850—59: 129, Will Record 4: 202; Walton C. Clark of Chevy Chase, Maryland, who is a grandson of Mrs. Sarah Jane Echols, in a letter to the author dated 27 November 1972; Mrs. Charles S. Thompson and Mrs. Ralph L. Turner of Atlanta (née Sarah and Bonner Simms, respectively, of Covington) in a conversation with the author on 27 January 1971; tombstones, Covington City Cemetery.

25. *The Semi-Weekly Enterprise*, 9 February 1906; A. D. Meador, "The History of Covington," *The Covington News*, 20 October 1915; Deed Records E: 514, T: 243, X: 503.

26. Meador, "The History of Covington," *ibid.*; Edgar Wood in a conversation with the author on 13 September 1972.

27. Bryan, *Georgia Official & Statistical Register, op. cit.*, p. 869; "History of Brick Store Community," a booklet apparently authored by Mrs. Walter C. Emmel, 1964; Will Record 4: 23—25.

28. Major General Robert J. Travis, *The Travis (Travers) Family And Its Allies. . .* (Savannah: 1954), p. 96; Deed Record 22: 228.

29. Deed Record 22: 228; Edgar Wood, *op. cit.*

30. Deed Record 27: 266; Edgar Wood, *ibid.*; tombstones, Covington City Cemetery.

31. *The Covington News*, 11 November 1920; Will Record 4: 472—473; Walton C. Clark, *op. cit.*, in a letter dated 10 October 1972; Mrs. Odum, *op. cit.*

32. Deed Record W: 527.

33. Deed Record 20: 345.

34. Conversations with Mrs. William B. Williford on 28 October 1970 and 26 June 1972, and with N. S. Turner on latter date.

35. Deed Record 24: 508–509; N. S. Turner, *ibid.*

36. Deed Record 29: 279.

37. *The Covington News*, 21 September 1939; Marriage Record 3: 364; conversation with Mrs. William B. Williford on 4 August 1972; tombstones, Covington City Cemetery.

38. Mrs. Williford and Robert Fowler in conversations with the author on 1 November 1972 and 21 November 1971, respectively.

VIII: *THE FLOYD HOUSE*

1. E. Merton Coulter, *College Life In The Old South* (Athens: 1951), p. 160; A. L. Hull, *A Historical Sketch of The University of Georgia* (Atlanta: 1894), Mrs. D. L. Wilson of Macon in a letter to the author dated 15 December 1970 and Mrs. Cullen Gosnell of Atlanta in a conversation with the author on 9 Dec. 1970—both ladies being great-granddaughters of Judge Floyd. Joseph A. Waddell, *Annals of Augusta County, Virginia, From 1726 to 1871* (Bridgewater, Va.: 1958), pp. 209–210, indicates that Judge John J. Floyd was closely related to Virginia Governors John and John Buchanan Floyd, *père et fils.*

2. Deed Record D: 582.

3. Medora Field Perkerson, *White Columns In Georgia* (New York: 1952), p. 28; Mrs. Gosnell. *idem.*

4. Lucian Lamar Knight, *Georgia's Landmarks, Memorials and Legends* (Atlanta: 1914), II: 912–913; Wylly Folk St. John, "Old South Tour of Covington," *The Atlanta Journal Magazine*, 18 April 1948; Index card at State Department of Archives and History, in Atlanta.

5. James C. Bonner, ed., *The Journal of A Milledgeville Girl, 1861–1867* [by Anna Maria Green] (Athens: 1964), p. 9n; Mary Givens Bryan, comp., *Georgia Official & Statistical Register, 1957–1958* (Hapeville: 1958), p. 999; Warren Grice, *The Georgia Bench and Bar* (Macon: 1931), p. 154; Warren Grice and E. Merton Coulter, ed., *Georgia Through Two Centuries* (New York and Palm Beach: 1965), I: 445; Stephen F. Miller, *The Bench and Bar of Georgia* (Philadelphia: 1855), II: 374; Index card at State Department of Archives and History, in Atlanta.

6. Paul Murray, *The Whig Party in Georgia, 1825–1853* (Chapel Hill: 1948), pp. 108, 158, 160.

7. Grice and Coulter, *Georgia Through Two Centuries, idem.*

8. Marriage Record A: 283; Mrs. Gosnell, *idem.*; Mrs. John B. Reeves of Brevard, N.C. (the former Sarah Graves, granddaughter of Iverson and Sarah Dutton Graves) in a conversation with the author on 27 July 1971.

9. James I. Robertson, Jr., ed., *The Diary of Dolly Lunt Burge* (Athens: 1962), p. 118 (*see also viii–xi*); Dutton Morehouse (great-grandson of "Dolly") and Mrs. Morehouse in conversations with the author on 2 Dec. 1970 and 14 Dec. 1971; Mrs. Reeves, *idem.*

10. Dorothy Orr, *A History of Education in Georgia* (Chapel Hill: 1950), p. 155; the Rev. George White, *Historical Collections of Georgia* (New York: 1854; reprint Danielsville, Ga.: 1968), p. 574; *Masonic Messenger*, a publication of the Grand Lodge of Georgia, April-Sept. 1938; *The Covington Star*, 9 Sept. 1927; Marriage Records 1850–1859: 101 and 1867–74: 139; Mms. Gosnell and Wilson, *idem*. Stewart Floyd is not listed by Mrs. Gosnell, but he is included in data provided by Mrs. Wilson and in the "Reminiscences" of L. L. Cody which appeared in *The Covington News* in 1932.

11. Rebecca Latimer Felton, *Country Life in Georgia In the Days of My Youth* (Atlanta: 1919), pp. 28, 57, 71, 72; Lucian Lamar Knight, *A Standard History of Georgia and Georgians* (Chicago and New York: 1917), IV: 2098–2101; Bernice McCullar, *This Is Your Georgia* (Montgomery, Ala.: 1968), pp. 615–618.

12. United States Census 1860–Gerogia–Newton County, p. 16; Military Record at State Department of Archives and History; Mrs. Gosnell, *idem*.

13. Bonner, *Journal of a Milledgeville Girl, ibid.*, pp. 10–14, 38.

14. *Ibid.*, pp. 2, 6; Nelle Womack Hines, *A Treasure Album of Milledgeville and Baldwin County, Georgia* (reprint Macon: 1949), pp. 23–24.

15. Mrs. John B. Davis, "History of Covington U. D. C.," a copy of which was made available to the author through the courtesy of Miss Sarah Mobley.

16. Index card at State Department of Archives and History, in Atlanta.

17. Dolly Sumner Lunt (Mrs. Thomas Burge), *A Woman's Wartime Journal* (New York: 1918), pp. 4–5. This portion of Mrs. Burge's diary appears on pp. 91–92 of the enlarged edition edited by James I. Robertson, Jr. under the title *The Diary of Dolly Lunt Burge* (Athens: 1962).

18. Anita B. Sams, *Wayfarers in Walton* (Monroe, Ga.: 1967), p. 102.

19. I. W. Avery, *The History of The State of Georgia From 1850 to 1881* (New York: 1881), pp. 341, 348, 389–390.

20. *Masonic Messenger, idem.*, May 1938.

21. *The Georgia Enterprise*, 16 Mar. 1883; Will Book III: 177–179.

22. Mrs. Gosnell, *idem.*; tombstones, Covington City Cemetery.

23. Deed Record 13: 191.

24. John H. McIntosh, *The Official History of Elbert County 1790–1935* (Elberton: 1940; reprint Atlanta: 1968), pp. 444–446; data from the Bible of Fitz Herbert Heard, obtained through the courtesy of Miss Sarah Mobley.

25. L. Wilson Jarman, "A Walk Around The Square [In 1889]," *The Covington News* 14 May 1953; Mrs. Charles S. Thompson and Mrs. Ralph L. Turner of Atlanta, nieces of Mrs. Edward Heard, in a conversation with the author on 11 Jan. 1971; tombstone, Covington City Cemetery.

26. *The Covington News*, 16 June 1960; Will Record 4: 269–270; tombstones, Covington City Cemetery.

27. Deed Records 54: 608 and 55:37; Will Record 6: 53–56; Mrs. William B. Williford in a conversation with the author on 6 Nov. 1971.

28. Mrs. Williford, *idem.*; Mrs. Robert Wharton of St. Simons Island in a conversation with the author on 24 June 1972.

29. *The Covington News,* 16 June 1949.

30. Deed Record 77: 272, 303; tombstones in Covington City Cemetery.

31. Conversation with Mrs. W. H. Thompson, 8 Jan. 1972.

32. Richard Barksdale Harwell, ed., *Louisiana Burge: The Diary of a Confederate Girl,* n.p., n.d., reprinted from *The Georgia Historical Quarterly,* XXXVI: 144—163 (June 1952); Cornelia Gray Lunt, *Sketches of Childhood and Girlhood* (Evanston, Ill.: *c.* 1925), pp. 44—46; Dorothy G. Bolton, ed., *Little Sadai: Journal of Miss Sadai C. Burge, 1874* (Atlanta: n.d.), pp. 1—8; James I. Robertson, Jr., ed., *The Diary of Dolly Lunt Burge* (Athens: 1962), pp. vii—xv; "Georgia Genealogical Library: Newton County, Georgia, Bible Records and Family Histories, Etc.," available on microfilm at Washington Memorial Library in Macon; Deed Records 69: 309, 91: 142, 97: 243, 106: 230; Marriage Record A, 1822—1835: 171; Dutton Morehouse, *op. cit.,* and Mrs. Morehouse in conversations with the author on 2 Dec. 1970 and 14 Nov. 1971; Burge and Bolton tombstones on what was originally a part of *Burge Plantation,* and Parks and Gray tombstones in the cemetery at Oxford.

IX: THE CARR - CODY - CORLEY HOUSE

1. Deed Record S: 404.

2. *Historic American Buildings Survey* (Washington: 1941), p. 86; data submitted to the National Park Service by Harold Bush-Brown, District Officer, H.A.B.S. (and a distinguished architect), 1 Dec. 1936.

3. Latter citation, *ibid.,* citing as source for portion of data the late Mrs. Corrie Carr Wright.

4. Lucian Lamar Knight, *Georgia's Landmarks, Memorials and Legends* (Atlanta: 1913, 1914), I: 510; *The Covington Star,* 18 Feb. 1896, 14 Jan. 1902; United States Census 1860—Georgia—Newton County, p. 27; the same, 1870: pp. 77, 89; Deed Record U: 28; Marriage Record 1849—55: 38; "Georgia D. A. R. Genealogical Library: Newton County, Georgia, Bible Records and Family Histories, Etc., Vols. 1 & 2," available on microfilm at Washington Memorial Library in Macon; Index cards at State Department of Archives and History in Atlanta; Carr Family data provided by Bates Block of Atlanta, 15 Dec. 1971; tombstones, Covington City Cemetery.

5. *The Covington News,* 3 Mar. 1921; Deed Records U: 515—516, W: 569—570, 4: 162, 8: 305—306, 25: 242, 28: 338, 32: 183; Marriage Records 1874—84: 423, 1884—1894: 502; Will Record III: 287—290; Mrs. Wendell Crowe and Edgar Wood in conversations with the author on 1, 7 Nov. 1972, respectively; tombstones, Covington City Cemetery.

6. Tombstones, Covington City Cemetery.

7. Deed Record N: 48.

8. *Idem.;* Knight, *Georgia's Landmarks, op. cit.,* II: 569; "Georgia D. A. R. Genealogical Library," *idem.;* tombstones, Covington City Cemetery.

9. A. L. Hull, *A Historical Sketch of The University of Georgia* (Atlanta: 1894), "Alumni" listing in back of book.

10. "Georgia D. A. R. Genealogical Library," *idem.;* L. L. Cody, "Reminiscences,"

The Covington News, 21 May 1953, *et sequel.* Mr. Cody, son of Dr. J. M. Cody and his first wife, lived in Macon.

11. Franklin M. Garrett, *Atlanta and Environs* (New York: 1954), I: 638–639, II: 127; Lodowick Johnson Hill, *The Hills of Wilkes County, Georgia, and Allied Families* (Atlanta: 1922), p. 197; Lucian Lamar Knight, *A Standard History of Georgia and Georgians* (New York: 1917), VI: 2852–2853; Thomas H. Martin, *Atlanta and Its Builders* (n.p.: 1902), II: 687; *The Atlanta Journal*, 17 Aug. 1882; Deed Records S: 614, T: 82–84; Marriage Record 1849–1855: 16; Fulton County Will Book B: 95–97, available at Fulton County Courthouse in Atlanta; Index card on Augustus H. Lee at State Department of Archives and History, in Atlanta.

12. Deed Records, *idem.*, and U: 416–417.

13. *The Augusta Chronicle*, 21 Dec. 1890; "History of First Baptist Church of Covington Georgia," *The Covington News*, 13 Aug. 1926; L. Wilson Jarman, "A Walk Around The Square [In 1889]," *The Covington News*, 14 May 1953; *The Covington Star*, 5 Nov. 1895; cornerstone, Newton County Courthouse; tombstones, Covington City Cemetery.

14. Marriage Record 1874–84: 17, 459; Will Book 3: 385–387; Corley family data provided the author by William Herbert Corley of Starrsville through his son Starr Corley of Covington, 19 Dec. 1971. Mr. Corley listed a Corley daughter named Tybe who married Robert Buckhannon, but the name used here is taken from a grave next to that of James T. Corley in the Covington City Cemetery, which records that Martha Vashti, wife of B. H. Buchanan, died 13 Oct. 1891, aged 29 years. For additional data on the Corley and Middlebrooks families, see Marguerite Starr Crain and Janell Turner Wenzl, *They Followed The Sun: The Story of James Penn Starr and Georgianna Theus, Their Ancestors and Their Progenies* (n.p.; n.d. Dallas: 1969?), p. 81, and Major General Robert J. Travis, *The Travis (Travers) Family And Its Allies. . .* (Savannah: 1954), p. 115.

15. *Historic American Buildings Survey*, 1936, *et sequel*; Mrs. W. S. Cook, Sr. (née Sallie Mae Pickett) in a conversation with the author on 3 Nov. 1971.

X: *THE PRESIDENT'S HOUSE*

1. Deed Record E: 651.

2. Roe Herring Hendrick, *Lineage and Tradition of the Herring, Conyers, Hendrick, Boddie, Perry, Crudup, Denson and Hilliard Families* (Published Privately: 1916), p. 115.

3. *Idem.*; Mary Givens Bryan, comp., *Georgia Official & Statistical Register 1957–1958* (Hapeville: 1958), p. 999; Will Record 2: 97; tombstone in Williamson-Conyers family cemetery at rear of 5183 N. West Street in North Covington. The quotation is from the last.

4. Hendrick, *Lineage and Tradition*, p. 115; Deed Record M: 427–428; Marriage Record A: 231; Will Record 2: 97; tombstones in Williamson-Conyers Family Cemetery, *op. cit.*, and in Covington City Cemetery.

5. Deed Record E: 651.

6. *Idem.*

7. Deed Record O: 34–35.

8. *The Covington Star*, 19 Jan. 1892; G. C. Adams, "Chronicles of Newton," *The Covington News*, 21 Oct. 1927; Deed Record F: 424.

9. Deed Record I: 41.

10. Bryan, *Georgia Official & Statistical Register, op. cit.*, p. 118; *The Georgia Enterprise*, 19 Aug. 1883; "William White Clark's Family Bible Records," copied in 1935 by Mrs. A. L. Loyd for the Sergeant Newton Chapter, DAR, and made available to the author on 2 Oct. 1972 by Mrs. Harry Dietz from a copy filed in the Office of the Court of Ordinary in the Newton County Courthouse.

11. Deed Record L: 507.

12. Henry Morton Bullock, *A History of Emory University* (Nashville: 1937; reprint Atlanta: 1972), p. 35, citing *Southern Christian Advocate*, 1 Feb. 1839; Dorothy Orr, *A History of Education in Georgia* (Chapel Hill: 1950), p. 155; Adiel Sherwood, *A Gazetteer of Georgia* (Atlanta: 1860; reprint Atlanta: 1970), p. 103; Annette McDonald Suarez, ed., *The Journal of Andrew Leary O'Brien* (Athens: 1946), p. 71; Mrs. A. D. Williams and Carrie Williams, "Southern Female College," an article from an unidentified newspaper filed at the State Department of Archives and History in Atlanta. Deed Record F: 820 reveals that on 6 May 1842 Green B. Turner had acquired from Allen Turner Lots 22 and 23 in Square D, as well as Lot 24. The last included the entire block to the south of the other lots (present block beginning at southeast corner of Conyers and Davis streets).

13. I. W. Avery, *The History of Georgia From 1850 to 1881* (New York: 1881), p. 181; Lucian Lamar Knight, *A Standard History of Georgia and Georgians* (New York: 1917), IV: 1872, V: 689; Robert Manson Myers, ed., *Children of Pride. A True Story of Georgia and the Civil War* (New Haven: 1972), p. 1502; William Bailey Williford, *Americus Through The Years* (Atlanta: 1960), pp. 16, 27; *Masonic Messenger*, a publication of the Grand Lodge of Georgia, September 1938.

14. *Code of Georgia Annotated* (Atlanta: 1966), p. 163; Dorothy Orr, "Gustavus John Orr: Georgia Educator, 1819–1887," *The Atlanta Historical Bulletin,* Fall-Winter 1971, Vol. XVI, No. 3-4, p. 105, citing Ordinary Minutes 1864–1869; Map of Covington, 1832 (*see Frontispiece*), a copy of which was made available to the author by City Manager Frank B. Turner.

15. The Rev. George White, *Historical Collections of Georgia* (New York: 1854; reprint Danielsville, Ga.: 1968), p. 574.

16. *Masonic Messenger, op. cit.*, April 1938.

17. Bullock, *Emory, op. cit.*, p. 32; Allen D. Candler and Clement A. Evans, eds., *Cyclopedia of Georgia* (Atlanta: 1906), II: 552.

18. Mrs. John B. Reeves of Brevard, North Carolina (the former Sarah Graves of *Mt. Pleasant*), in a conversation with the author on 27 July 1971. She said it was absurd to say that *Orna Villa*, as the Means' home in Oxford is called, antedates the town, as has sometimes been claimed.

19. *Masonic Messenger, idem.*, and May 1938.

20. Latter citation.

21. Williams, "Southern Female College," *idem.*

22. *Masonic Messenger*, May 1938.

23. *Idem.*

24. Dorothy Orr, "Gustavus John Orr," *op. cit.*, pp. 105, 106, 126; *Masonic Messenger*, May 1938. Quote is from the latter.

25. Candler and Evans, *Cyclopedia of Georgia, op. cit.*, III: 41—45.

26. *Masonic Messenger*, June 1938.

27. The Rev. James Stacy, DD, *The Presbyterian Church. A History of the Presbyterian Church in Georgia* (Elberton: 1912), pp. 222, 356, 365, 366; *The Covington News*, 2 July 1959.

28. *The Covington Star*, 22 January 1895; Marriage Record 1860—65: 459; Donald Stephenson in a conversation with the author on 8 August 1972; tombstones in Covington City Cemetery.

29. "Old Homes of Covington," a booklet prepared by the Covington Garden Club, 1969, p. 4; Mrs. William B. Williford in a conversation with the author on 11 January 1971.

30. *Masonic Messenger*, August 1938.

31. *Idem.*; Deed Record Z: 53—54, referring to T: 607.

32. Former citation.

33. Williams, "Southern Female College," *idem.*; Mrs. Charles S. Thompson of Atlanta in a conversation with the author on 9 December 1970.

34. Mary Sessions Mallard in *The Covington News*, 29 February 1958; *The Georgia Enterprise*, 30 March 1900; plaque on Municipal Building.

35. Deed Record 7: 1.

36. *The Covington Star*, 12 April and 24 May 1892; Will Record 4: 253.

37. *The Covington Star*, 28 June 1892, which lists the bride as Julia E. Scott, and Marriage Record 1884—1894: 471, which lists her as J. E. Glenn. The quotation is from G. C. Adams, "Chronicles of Newton," which appeared in *The Covington News* on 21 October 1927.

38. Marriage Record 1: 506; Tandy E. Bush of Tampa, Florida, in a letter to the author dated 26 June 1972; conversation with Mrs. William B. Williford on 2 August 1972; tombstones in Covington City Cemetery.

39. Deed Record 63: 332.

40. Charles D. Strickland in a conversation with the author on 6 June 1972.

XI: *USHER HOUSE*

1. Personal observation of the author, courtesy of the present owners, Dr. and Mrs. Robert L. Faulkner. An 1848 deed (I: 593) mentions the Usher property.

2. Henry Branham in *The Atlanta Journal*, 25 Sept. 1932, and *The Covington News*, 18 Nov. 1932; Deed Record G: 4.

3. Marriage Record B, 1835—43: 145; a Mrs. Bass of Savannah, a great-great-granddaughter of Robert Usher and of Cary Wood, in a conversation with the author at the home built for the latter, on 22 April 1972; data provided by Clifford Henderson of Ormond Beach, Fla., a grandson of Mr. Usher, and the former's niece Mrs. David D. Harvey of Rome, on 16 June 1971; Mrs. D. L.

Wilson of Macon in a letter to the author dated 15 Dec. 1970; tombstone in old (Methodist) portion of Covington City Cemetery.

4. Tombstones in Covington City Cemetery.

5. Will Record 2: 131–133.

6. Harry H. Stone, "Oxford In The Olden Days," *The Covington News*, 8 Oct. 1927.

7. Georgia Historical Commission Marker (No. 107-3) on the north side of Covington.

8. Mrs. Charles S. Thompson of Atlanta in a conversation with the author on 7 Jan. 1971.

9. United States Census 1860—Georgia—Newton County, p. 26; Deed Record S: 240–241; Will Record 3: 394–397; letter from Mrs. Wilson, *idem.*; tombstones in Covington City Cemetery.

10. *The Covington Star*, 18 Feb. 1896; tombstone, Covington City Cemetery.

11. L. L. Cody, "Reminiscences," *The Covington News*, 21 May 1953; Will Record 3: 394–397; Mrs. William B. Williford in a conversation with the author on 18 June 1971.

12. Deed Record T: 365; Marriage Record 1874–84: 148; Mrs. William B. Williford, *idem.*

13. Lodowick Johnson Hill, *The Hills of Wilkes County, Georgia, And Allied Families* (Atlanta: 1922), p. 197; Lucian Lamar Knight, *A Standard History of Georgia and Georgians* (New York: 1917), VI: 2852–2854; *The Covington Star*, 18 Feb. 1896; *The Georgia Enterprise*, 30 Mar. 1900, 27 Jan. 1905; Marriage Record 1867–74: 135; Record of Charters I: 23–25, available in office of the Clerk of Newton Superior Court; David Butler in a conversation with the author on 9 Mar. 1970.

14. Knight, *A Standard History, idem.*; *The Covington News*, 26 Apr. 1917; Will Record 4: 247–248. Quotation is from obituary in the *News*.

15. Hill, *The Hills of Wilkes County, idem.*; Knight, *A Standard History, idem.*; tombstones, Covington City Cemetery.

16. Hill, *The Hills of Wilkes County, idem.*; *The Georgia Enterprise*, 18 Aug. 1899; Marriage Record 1894–1904: 212; Mrs. N. S. Turner in a conversation with the author on 21 Nov. 1972.

17. *The Covington News*, 14 June 1917.

18. *The Covington News*, 4 Nov. 1927; Will Record 5: 56, 57; tombstones, Covington City Cemetery.

19. *The Covington News*, 29 July 1926.

20. Deed Record 27: 515; tombstone, Covington City Cemetery.

21. Marriage Record 1874–84; 79; conversations with Dutton Morehouse of *Burge Plantation*, a nephew of Mrs. Bolton, on 14 Nov. 1971; with Mrs. Morehouse on 2 Dec. 1970, and with Mrs. William B. Williford on 28 Oct. 1970.

22. Dutton Morehouse, *idem.*; Mrs. Hampton Flowers of Atlanta in a conversation with the author on 22 Apr. 1971.

23. *Idem.*

24. Dutton Morehouse in conversations with the author on 14 Nov. 1971 and 28 Apr. 1972. The sisters' compromise is mentioned in Medora Field Perkerson, *White Columns In Georgia* (New York: 1952), pp. 16–17; see also pp. 23–24.

25. *Idem.; The Covington News*, 13 Aug. 1959, 2 July 1964.

26. Mrs. Leon Cohen and Mrs. William B. Williford in conversations with the author on 1 Apr. 1972.

27. Mrs. Williford, 8 May 1972.

28. *Ibid.*, 12 May 1972.

29. Bulletin, The Church of The Good Shepherd, 12 Apr. 1970.

30. *The Covington News*, 10, 13, 27 Sept. 1951; Mrs. Leslie J. Moore and Mrs. William B. Williford in a conversation with the author on 21 May 1972.

31. *Idem.*; plaque in vestibule of The Church of The Good Shepherd.

32. Deed Record 50: 43; Mrs. William B. Williford, 8 May 1972.

33. *The Covington News*, 17 June 1971; Mrs. Williford, *idem*.

34. *The Covington News*, 17 June 1971.

35. *Ibid.*, 13 Aug. 1959.

36. *Ibid.*, 17 June 1971; Will Book 7: 195–202.

37. Deed Record 110: 205.

38. Dr. Robert L. Faulkner in a conversation with the author on 19 Jan. 1972.

39. *Ibid.*, and Mrs. Faulkner, 25 Sept. 1972.

40. *Idem.*

XII: THE BATES - TERRELL HOUSE

1. *The Georgia Enterprise*, 5, 12 January 1883; Mrs. Willie Conyers Cook, "Clement Bates, Englishman, Emigrated to New England With Family in 1635," *The Sunday American*, Atlanta, 11 September 1932; tombstones in Covington City Cemetery.

2. Mary Givens Bryan, comp., *Georgia Official & Statistical Register 1957–1958* (Hapeville: 1958), pp. 999, 1188; George White, *Statistics of the State of Georgia* (Savannah: 1849), p. 451; *The Georgia Enterprise*, 6 April 1883, 24 August 1900; Fitzhugh Lee, "Newton County History," clipping from an unidentified newspaper dated 30 November 1934, available at State Department of Archives and History, in Atlanta; Deed Records A: 94, F: 376; tombstone, Covington City Cemetery.

3. First Methodist Church Bulletin for Homecoming Service, 13 June 1954, p. 3, citing Deed Records A: 357, C:110. The author is indebted to Miss Martha Ramsey for a copy of this bulletin.

4. Deed Record F: 555, 18 January 1840, refers to purchase by John Harris of a 24-acre tract adjoining Dr. Bates' property on the north. See also D: 341 (purchase by Bates, 6 September 1832, of Lot 20 for $30.50); 3: 247 (sale by daughter of Lot 19); 3: 248 (*ibid.*, Lot 17).

5. Mrs. Cook, "Clement Bates, Englishman," *op. cit.*; Sarah Simms Edge, "Joel Hurt," *The Atlanta Historical Bulletin*, 1955, pp. 9–21, and conversations by the present author with that author (by then Mrs. Fred Fletcher of Atlanta) on 9 December 1970 and 30 November 1971. Mrs. Fletcher is a daughter of Arthur Benjamin Simms, Jr., of Covington and Atlanta, and a granddaughter of Joel Hurt of Atlanta.

6. *Idem.* (Mrs. Cook errs in the date of marriage, which she says was *11* May, and in saying that he was a colonel, when actually he was only *acting* in that capacity when killed.); *Masonic Messenger*, September 1938; Deed Record K: 211; Marriage Record 1860—65: 51; tombstones in Williamson-Conyers Family Cemetery in North Covington.

7. Roe Herring Hendrick, *Lineage and Tradition of the Herring, Conyers, Hendrick, Boddie, Perry, Crudup, Denson and Hilliard Families* (Published Privately: 1916), pp. 27, 111.

8. Bowling C. Yates, *History of the Georgia Military Institute [of] Marietta, Georgia...* (Marietta, Georgia: 1968), pp. 24, 26; UDC record on Major William D. Conyers, Jr., a copy of which was kindly loaned to the author by Miss Sarah Mobley.

9. *Idem.*

10. Letter from Conyers' brother-in-law, Major James P. Simms, which is quoted on pages 58—59.

11. Mrs. Cook, "Clement Bates, Englishman," *idem.*; Will Record 3: 72—74; tomb of Rebecca E. Conyers in the Williamson-Conyers Family Cemetery.

12. Mrs. Cook, "Clement Bates, Englishman," *idem.* (which incorrectly states that he died *13* May); Fitzhugh Lee, "Newton County History," *idem.*; letter cited in next Source Note; tombstone in Williamson-Conyers Family Cemetery.

13. A typed copy of this letter was loaned to the author by Miss Sarah Mobley. It probably was made from the original by her late aunt, Miss Sallie Mae Sockwell, who was a friend and UDC associate of Major Conyers' widow. The letter appears in Hendrick, *Lineage and Tradition, op. cit.*, pp. 29—30. Identification of Brigadier General William Tatum Wofford is established in Ezra J. Warner, *Generals In Gray. Lives of the Confederate Commanders* (Baton Rouge: 1959); pp. 343—344.

14. Mrs. Cook, "Clement Bates, Englishman," *op. cit.*; Will Records 2: 300—303, 3: 72—74.

15. A brief history of the Covington Chapter, UDC, by Miss Sallie Mae Sockwell in *The Covington News*, 21 October 1927.

16. *The Georgia Enterprise*, 5 January 1884 and 24 August 1900; tombstones in Covington City Cemetery.

17. Deed Record 3: 247, 248; Will Record 2: 169—177.

18. *The Covington News*, 21 October 1920, quoting *The Atlanta Constitution* of 18 October; Mrs. Cook, "Clement Bates, Englishman," *op. cit.*; tombstone, Covington City Cemetery.

19. Deed Record 6: 560.

20. *The Covington News*, 9 March 1928; tombstone, Covington City Cemetery.

21. *The Covington News*, 26 January 1922; Marriage Record 1874—84: 222; Will Record 5: 11—13; tombstones, Covington City Cemetery.

22. Mrs. Charles S. Thompson of Atlanta (née Sarah Simms of Covington) told the author on 14 November 1971 that the Bates cottage was the nucleus of the present columned mansion. Colonel William G. Borella, the present owner, told the author on 6 August 1972 that he had seen the beams under a portion of the house and

that Mrs. Mary Sockwell Biggers had told him that her father had covered the original wide pine flooring with hardwood.

23. *The Covington News*, 9 March 1928; tombstones, Covington City Cemetery.

24. G. C. Adams, "Chronicles of Newton," *The Covington News*, 21 October 1927; the same newspaper, 24 April 1941; Marriage Record 1884–1894: 225; Miss Sarah Mobley, Mr. Sockwell's niece, in a conversation with the author on 16 November 1971; tombstones, Covington City Cemetery.

25. *The Covington News*, 27 August 1959; Miss Mobley, *idem*.

26. *The Covington News*, 24 April 1941; clipping from the same, date unknown, which is an advertisement for the Bank of Covington. Latter examined courtesy of Miss Sarah Mobley.

27. *The Covington News*, 27 August 1959; tombstone, Covington City Cemetery.

28. Deed Record 87: 149.

29. Conversation with Lieutenant Colonel William G. Borella, 6 August 1972.

30. *Idem.*

XIII: *DIXIE MANOR*

1. Deed Record B: 255, 540–541.

2. Deed Record F: 554, 556.

3. "Old Homes of Covington," a booklet prepared by the Covington Garden Club (1969), p. 4; Dr. J. R. Sams in a conversation with the author on 28 Oct. 1971.

4. Lucian Lamar Knight, *Georgia's Landmarks, Memorials and Legends* (Atlanta: 1913, 1914), I: 836; Anita B. Sams, *Wayfarers In Walton* (Monroe, Ga.: 1967), p. 51; The Rev. George White, *Historical Collections of Georgia* (New York: 1854; reprint Danielsville, Ga.: 1968), p. 578; "The Southern Masonic Female College," *Masonic Messenger*, a publication of the Grand Lodge of Georgia, April 1938; bronze tablet at Brick Store, placed there in 1933 by Sergeant Newton Chapter, DAR.

5. I. W. Avery, *The History of the State of Georgia From 1850 to 1881* (New York: 1881), pp. 107–109; *The Georgia Enterprise*, 8 Mar. 1872; Marriage Record B, 1835–43: 127; Index card at State Department of Archives and History, in Atlanta.

6. Deed Records M: 610, O: 162.

7. Marriage Record C, 1843–48: 106; Will Record 1850–1871: 279–281 (will of Mrs. Sarah Ann Sanders, which mentions her grandchildren Corinne, Sallie and Osborn Rogers); Family Record of Louise Haygood (Mrs. Hugh H.) Trotti of Decatur, which she kindly made available to the author on 2 January 1972 (most of these data are filed at the State Archives, to which they were given by Mrs. Trotti); tombstone, old (Methodist) portion of Covington City Cemetery.

8. Louise McHenry Hicky, *Rambles Through Morgan County* (Madison, Ga.: 1971), pp. 39, 42, 52, 100–106; United States Census 1860–Georgia–Newton County, p. 26; the same, 1870, p. 77; Family Record of Mrs. Trotti, *op. cit.*, citing family Bible records and Marriage Record 1855–61: 422.

9. Mrs. John B. Davis, "History [of] Covington U. D. C.," *The Covington News.*

Clipping examined through the courtesy of Miss Sarah Mobley; undated, but probably 13 Oct. 1926.

10. *Idem.*

11. *Idem.*

12. Mary Givens Bryan, comp., *Georgia Official & Statistical Register 1957–1958* (Hapeville: 1958), p. 1189; Lucian Lamar Knight, *A Standard History of Georgia and Georgians* (New York: 1917), IV: 2245–2246; *The Covington News*, 15 July 1926; Marriage Record 1869–74: 148; Family Record of Mrs. Trotti, *idem.*

13. *Masonic Messenger, op. cit.*, Aug. 1938; Family Record of Mrs. Trotti.

14. Knight, *Georgia's Landmarks, op. cit.*, II: 912–913, quoting Mrs. Thad Horton of Atlanta.

15. Deed Record S: 492–493.

16. *The Covington Star*, 28 June 1896; Family Record of Mrs. Trotti, *op. cit.*

17. Deed Record Y: 58.

18. Deed Records X: 415–416, Z: 567–568.

19. *The Covington Star*, 30 Nov. 1897.

20. Sarah Anderson Dixon, *Newton County Georgia Cemeteries* (Starrsville, Ga.: 1968), p. 72; Letters Testamentary I: 390; Will Record 4: 23–25.

21. Mrs. William B. Williford in a conversation with the author on 25 July 1972. Wright Adams was a close friend of her first husband, Thomas C. Swann.

22. Superior Court Minutes For 1900: 251–254. Sources for data on Mrs. Cynthia (Colley) Purington: *The Covington Star*, 5 April 1892, 12 January 1897; Marriage Records A: 278, C: 158, and 1850–59: 200; Will Records 1: 180–181, 2: 86–98; Inventory and Appraisement A: 10, 11; tombstones in Covington City Cemetery and in Colley Family Cemetery on Alcovy Road, near the river and the railroad tracks.

23. Deed Record 3: 473–474.

24. Carr family data made available to the author by Bates Block of Atlanta, 15 Dec. 1971; Military Record at State Department of Archives and History, in Atlanta; tombstones in Covington City Cemetery.

25. "Georgia D. A. R. Genealogical Library: Newton County, Georgia, Bible Records and Family Histories, Etc., Vols 1 & 2," available on microfilm at Washington Memorial Library in Macon; Miss Julia Aiken and Mrs. William B. Williford in conversations with the author on 3 Oct. 1971 and 2 Aug. 1972, respectively; tombstones in Covington City Cemetery.

26. Medora Field Perkerson, *White Columns In Georgia* (New York: 1952), p. 30; *The Atlanta Constitution*, 1 July 1928.

27. Dolly Sumner Lunt (Mrs. Thomas Burge), *A Woman's Wartime Journal* (New York: 1918), p. 8; *Memoirs of Georgia, Historical and Biographical* (Atlanta: 1895), II: 653; Mrs. W. C. Clark, "Covington During The Sixties," *The Covington News*, 21 Oct. 1927; Wylly Folk St. John, "Old South Tour of Covington," *The Atlanta Journal Magazine*, 18 Apr. 1948; Mrs. Lee Stephenson in a conversation with the author on 27 July 1972; tombstone, Covington City Cemetery.

28. *The Covington Star*, 26 Jan. 1900; *The Georgia Enterprise*, 12 Jan. 1900.

29. L. L. Cody, "Reminiscences," *The Covington News*, 1932 and 21 May 1953; tombstone, Covington City Cemetery.

30. *The Covington News*, 18 Feb. 1954; Deed Records 32: 79, 39: 438; Will Record 5: 163–164; tombstones, Covington City Cemetery.

31. *Historic Beaufort: A Guide to the Gracious Old Homes, Churches and Other Points of Interest in Beaufort, South Carolina* (Beaufort: 1970), pp. 56–57, 62–63, 86–87, 94–95; *The Covington News*, 5 June 1969; Dr. J. R. Sams in a conversation with the author on 5 August 1972.

32. Dr. Sams, *idem.*

33. *Idem.*; St. John, "Old South Tour," *op. cit.*

34. *The Covington News*, 5 June 1969.

35. Dr. Sams, *idem.* and 9 Oct. 1972.

36. *Idem.*; *The Covington News*, 5 Oct. 1972.

XIV: *WHITEHALL*

1. Deed Record F: 555. Flanegan-Neal transaction is in Deed Record B: 540–541; Flanegan-Dickson is mentioned in F: 551.

2. N. S. Turner in a conversation with the author on 11 May 1970.

3. Fitzhugh Lee, "Newton County History." *The Covington News*, 27 April 1937; United States Census, 1860–Georgia–Newton County, p. 13; the same, 1870, p. 95; Index card at State Department of Archives and History, in Atlanta (citing data provided by Mrs. O. W. Porter of Covington); tombstones in Covington City Cemetery.

4. Mary Givens Bryan, comp., *Georgia Official & Statistical Register 1957–1958* (Hapeville: 1958), pp. 869, 1188; Lodowick Johnson Hill, *The Hills of Wilkes County, Georgia, and Allied Families* (Atlanta: 1922), pp. 196–197; Lucian Lamar Knight, *A Standard History of Georgia and Georgians* (New York: 1917), VI: 2852.

5. Bryan, *Georgia Official & Statistical Register, op. cit.*, pp. 999, 1188; Lucian Lamar Knight, *Georgia's Landmarks, Memorials and Legends* (Atlanta: 1913, 1914), II: 911; *Masonic Messenger*, a publication of the Grand Lodge of *Georgia*, April, May, June and August 1938; Index card at State Department of Archives and History.

6. Medora Field Perkerson, *White Columns In Georgia* (New York: 1952), p. 30.

7. United States Census, 1860, *op. cit.*, p. 13; the same, 1870, p. 95; Deed Record U: 65; Will Record 3: 93–94.

8. United States Census, 1860, *idem.*; Will Record 3: 93–94. John Harris' will clearly refutes the statement appearing in Annie Hornady Howard, *Georgia Homes and Landmarks* (Atlanta: 1929), p. 94, that "Isaac P. Henderson [Harris] inherited this historic place and reared his family there. . ."

9. Military record at State Department of Archives and History, in Atlanta. Partnership mentioned in Deed Record C: 270; home mentioned in 3: 480 and 4: 156, 385.

10. Marriage Records 1860–65: 9, 1865–69: 97, 1869–74: 93, 1884–94: 50; Mrs. Fulton E. DeVane of Quitman (née Eleanor Butler of Covinton) in a letter to the

author, 1 January 1972, re Anderson and allied families; tombstones in Covington City Cemetery.

11. Will Record IV: 66–67.

12. Historical marker at intersection of Highways 278 and 142, east of Covington.

13. *Memoirs of General William T. Sherman* (New York: 1875), II: 180–181.

14. *Ibid.*, pp. 175–176.

15. Brevet Major George Ward Nichols, *The Story of The Great March. From The Diary of A Staff Officer* (New York: 1865), pp. 59–62.

16. M. A. DeWolfe Howe, ed., *Marching With Sherman. Passages From The Letters and Campaign Diaries of Henry Hitchcock* (New Haven: 1927), pp. 66, 69, 72.

17. Tombstones, Covington City Cemetery.

18. Deed Records T: 365, U: 65; deed to portion of *Harris' Quarters* in possession of Miss Sarah Mobley, granddaughter of J. W. Sockwell.

19. Marriage Record 1874–84: 148; Mrs. William B. Williford in a conversation with the author on 11 November 1969.

20. Both sales are recorded in Deed Record T: 678. The latter transaction excluded a one-acre tract "on which Shiloh Church is located."

21. Deed Record Z: 310–311.

22. Miss Marjorie Weldon of Atlanta, granddaughter of Mr. and Mrs. Franklin Wright, in letters to the author dated 22 June 1971 and 27 May 1972, and in conversations with him on 11, 25 May 1972.

23. *Idem.*

24. *Idem.*

25. *Idem.*, (letters).

26. *Idem.*

27. *The Atlanta Constitution*, 18 October 1894. A similar account appeared in *The Covington Star*, 23 October 1894. See also Marriage Record 1894–1904: 21.

28. *Idem.* (For Dr. Isaac Stiles Hopkins, see Henry Morton Bullock, *A History of Emory University* [Nashville: 1936; reprint Atlanta: 1972], pp. 174, 177.)

29. *Idem.*; Miss Weldon, *op. cit.*, in a conversation with the author on 25 May 1972, and clippings and letters in her father's scrapbook.

30. Bryan, *Georgia Official & Statistical Register, op. cit.*, pp. 868, 1206; Allen D. Candler and Clement A. Evans, eds., *Cyclopedia of Georgia* (Atlanta: 1906), III: 634–638, 640–641; Mrs. Willie Conyers Cook, "Clement Bates, Englishman, Emigrated to New England With Family in 1635," *The Sunday American* (Sunday issue of *The Atlanta Georgian*), 11 September 1932; Miss Weldon, *op. cit.*, letter, 22 June 1971.

31. Miss Weldon, letter, 22 June 1971; tombstones, Covington City Cemetery.

32. Deed Record 5: 115–117; Miss Weldon, conversation, 25 May 1972.

33. *The Covington News*, 13 November 1931; *The Georgia Enterprise*, 30 March 1900; Record of Charters I: 23–25, in office of Clerk of Superior Court; conversation with Mrs. William B. Williford (widow of Thomas C. Swann [Jr.]) and David Butler on 9 March 1970, and with Mrs. Charles S. Thompson of Atlanta (née Sarah Simms of Covington) on 9 December 1970; letters and other papers of the senior

T. C. Swann, which were examined through the courtesy of his daughter-in-law Mrs. Williford.

34. *Moody's Industrial Manual* (New York: 1958), July 1958: 1450; *The Atlanta Constitution*, 10 February 1953; *The Atlanta Journal*, 11 December 1963; *The Semi-Weekly Enterprise,* 9 February 1906; *The Weekly Enterprise*, 10 August 1906.

35. *The Covington News*, 13 November 1931; Will Record 5: 17.

36. *Idem.*; the late Mrs. E. B. Rogers (née Natalie Turner) in a conversation with the author on 29 September 1969.

37. *The Covington News*, 21 March 1930; Marriage Record 3: 239.

38. Mrs. Thompson and Miss Weldon, *idem.*, conversations on 9 December 1970 and 22 June 1971, respectively.

39. Mrs. Williford, *idem.*, conversation on 10 July 1970.

40. *The Atlanta Constitution,* 10 December 1959; Mrs. N. S. Turner in a conversation with the author on 15 July 1972; tombstone, Covington City Cemetery.

41. Deed Record 46: 188.

42. *The Covington News*, 2 August 1956; Marriage Record 7: 217.

XV: HOME OF "THE HONEST MAN"

1. Deed Record R: 224.

2. *Idem.*; *The Covington Star*, 2 July 1889; Deed Record M: 480, 481; Mrs. R. H. Patterson in impromptu remarks at a meeting of the Newton County Historical Society on 21 May 1972; Mrs. Lee Stephenson (quoting her late father-in-law John Stephenson re DeWald in Atlanta) in a conversation with the author on 19 July 1972.

3. Deed Record R: 246–247.

4. United States Census 1860–Georgia–Newton County, p. 26; the same, 1870, p. 91; Mrs. David Butler of Covington and Robert R. Wood 3rd of Atlanta, great-grandchildren of Cary Wood, in conversations with the author on 9 Mar. 1970 and 8 Aug. 1971, respecitvely; tombstones, Covington City Cemetery.

5. Lillian Henderson, *Roster of the Confederate Soldiers of Georgia 1861–1865* (Hapeville: 1960), p. 509.

6. I. W. Avery, *The History of Georgia From 1850 to 1881* (New York: 1881), pp. 324–330.

7. *Ibid.*, 326, 329.

8. *Ibid.*, 329.

9. *Ibid.*, 331–332; C. Mildred Thompson, *Reconstruction In Georgia; Economic, Social, Political; 1865–1872* (New York: 1915; reprint Atlanta: 1971), p. 41.

10. *Ibid.*, Thompson.

11. *The Georgia Enterprise*, 2 Sept. 1870.

12. Deed Record T: 232.

13. *The Covington News*, 8 May 1903; Will Record 3: 47, 169–177; tombstones, Covington City Cemetery.

14. Deed Record X: 500.

15. Marriage Record 1869–74: 182; tombstones, Covington City Cemetery.

16. *The Georgia Enterprise*, 29 Apr. 1904; Mrs. Annie Laura (Robinson) Dodson of Oxford and Mrs. Charles S. Thompson of Atlanta in conversations with the author on 24 Oct. 1972 and 9 Dec. 1970, respectively; Mrs. Anita Stewart Armstrong of Atlanta in a letter to the author dated 23 Nov. 1971 and also in an earlier conversation with him.

17. ,*The Atlanta Constitution*, 24 Aug. 1927; *The Georgia Enterprise*, 29 Apr. 1904; Fulton County Will Book I: 127; Franklin Anderson in a conversation with the author on 12 Nov. 1971; tombstone, Covington City Cemetery.

18. J. O. Martin, "Newton Memories," *The Covington News*, 13 May 1954, *et sequel; The Georgia Enterprise*, 21 Oct. 1904; Marriage Record 1869–1874: 55; Will Records 3: 323–324, 330–335; tombstones, Covington City Cemetery.

19. Nelle Womack Hines, *A Treasury Album of Milledgeville and Baldwin County, Georgia* (Macon: 1949), p. 5; *The Atlanta Constitution*, 22 Nov. 1963; *The Covington Star*, 11 Jan., 15 Nov. 1898; *The Georgia Enterprise*, 21 Oct. 1904; Martin, "Newton Memories," *op. cit.*; Deed Record W: 569–570; Mrs. William B. Williford in a conversation with the author on 26 Oct. 1972.

20. Miss Annie Pauline Anderson and her brother Franklin in conversations with the author on 25 Oct. 1970, 12 Nov. 1971 and 2 Oct. 1972.

21. *Memoirs of Georgia, Historial and Biographical* (Atlanta: 1895), II: 641–642; *The Covington News*, 17 Jan. 1912; *The Georgia Enterprise*, 6 Feb. 1903; Deed Records W: 569–570, 4: 230.

22. Deed Record 13: 519.

23. *The Covington News*, 16 Nov. 1961.

24. *Idem.*

25. *The Covington News*, 3 Mar. 1938, 23 May 1963, Marriage Record 3: 557.

26. Deed Record 60: 327.

27. Mrs. Everett Pratt in a conversation with the author on 11 Nov. 1972.

XVI: *POVERTY HILL* AND OTHERS

1. Deed Record K: 361.

2. *The Georgia Enterprise*, 21 Apr. 1871; Deed Records A: 19, 51 and K: 359; attachment to a letter to the author from Mrs. Fulton B. DeVane of Quitman, Ga. (née Eleanor Henry Butler of Covington), dated 1 Jan. 1972.

3. Letter from Mrs. DeVane, *op. cit.*

4. Henry Morton Bullock, *A History of Emory University* (Nashville: 1936; reprint Atlanta: 1972), pp. 75–89, 92–100; Deed Record K: 359.

5. *Idem.*; Dr. Charles C. Jarrell, *Oxford Echoes* (Oxford, Ga.: 1967), p. 50; *The Atlanta Journal*, 25 Sept. 1932; *The Covington News*, 2 Sept., 18 Nov. 1932. Deed Record G: 4 (9 Mar. 1842) refers to "Robert O. Usher and Joseph S. Anderson, Merchants trading under the name and style of Usher & Anderson."

6. Henry Branham, "Bank Occupies Stanch Old Covington House That Started As Hotel In Another Town," *The Atlanta Journal*, 25 Sept. 1932; *The Georgia Enterprise*, 4 Jan. 1884.

7. *The Georgia Enterprise*, 6 Feb. 1885.

8. *Idem.; The Atlanta Journal, op. cit.*

9. Letter from Mrs. DeVane, *idem.*; Will Record 3: 1–5.

10. *Idem.; The Weekly Enterprise* [weekly edition of *The Georgia Enterprise*, which sometimes published twice weekly], 5 Apr. 1907; Marriage Record B, 1835–1843: 212 and 1865–69: 97.

11. Ezra J. Warner, *Generals in Gray. Lives of the Confederate Commanders* (Baton Rouge: 1959), pp. 6–7; letter from Mrs. DeVane, *op. cit.*

12. I. W. Avery, *The History of the State of Georgia From 1850 to 1881* (New York: 1881), p. 215; Douglas Southall Freeman, *Lee's Lieutenants* (New York: 1950), II: 63, 181(n50), 204, 209–210, 217, 218n, 220n, 256, 264, 266 and III: 190n, 195n, 197, 204, 223–224 and n50, 361, 364, 554, 591, 623, 766; Franklin M. Garrett, *Atlanta and Environs* (New York: 1954), I: 875–876; Lucian Lamar Knight, *A Standard History of Georgia and Georgians* (New York: 1917), IV: 1996–1997; James Longstreet, *From Manassas To Appomattox*, ed. by James I. Robertson, Jr. (Bloomington, Ind.: 1960), pp. 174, 220, 222–223, 226–227, 242–243, 245, 247, 249, 253, 368, 370–372, 395, 428, 462, 482, 502, 506, 562, 617; Anita B. Sams, *Wayfarers in Walton* (Monroe, Ga.: 1967), pp. 120, 126, 133–134, 135–136, 138, 139, 143, 148–149, 151, 152, 156, 157, 158–162, 165–166; *War of the Rebellion: A Compilation of the Official Records of the Union and Confederate Armies* (Washington: 1880–1901), Series 19, Part 1, pp. 908–909; Warner, *Generals In Gray, op. cit.*; Bell Irwin Wiley and Hirst D. Milhollen, *Embattled Confederates* (New York: 1964), p. 276; A. R. Kuykendall, Jr., in *West End Star*, Atlanta, 1 Mar. 1962; copies of General Anderson's Oath of Allegiance and Presidential Pardon at State Department of Archives and History, in Atlanta, to which they were presented by his grandniece Miss Rose Rheburgh of Atlanta and Covington.

13. Freeman, *Lee's Lieutenants, op. cit.*, III: 774, 778; Garrett, *Atlanta and Environs, idem.*; Sams, *Wayfarers In Walton, op. cit.*, p. 120; Warner, *Generals In Gray, idem.*; Kuykendall in *West End Star, op. cit.*; "Newton County's Four Generals," *The Covington News*, 20 Apr. 1961.

14. *Memoirs of General William T. Sherman* (New York: 1875), II: 180; *Register of Graduates and Former Cadets United States Military Academy* (New York: 1954), pp. 154–157; letter to the author from Philip A. Farris of the Association of Graduates of the United States Military Academy, dated at West Point, 22 June 1971. One of the innumerable published references to the local legend that Sherman spared Covington because of friendship appeared in a column by Evelyn Hanna [later Mrs. Robert Somerville of Roswell], who wrote in *The Atlanta Constitution* in 1942 that he did this because "in his youth he had known at West Point *two* fellow-cadets from Covington, Ga., who were later generals in the Confederate Army..."

15. M. A. DeWolfe Howe, ed., *Marching With Sherman. Passages From The Letters and Campaign Diaries of Henry Hitchcock* (New Haven: 1927), p. 69.

16. *The Covington Star*, 29 Oct. 1895; *Masonic Messenger*, a publication of the Grand Lodge of Georgia, issues of Aug. and Sept. 1938; United States Census

1870–Georgia–Newton County, p. 88; letter from Mrs. DeVane, *op. cit.*; tombstone, Covington City Cemetery. William P. Anderson is not mentioned in the will of his father, Joseph S. Anderson (Will Record 3: 1–5), but that document does mention the testator's son George T. Anderson. The obituary of William P. Anderson in *The Covington Star*, 29 Dec. 1895, states that he "was a brother of General Tige Anderson. . .."

17. Archel Camp, *Uncle Charlie And His Rifle* (Boulder, Colo.: 1960), pp. 54–56; Deed Records I: 289, 544 and K: 233; Marriage Record C, 1843–48: 179; cornerstone of First Baptist Church. Mrs. Anderson's parentage is established in her obituary in *The Covington Star*, 4 Oct. 1898.

18. *The Covington News*, 29 July 1920; *The Georgia Enterprise*, 3 Feb. 1905; Will Record 5: 93; Mrs. Charles S. Thompson of Atlanta (née Sarah Simms of Covington) and Mrs. William B. Williford in conversations with the author on 27 Jan. 1971; tombstones, Covington City Cemetery.

19. *The Covington Star*, 3 Apr. 1888, 4 June 1894; United States Census 1860–Georgia–Newton County, p. 134; the same, 1870, p. 88 (the latter lists Susan, whose name does not appear in the next source cited. Neither census lists Inez nor Lucy); Miss Rose Rheburgh, granddaughter of Mr. and Mrs. William P. Anderson, in a letter to the author dated 19 Nov. 1971. Deed Record K: 233 (sale of Anderson's Floyd Street residence in Nov. 1852) establishes the approximate date of completion of his new home.

20. Deed Record U: 459; Marriage Record 1874–84: 2; Mrs. Charles S. Thompson, *op. cit.*, in a letter to the author dated 7 May 1972 and in a conversation with him at his home on 14 Nov. 1971; Mrs. Leon Cohen and Mrs. John F. Meacham in conversations with the author on 29 Oct. 1971 and 4 Oct. 1972, respecitvely.

21. Marriage Record 1894–1904: 66; David Butler, grandson of William P. Anderson's sister Mrs. Henry, in a conversation with the author on 9 Mar. 1970; Mrs. Leon Cohen in conversations with the author on 29 Oct. 1971 and 8 May 1972; tombstones, Covington City Cemetery. Year of Columbian Exhibition established in *The World Almanac* (New York: 1965), p. 569.

22. Deed Record 13: 7; Mrs. John F. Meacham (née Elsie Rheburgh, daughter of S. C. Rheburgh and his second wife), Miss Sarah Mobley (daughter of Mr. and Mrs. R. M. Mobley), and Mrs. William B. Williford (quoting Mrs. Moody Summers, Sr.) in conversations with the author on 9 May 1972, 16 Nov. 1971, and 21 May 1972, respectively.

23. Deed Record O: 191–192; Will Record 3: 203–204; letter from Mrs. DeVane, *op. cit.*

24. Deed Records V: 387–389 and Y: 112. For data on the Sibleys see Lucian Lamar Knight, *A Standard History, op. cit.*, VI: 3224–3226.

25. *The Covington Star*, 22, 29, Oct. 1895 and 4 Oct. 1898.

26. Tombstones, Covington City Cemetery.

27. *The Covington News*, 7 Sept. 1928, 13 June 1930; G. C. Adams, "Chronicles of Newton," *The Covington News*, 21 Oct. 1927; Will Book 3: 208–211; "Georgia D. A. R. Genealogical Library: Newton County, Georgia, Bible Records

and Family Histories, Etc., Vols. 1 & 2," p. 110, available on microfilm at Washington Memorial Library in Macon; card file on "Harper Guards" (Co. E, 42nd Rgt. Ga. Vol. Inf.) at State Department of Archives and History, in Atlanta; tombstones, Covington City Cemetery.

28. [Sam Boykin,] *History of the Baptist Denomination in Georgia* (Atlanta: 1881), "Biographical Compendium," pp. 78–79; Major General Robert J. Travis, *The Travis (Travers) Family And Its Allies...* (Savannah: 1954), p. 22; *The Covington News*, 7 Sept. 1928; *The Georgia Enterprise*, 19 Dec. 1869, 17 June 1904; "Georgia D. A. R. Genealogical Library," *idem.*; Deed Records S: 594, T: 316–317, 6: 176; letter from Mrs. DeVane, *op. cit.*; tombstones, Covington City Cemetery.

29. Deed Records Y: 577–578, Z: 401.

30. L. Wilson Jarman, "A Walk Around The Square [in 1889]," *The Covington News*, 21 May 1953.

31. *Idem.*

32. Deed Records 1: 128, 3: 287–288, 10: 247–248; David Butler in a conversation with the author on 9 Mar. 1970.

33. Deed Record X: 305; "Muster Roll of Captain Henry T. Henry's Company...," which was examined through the courtesy of Captain Henry's grandson, David Butler; letter from Mrs. DeVane, *idem.* Dr. Henry, whose obituary appeared in *The Covington Star* on 22 Nov. 1892, died and was buried at Troup; his wife was buried in Covington City Cemetery.

34. Eleanor Stuart Henry, *Memoirs* (published privately, n.p.: 1956), a copy of which was examined by the author through the courtesy of her nephew David Butler; letter from Mrs. DeVane, *idem.*; tombstones, Covington City Cemetery.

35. Henry, *Memoirs, idem.; The Covington News*, 27 Dec. 1929; *The Covington Star*, 29 Oct. 1895; Mrs. David Butler in a conversation with the author on 9 Mar. 1970.

36. Deed Records 23: 301, 302 and 24: 461; letter from Mrs. DeVane, *idem.*; David Butler, *idem.*

37. Deed Record 27: 472.

38. Marriage Record 3: 146.

39. Personal knowledge of the author.

40. "Old Homes of Covington," a booklet prepared by the Covington Garden Club, 1969, p. 3.

41. *History of Peach County, Georgia*, compiled by Governor Treutlen Chapter, DAR, Fort Valley (Atlanta: 1972), p. 272.

42. *The Covington News*, 23 June 1966; Marriage Record 8: 265.

XVII: *THE COTTAGE*

1. Medora Field Perkerson, *White Columns In Georgia* (New York: 1952), p. 29; Katherine Pierce, "Covington's Tour of Homes," *The Atlanta Journal Magazine*, 24 April 1949; "Plantation Ghosts and Southern Hospitality," *The Atlanta Journal-Constitution Magazine*, 5 April 1953; Wylly Folk St. John, "Old South Tour of

Covington," *The Atlanta Journal Magazine*, 18 April 1948; "Old Homes of Covington," a booklet prepared by the Covington Garden Club, 1969, p. 2.

2. Deed Record K: 438; Marriage Record 1852–1861: 101; Mrs. D. L. Wilson of
Macon, a grandniece of Mrs. Neel, in a letter to the author dated 15 December
1970.

3. Deed Record M: 418.

4. A map on the back of a deed to property sold by William P. Anderson to
Henry T. Henry, 15 August 1863 (Deed Record X: 305), indicates that Judge
Floyd owned land on the north side of the Covington-Madison road (now Floyd
Street), extending west from the present Butler Avenue. The Act giving married
women the right to own property in their own name is recorded in *Georgia Laws
1866*, p. 146.

5. Henry Morton Bullock, *A History of Emory University* (Nashville: 1936; reprint
Atlanta: 1972), pp. 55, 59, 60; Deed Record E: 282; Will Records I: 231–236 and
1850–1871: 279–281.

6. "Old Homes of Covington," *idem.*; Miss Geniveve Scully of Atlanta, granddaughter of Mr. Neal's half-sister Emma Sanders, in a conversation with the author
on 22 April 1972.

7. *Idem.*

8. Edward Mayes, *Lucius Q. C. Lamar: His Life, Times, and Speeches 1825–1893*
(Nashville: 1896), pp. 101–102; military record cards at State Department of
Archives and History, in Atlanta; letter from Major James P. Simms to his mother,
23 September 1862, which is reproduced on page 59 of the present work;
tombstone, Williamson-Conyers Family Cemetery in North Covington.

9. Mrs. John B. Davis, "History of Covington U. D. C.," a newspaper clipping of
which was made available to the author by Miss Sarah Mobley.

10. Major Simms, letter, *idem.*

11. United States Census, 1860–Georgia–Newton County, p. 17; the same, 1870:
154.

12. *The Covington Star*, 5 March 1889; *The Georgia Enterprise*, 1 May 1903.
Quotation is from the latter.

13. Davis, "History of Covington U. D. C.," *op. cit.*

14. *Idem.*

15. *The Atlanta Journal*, 28 June 1915; *The Covington Star*, 4 October 1892, 3
May 1898; Marriage Record 1884–1894: 486 and 1894–1904: 202; Fulton County
Will Book E: 648; Mrs. D. L. Wilson of Macon in a letter to the author dated 15
December 1970; Mrs. Cullen Gosnell of Atlanta in a conversation with the author
on 9 December 1970. The two ladies are great-granddaughters of Judge John J.
Floyd and grandnieces of Mrs. McCormick Neal.

16. Tombstones, Covington City Cemetery.

17. *Atlanta City Directories* 1901: 1339, 1904: 1121, 1910: 1484, 1912: 1428,
1915: 1562, 1923: 1065, 1940: 1281; *The Atlanta Journal*, 28 June 1915; *The
Covington Star*, 26 July 1898, 22 January 1904; Marriage Record 1894–1904: 412.

18. *The Weekly Enterprise*, 23 March and 13 April 1906.

19. *The Georgia Enterprise*, 25 August 1899.

20. *Atlanta City Directory 1910*, pp. 1248, 1484; *The Atlanta Journal*, 18 August 1902, 28 June 1915; Marriage Record 1867–74: 90; tombstone, Covington City Cemetery.

21. *The Atlanta Journal*, 28 June 1915; tombstone, Covington City Cemetery.

22. *Atlanta City Directory 1910*, p. 1248, and *1915*, p. 1332; Mrs. Charles S. Thompson of Atlanta (née Sarah Simms of Covington) in a conversation with the author on 9 December 1970.

23. *The Covington News*, 18 October 1935; *The Semi-Weekly Enterprise*, 29 December 1905; Deed Record 32: 360; Miss Scully, *idem*.

24. Mrs. Thompson, *idem*.

25. Major General Robert J. Travis, *The Travis (Travers) Family And Its Allies...* (Savannah: 1954), p. 21; *The Covington Star*, 9, 30 November 1897 and 15 February 1898; Mrs. William W. Aiken in a conversation with the author on 23 May 1972.

26. *The Covington Star*, 30 November 1897.

27. Walter G. Cooper, *The Story of Georgia* (New York: 1938), III: 421; Franklin M. Garrett, *Atlanta and Environs* (New York: 1954), II: 205–206, 556; Lucian Lamar Knight, *A Standard History of Georgia and Georgians* (New York: 1917), VI: 2935; Travis, *The Travis (Travers) Family, op. cit.*, pp. 95, 96, 102; Deed Record A: 253; William D. Travis, 3rd., in a conversation with the author on 26 August 1971.

28. Travis, *The Travis Family, op. cit.*, pp. 104–105, 157–158 (citing Will Record I: 102).

29. *Ibid.*, pp. 95, 156–157; *The Covington Star*, 15 May 1888, 8 April 1890; Will Record 3: 284–287; William D. Travis, 3rd., *idem*. Deed Record S: 240–241 refers to "Robert Livingston's Corner ... across branch ... to lower corner of J. N. Bradshaw's land ... on Academy Street."

30. Travis, *The Travis Family*, pp. 21–22; William D. Travis, 3rd., *idem*.

31. Will Record 4: 458–460; William D. Travis, 3rd., *idem*.

32. Travis, *The Travis Family*, p. 21.

33. Will Records 5: 214, 241–242 and 6: 176; Mrs. William B. Williford in a conversation with the author on 18 August 1971.

34. William D. Travis, 3rd., *idem*.

35. Deed Records 1: 162, 4: 387; Mortgage Deeds 1: 294, 563.

36. *The Georgia Enterprise*, 29 January 1869; "Georgia D. A. R. Genealogical Library: Newton County, Georgia, Bible Records and Family Histories, Etc., Vols. 1 & 2," available on microfilm at Washington Memorial Library in Macon; Marriage Record 1865–69: 267; Will Records 3: 208–211, 4: 226; Miss Virginia Merck, granddaughter of R. W. Clarke, in a conversation with the author on 29 June 1972; tombstones, Covington City Cemetery.

37. *The Covington Star*, 4 December 1888; *The Georgia Enterprise*, 10 April 1903; Deed Record 15: 301; Will Record 4: 226; tombstones, Covington City Cemetery.

38. Deed Record 15: 301.

39. Tandy E. Bush of Tampa, Florida, son of the second Mrs. R. W. Milner, in a letter to the author dated 26 June 1972.
40. *Idem.*; tombstones, Covington City Cemetery.
41. *Idem.*
42. Tandy E. Bush, *idem.*; Mrs. Robert Wharton of St. Simons Island, niece of John T. Swann, in a conversation with the author on 24 June 1972.
43. Paul Swann of Dalton, nephew of Jack Swann, in a conversation with the author on 2 September 1972.
44. Tandy E. Bush, *idem.*; Deed Record 22: 558.
45. Marriage Record 3: 461; Mrs. Patterson, *idem.* and 18 June 1972.
46. Katherine Pierce, "Hostesses in Hoop Skirts at Covington's Tour of Homes," *The Atlanta Journal Magazine*, 24 April 1949; Wylly Folk St. John, "Covington's Tour of Homes Offers Plantation Ghosts and Southern Hospitality," *The Atlanta Journal-Constitution Magazine*, 5 April 1953; the same author, "Old South Tour of Covington," *The Atlanta Journal Magazine*, 18 April 1948.
47. Deed Records M: 418, 11: 255, 17: 515; Mrs. R. H. Patterson in a conversation with the author on 1 April 1972.
48. *Historic American Buildings Survey*, compiled and edited by Historic American Buildings Survey of the National Parks Service (Washington: 1941), p. 86. The Neal-Patterson "cottage" is identified here as the Downs House.

XVIII: DR. ARCHIBALD CAMP'S HOME

1. Deed Record S: 599—600.
2. Archel Camp, *Uncle Charlie And His Rifle* (Boulder, Colo: 1960), 41, 54—56; *The Covington Star*, 4 October 1898; Deed Record N: 275—276; Marriage Record C: 179; Fitzhugh Lee, "Newton County History," *The Covington News*, 27 May 1937; O. Grant Gooden of Springfield, Pennsylvania, a great-grandson of Dr. Camp, in a letter to the author dated 8 October 1972.
3. Camp, *Uncle Charlie, ibid.*, pp. 55—56; Lee, "Newton County History," *idem.*; Gooden, *idem.*
4. Camp, *Uncle Charlie, ibid.*, p. 54; Gooden, *idem.*; Index card at State Department of Archives and History, in Atlanta (data provided by Miss Charles Josephine Camp-Porter of Covington).
5. I. W. Avery, *The History of Georgia From 1850 To 1881* (New York: 1881), pp. 149—157; Camp, *Uncle Charlie, ibid.*, 55—56; Lucian Lamar Knight, *Georgia's Landmarks, Memorials and Legends* (Atlanta: 1913, 1914), II: 558—570.
6. Knight, *Landmarks, ibid.*, II: 121—130; Frederick W. Seward, *William H. Seward: An Autobiography, with a Memoir of His Life and Selections from His Speeches* (New York: 1891), pp. 36—43; Mrs. John B. Reeves of Brevard, North Carolina (née Sarah Graves of *Mt. Pleasant*), in a conversation with the author on 24 August 1972.
7. Camp, *Uncle Charlie*, pp. 11—12, 68, 85.
8. *Ibid.*, pp. 56, 65.
9. *Ibid.*, pp. 72, 96—97.
10. *Ibid.*, pp. 85—88, 95.

11. *Ibid.*, p. 82.

12. *Ibid.*, pp. 26, 104–106, 111–112; Marriage Records 1860–65: 329, 1867–74: 45; tombstones, Covington City Cemetery.

13. Mrs. Reeves, *op. cit.*

14. Gooden, *op. cit.*; Mrs. P. W. Pratt, Sr., present owner of the Camp house, in a conversation with the author on 8 August 1970, citing as her authority a statement made several years earlier by the previously-mentioned Mr. Gooden in the course of a visit to the house.

15. Camp, *Uncle Charlie, op. cit.*, p. 103.

16. *Ibid.*, pp. 99, 108–111; Marriage Record 1867–74: 240.

17. Deed Record S: 599–600, 600–601.

18. [Sam Boykin,] *History of the Baptist Denomination in Georgia* (Atlanta: 1881), "Biographical Compendium," pp. 61–62.

19. A. L. Hull, *A Historial Sketch of the University of Georgia* (Atlanta: 1894), "List of Graduates."

20. [Boykin,] *History of the Baptist Denomination, idem.*

21. *Ibid.*, p. 62.

22. M. L. Brittain, *The Story of Georgia Tech* (Chapel Hill: 1948), pp. 13, 20, 93–94; Henry Morton Bullock, *A History of Emory University* (Nashville: 1936; reprint Atlanta: 1972), p. 177; Clark Howell, *History of Georgia* (Chicago: 1926), IV: 20–22; Lucian Lamar Knight, *A Standard History of Georgia and Georgians* (New York: 1917), IV: 2155–2158; Dorothy Orr, *A History of Education in Georgia* (Chapel Hill: 1950), pp. 387–388.

23. *The Covington News*, 3 January, 14 February 1912; Deed Records I("eye"): 544, 4; 384; cornerstone of First Baptist Church.

24. Knight, *A Standard History, ibid.*; *The Covington News*, 3 January, 14 February 1912 (tribute quoted from latter); *The Covington Star*, 8 October, 24 December 1889.

25. Mrs. Harry Dietz in a conversation with the author on 2 October 1972.

26. *Idem.*

27. *Idem.*; Deed Records 17: 217, 18: 115 and 559, 20: 54.

28. *The Covington News*, 12 June 1958; Will Record 5: 386–387; tombstones, Covington City Cemetery.

29. Deed Records 20: 310, 21: 310.

30. Bullock, *History of Emory, op. cit.*, pp. 219–220, 229, 234, 237, 238, 239, 285–292, 295, 297.

31. Mrs. Williford, *idem*; Mrs. Lowry Hunt of Madison, daughter of Mr. and Mrs. Charles Candler, in a conversation with the author on 6 June 1972.

32. Deed Record 31: 59.

33. Louise McHenry Hicky, *Rambles Through Morgan County* (Madison, Georgia: 1971), pp. 17, 50, 52, 138–140, 194; *The Covington News*, 13 August 1926; *The Georgia Enterprise*, 9 November 1900; a brief history of the Covington Chapter, UDC, by Miss Sallie Mae Sockwell, examined through the courtesy of her niece Miss Sarah Mobley; Deed Records F: 820, U: 209, 6: 505; Mrs. William B. Williford in a

conversation with the author on 1 October 1972.

34. *The Covington News*, 21 April 1955; tombstone, Covington City Cemetery.

35. *The Covington News*, 25 December 1958, 23 May 1963; Marriage Record 7: 360.

XIX: THE LEE - ROGERS HOUSE

1. Deed Record B: 540—541, 4: 498; Miss Dorothy Lee in a conversation with the author on 23 June 1972.

2. *The Covington News*, 10 Jan. 1912; *The Georgia Enterprise*, 18 June 1901; Miss Lee, *idem.*

3. Deed Record 4: 498, 501. T. J. Shepherd apparently was a son of Thomas Shepherd, as Deed Record R: 504—505 cites gift of land by the latter to his grandson William B. Shepherd, who is known to have been a son of the former.

4. *Memoirs of Georgia, Historical and Biographical* (Atlanta: 1895), II: 641—642; G. C. Adams, "Chronicles of Newton," *The Covington News*, 21 Oct. 1927; "Georgia D. A. R. Genealogical Library: Newton County, Georgia, Bible Records and Family Histories, Etc., Vols. 1 & 2," available on microfilm at Washington Memorial Library in Macon; Marriage Record 1874—84: 518; tombstones, Covington City Cemetery.

5. L. Wilson Jarman, "A Walk Around the Square [In 1889]," *The Covington News*, 14 May 1953.

6. *The Covington News*, 17 Jan. 1912; *The Covington Star*, 20 Dec. 1898.

7. *The Covington News*, 13 June 1930; Jarman, "A Walk Around The Square," *idem.*; Will Record 4: 455—457; Miss Dorothy Lee in a conversation with the author on 10 Oct. 1972.

8. *The Covington Star*, 2 Mar. 1897, 3 Sept. 1901; Deed Records Y: 563, 4: 384 and 498, 25: 65.

9. *The Georgia Enterprise*, 22 Jan. 1904; Marriage Record 3: 173; Will Record 5: 17.

10. *The Covington News*, 24 Aug. 1950; Marriage Record 6: 171.

11. Will Record 7: 104—109.

12. Deed Records 91: 142, 143 and 97: 243.

XX: THE PORTER - ROGERS - TUCK HOUSE

1. Deed Records A: 94, R: 14, T: 14; Miss Louis Gray, Historian of the First Baptist Church, in a conversation with the author on 17 Nov. 1972 (citing Deed Record S: 552 as source for sale by Corley to deacons of the Church); Miss Mary Willingham, daughter of Wilkins Willingham, in a conversation with the author on 12 Nov. 1972.

2. Entry in the Swann Family Bible, now owned by the Swanns' daugher-in-law, Mrs. William B. Williford, and that lady herself in a conversation with the author on 18 Nov. 1969.

3. Archel Camp, *Uncle Charlie And His Rifle* (Boulder, Colo: 1960), pp. 104—106; Allen D. Candler and Clement A. Evans, eds., *Cyclopedia of Georgia* (Atlanta: 1906), IV: 251—252; Walter G. Cooper, *The Story of Georgia* (Atlanta: 1938), IV: 78—79; *The Georgia Enterprise*, 14 May 1901; *The Macon Telegraph*, 13 June 1949; Program for Commencement Exercises at Lucy Cobb Institute, 14 June 1893, a copy of which is owned by the author; Swann Family Bible, *idem.*

4. Cooper, *The Story of Georgia, idem.; Garden History of Georgia* (Atlanta: 1933), pp. 333–334; *The Macon Telegraph, idem.*
5. *Chapter Histories/Daughters of The American Revolution In Georgia. 1891–1931* (Augusta: 1932?), p. 145; Cooper, *The Story of Georgia, idem.*; Frank F. Jones, *Biographies of The Members of The Rotary Club of Macon, Georgia, 1938–1942; Register of the Georgia Society Colonial Dames of America* (Savannah: 1926), p. 162; *Register of the Georgia Society Colonial Dames of America* (Baltimore: 1937), p. 130; Dr. Thaddeus Brockett Rice and Carolyn White Williams, *History of Greene County Georgia 1786–1886* (Macon: 1961), p. 313; Ida Young, Julius Gholson, and Clara Nell Hargrove, *History of Macon, Georgia* (Macon: 1950), pp. 700–701; *The Atlanta Journal*, 3 Jan. 1972; *The Macon Telegraph*, 4 Aug. 1939 and 13, 14 June 1949; Bibb County Will Books K: 209 and N: 261–278; Bibb County Minutes QQ: 238 and YY: 509; plaques on specified buildings at Mercer and Wesleyan.
6. Lucian Lamar Knight, *A Standard History of Georgia and Georgians* (New York: 1917), VI: 2889–2890; Mortgage Record 28: 490–493.
7. Knight, *A Standard History, idem.; The Covington Star*, 5 Apr. 1892; tombstones, Covington City Cemetery.
8. *Idem.; The Covington Star*, 25 Dec. 1894; *The Weekly Enterprise*, 18 May 1906.
9. "Old Homes of Covington," a booklet prepared by the Covington Garden Club, 1969, p. 1; notes on history of Covington Chapter, United Daughters of the Confederacy, prepared by Miss Sallie Mae Sockwell and loaned to the author by her niece Miss Sarah Mobley; George Elliott in a conversation with the author on 25 Oct. 1971.
10. Deed Record 21: 134.
11. Knight, *A Standard History, op. cit.*, IV: 2205–2206.
12. *Idem.*; Mrs. William B. Williford in a conversation with the author on 11 Mar. 1971.
13. *The Covington News*, 28 Oct. 1920; Mrs. Williford, *idem.*; Deed Record 97: 773.
14. *The Covington News*, 22 May 1969; tombstones, Covington City Cemetery.
15. Deed Record 97: 773.

XXI: THE LEE - PORTER HOUSE

1. Deed Records R: 272, U: 209, 11: 230.
2. Mrs. William B. Williford in a conversation with the author on 11 Oct. 1970.
3. Deed Record 33: 139; Edgar Wood in a conversation with the author on 3 June 1971.
4. Miss Dorothy Lee in a conversation with the author on 10 Oct. 1972; Mrs. Williford, *idem.*
5. Deed Record 25: 10.
6. *The Covington News*, 27 Mar. 1947, 16 Nov. 1961, Will Record 4: 211 and 5: 185–187.
7. Deed Record 25: 11.
8. Wylly Folk St. John, "Old South Tour of Covington," *The Atlanta Journal Magazine*, 18 Apr. 1948; Mrs. Williford, *op. cit.*, 3 Oct. 1972.
9. *The Covington News*, 27 Aug. 1942.

10. *Idem.*; Mrs. Williford, *op. cit.*, 2 Mar. 1972.

11. *The Covington News*, 7 Apr. 1960; Deed Record 51: 554. (Deed Record 51: 41 records the sale by Mrs. Porter on 7 Aug. 1958 to R. Luke Savage and Ilene M. Savage of a plot of land at the rear of her home.)

12. *Polk's Covington City Directory 1971* (Richmond: 1971), p. 9; Deed Records 59: 250, 67: 384.

BIBLIOGRAPHY

BIBLIOGRAPHY

BOOKS

Atlanta City Directories. Various years.

Avery, I. W., *The History of the State of Georgia From 1850 to 1881,* New York, 1881.

Bonner, James C., ed., *The Journal of a Milledgeville Girl, 1861–1867* [by Anna Maria Green], Athens, 1964.

[Boykin, Sam,] *History of the Baptist Denomination in Georgia,* Atlanta, 1881.

Brittain, M. L., *The Story of Georgia Tech,* Chapel Hill, 1948.

Brooks, Robert Preston, *The University of Georgia Under Sixteen Administrations. From 1785–1955,* Athens, 1956.

Bryan, Mary Givens, comp., *Georgia Official & Statistical Register 1957–1958,* Hapeville, 1958.

Bullock, Henry Morton, *A History of Emory University,* Nashville, 1936; reprint Atlanta, 1972.

Burge, Dolly Lunt. See *Dolly Sumner Lunt* and *James I. Robertson, Jr.*

Burge, Louisiana. See *Richard Barksdale Harwell.*

Camp, Archel, *Uncle Charlie And His Rifle,* Boulder, Colo., 1960.

Candler, Allen D. and Clement A. Evans, eds., *Cyclopedia of Georgia,* 3 vols., Atlanta, 1906.

Chapter Histories. Daughters of The American Revolution In Georgia, 1891–1931, Augusta, 1932(?)

Clark, Walter A., *Under The Stars and Bars, or The Memories of Four Years Service,* Augusta, 1900.

Code of Georgia Annotated, Atlanta, 1966.

Cooper, Walter G., *The Story of Georgia,* 4 vols., New York, 1938.

Coulter, E. Merton, *College Life In The Old South,* Athens, 1951.

Crain, Marguerite Starr and Georgianna Theus, *They Followed The Sun: The Story of James Penn Starr and Georgianna Theus, Their Ancestors and Their Progenies,* n.p., n.d. (*Dallas, 1969?*).

Cumming, Kate. Richard Barksdale Harwell, ed., *Kate: The Journal of A Confederate Nurse,* Baton Rouge, 1959.

Dawson, William C., *Compilation of The Laws of the State of Georgia Passed By the General Assembly, Since The Year 1819 To The Year 1829, Inclusive,* Milledgeville, 1831.

Dictionary of International Biography, Vol. IX in 2 parts, London, 1972.

Directory of The Phi Delta Theta Fraternity, Oxford, Ohio, 1958.

Dixon, Sarah Anderson, *Newton County Georgia Cemeteries*, Starrsville, Ga., 1968.

Evans, Gen. Clement A., ed., *Confederate Military History*, Atlanta, 1899.

Felton, Rebecca Latimer, *Country Life in Georgia In The Days of My Youth*, Atlanta, 1919.

Freeman, Douglas Southall, *Lee's Lieutenants*, 3 vols., New York, 1950.

Garrett, Franklin M., *Atlanta and Environs*, 2 vols., New York, 1954.

Georgia Laws, 1866.

Grice, Warren, *The Georgia Bench and Bar*, Macon, 1931.

Harris, John B., *A History of the Supreme Court of Georgia*, Macon, 1948.

Harwell, Richard Barksdale, ed., *Louisiana Burge: The Diary of a Confederate Girl*, n.p., n.d.

Henderson, Lillian, *Roster of the Confederate Soldiers of Georgia 1861–1865*, Hapeville, 1960.

Hendrick, Roe Herring, *Lineage and Tradition of the Herring, Conyers, Hendrick, Boddie, Perry, Crudup, Denson and Hilliard Families*, n.p., 1916.

Hicky, Louise McHenry, *Rambles Through Morgan County*, Madison, 1971.

Hill, Lodowick Johnson, *The Hills of Wilkes County, Georgia, and Allied Families*, Atlanta, 1922.

Hines, Nelle Womack, *A Treasury Album of Milledgeville and Baldwin County, Georgia,* reprint Macon, 1949.

Historic American Buildings Survey, Washington, 1941.

Historic Beaufort: A Guide to the Gracious Old Homes, Churches and Other Points of Interest in Beaufort, South Carolina, Beaufort, 1970. Published by The Beaufort Historic Foundation.

History of Peach County Georgia, Atlanta, 1972. Compiled by The Governor Treutlen Chapter, Daughters of the American Revolution.

Hitchcock, [Major] Henry. See *M. A. DeWolfe Howe.*

Hoehling, A. A., *Last Train From Atlanta*, New York, 1958.

Howe, M. A. DeWolfe, ed., *Marching With Sherman. Passages From The Letters and Campaign Diaries of Henry Hitchcock*, New Haven, 1927.

Hull, A. L., *A Historical Sketch of the University of Georgia*, Atlanta, 1894.

Hull, Augustus Longstreet, *Annals of Athens, Georgia, 1801–1901*, Atlanta, 1906.

Jarrell, Dr. Charles C., *Oxford Echoes*, Oxford, Ga., 1967.

Kennedy, John F., *Profiles In Courage*, New York, 1961.

Knight, Lucian Lamar, *A Standard History of Georgia and Georgians*, 6 vols., New York, 1917.

Knight, Lucian Lamar, *Georgia's Bi-Centennial Memoirs and Memories*, 4 vols., Atlanta, 1932.

Knight, Lucian Lamar, *Georgia's Landmarks, Memorials and Legends*, 2 vols., Atlanta, 1913, 1914.

Knight, Lucian Lamar, *Reminiscences of Famous Georgians*, 2 vols., Atlanta, 1902.

Longstreet, Augustus Baldwin, *Georgia Scenes*, Augusta, 1835; reprint Atlanta, 1971.

Longstreet, James. James I. Robertson, Jr., ed., *From Manassas To Appomattox*, Bloomington, Ind., 1960.

Lunt, Cornelia Gray, *Sketches of Childhood and Girlhood*, Evanston, Ill., c. 1925.

Lunt, Dolly Sumner (Mrs. Thomas Burge), *A Woman's Wartime Journal*, New York, 1918.

McCullar, Bernice, *This Is Your Georgia*, Montgomery, Ala., 1968.

McIntosh, John H., *The Official History of Elbert County, 1790–1935*, Elberton, 1940; reprint Atlanta, 1968.

Marshall, Catherine, *A Man Called Peter*, New York, 1951.

Martin, Thomas H., *Atlanta and Its Builders*, n.p., 1902.

Mayes, Edward, *Lucius Q. C. Lamar: His Life, Times, and Speeches, 1825–1893*, Nashville, 1896.

Memoirs of Georgia, Historical and Biographical, 2 vols., Atlanta, 1895.

Miller, Stephen F., *The Bench and Bar of Georgia*, Philadelphia, 2 vols., 1855.

Moody's Industrial Manual, New York, 1958, 1960.

Murray, Paul, *The Whig Party In Georgia, 1825–1853*, Chapel Hill, 1948.

Myers, Robert Manson, ed., *Children of Pride. A True Story of Georgia and the Civil War*, New Haven, 1972.

Nichols, Brevet Major George Ward, *The Story of The Great March. From The Diary of A Staff Officer*, New York 1865.

Nichols, Frederick Doveton and Frances Benjamin Johnston, *The Early Architecture of Georgia*, Chapel Hill, 1957.

Orr, Dorothy, *A History of Education in Georgia*, Chapel Hill, 1950.

Perkerson, Medora Field, *White Columns In Georgia*, New York, 1952.

Polk's Covington City Directory, 1971, Richmond, 1971.

Rainer, Vessie Thrasher, *Henry County, Georgia. The Mother of Counties*, McDonough, Ga., 1971.

Register of the Georgia Society Colonial Dames of America, Baltimore, 1937.

Register of the Georgia Society Colonial Dames of America, Savannah, 1926.

Rice, Dr. Thaddeus Brockett and Carolyn White Williams, *History of Greene County, Georgia, 1786–1886*, Macon, 1961.

Robertson, James I., Jr., ed., *The Diary of Dolly Lunt Burge*, Athens, 1962.

Sams, Anita B., *Wayfarers In Walton*, Monroe, Ga., 1967.

Seward, Frederick W., *William H. Seward: An Autobiography, with a Memoir of His Life and Selections from His Speeches*, New York, 1891.

Sherman, General William T., Memoirs of, 2 vols., New York, 1875.

Sherwood, The Rev. Adiel, Gazetteer of Georgia, Macon, Griffin and Atlanta, 1860; reprint Atlanta, 1970.

Smith, George Gilman, D. D., The Story of Georgia and The Georgia People, Macon, 1900.

Stacy, The Rev. James, D. D., The Presbyterian Church. A History of the Presbyterian Church in Georgia, Elberton, Ga., 1912.

Stern, Philip Van Doren, Robert E. Lee: The Man and The Soldier, New York, 1963.

Suarez, Annette McDonald, ed., The Journal of Andrew Leary O'Brien, Athens, 1946.

Temple, Sarah Blackwell Gober, The First Hundred Years. A Short History of Cobb County in Georgia, Atlanta, 1935.

Thompson, C. Mildred, Reconstruction In Georgia; Economic, Social, Political; 1865–1872, New York, 1915; reprint Atlanta, 1971.

Travis, Maj. Gen. Robert J., The Travis (Travers) Family And Its Allies. . ., Savannah, 1954.

Waddell, Joseph A., Annals of Augusta County, Virginia, From 1726 to 1871, Bridgewater, Va., 1958.

Wade, John D., Augustus Baldwin Longstreet. A Study of the Development of Culture in the South, Athens, 1969.

War of the Rebellion: A Compilation of the Official Records of the Union and Confederate Armies, Washington, 1880–1901.

Warner, Ezra J., Generals In Gray. Lives of the Confederate Commanders, Baton Rouge, 1959.

White, The Rev. George, Historical Collections of Georgia, New York, 1854; reprint Danielsville, Ga., 1968.

White, George, Statistics of the State of Georgia, Savannah, 1849.

Who's Who in Commerce and Industry, New York, 1936.

Wiley, Belle Irwin and Hirst D. Milhollen, Embattled Confederates, New York, 1964.

Williford, William Bailey, Americus Through The Years. The First One Hundred and Twenty-Five Years of A Georgia Town and Its People, Atlanta, 1960.

Williford, William Bailey, Peachtree Street, Atlanta, Athens, 1962.

World Almanac, The, New York, 1965.

Yates, Bowling C., History of the Georgia Military Institute, Marietta, Georgia, Marietta, 1968.

Young, Ida and Julius Gholson and Clara Nell Hargrove, History of Macon, Georgia, Macon, 1950.

Newspapers, Magazines, and Booklets

Atlanta Constitution, The
Atlanta Journal, The

Augusta Chronicle, The
Covington News, The
Covington Star, The
Georgia Enterprise, The. Also published for a time as *The Weekly Enterprise* and *The Semi-Weekly Enterprise*.
Macon Telegraph, The
Southern Confederacy, The. Published in Atlanta, 1859–1864.
Sunday American, The. Sunday issue of *The Atlanta Georgian*.
West End Star, The. Atlanta neighborhood weekly.

Atlanta Historical Bulletin, The. Published by The Atlanta Historical Society.
Emory University, Bulletin of. Published by Emory Univeristy.
Garden Gateways. Published by The Garden Club of Georgia.
Georgia Historical Quarterly, The. Published by The Georgia Historical Society, Savannah.
Masonic Messenger. Publication of The Grand Lodge of Georgia.

Chrisler, Isabel, *Demorest In The Piedmont*, n.p., n.d. (Demorest?)
Henry, Eleanor Stuart, *Memories*. Published privately, 1956.
History of Brick Store Community. (By Mrs. Walter C. Emmel, c. 1964?)
Jones, Frank F., *Biographies of The Members of The Rotary Club of Macon, Georgia, 1938–1942*.
Old Homes of Covington. Compiled by The Covington Garden Club, 1969.
Year Book, Sergeant Newton Chapter, Daughters of The American Revolution, 1895–1970. Covington, 1970.

INDEX

INDEX

Adams, Charles F., 85, 150-151; D. J., 151; Ella, 151; Emma, 151; George C., 85; L. D., 85, 215; Mamie F. (Mrs. L. D.), 215; Ruth T. (Mrs. Wright), 151; Wright, 151.
Adamson, Robert L., 167.
Aiken, Parepa M. (Mrs. W. W.), 194, 211; William W., Dr., 211.
Alcovy Judicial Circuit, 3; River 7.
Alexander, Ada R. (Mrs. J. F.), 43; W. F., Major (CSA), 175.
Alford, Elizabeth G. (Mrs. Kelly, Jr.), 199; Kelly, Jr., 199.
Allen, George S., 14-15; J. O., Mr. and Mrs., 47; Judy, 15; Leonora B. (Mrs. George), 14-15; Louisa, 92; Nina, 15.
Anderson, Amanda B. (Mrs. J. C.), 230; Annie Pauline, 181; C. W., Mrs., 240; Catherine R. (Mrs. J. S.), 186; Ellen L. (Mrs. Robert), 38; Elizabeth, 186; Elizabeth H. (Mrs. W. H.), 190; Elizabeth R. (Mrs. G. T.), 187; Fannie, 190; Franklin, 181; George Thomas, Gen. (CSA), 186-187; Guards. See Newton Anderson Guards; Henry, 240; Horace, Dr., 156; Inez L., 190; J. A. B., Mrs., 159; J. C., Dr., 230; James L. B., 186; James R., 156; James W., 11-14; Jane F., 38, 186; Joseph P., 190; Joseph S., 4, 119, 122, 160, 183-184, 185, 186, 196, 201, 202; Leonora, 107; Lillian B. (Mrs. H. D.), 223; Lucy, 186, 190; Lucy C. (Mrs. J. S.), 184, 186; Lucy Catharine, 160; Martha K. (Mrs. J. R.), 156; Mary Frances, 186; Mary Virginia, 190; Minnie (Mrs. J. P.), 190; Miriam, 190; Newton, 230; Newton Z., Dr., 47, 180-181, 230; Newton Z., Mrs., 180; Robert, 38; Sam, 187; Samuel Smith, 187; Sarah Frances C. (Mrs. W. P.), 188, 190, 193, 217, 218, 224; Sarah H. (Mrs. J. W.), 12-13; Susan, 190; "Tige." See Geroge Thomas; Tommie, 230; William H., 190; William M., 14; William P., 18, 49, 113, 118, 183, 185, 186, 188, 190, 193, 197, 199, 200, 218, 224.
Andrew, James O., Bishop, 40.
Andrews, Gertrude, 65; W. A., Mr. and Mrs., 65.
Anthony, Samuel, Rev., 71.
Armstrong, Mrs. Anita S., 179.
Arnold, David, 169; Eugenia, 169; Florence T. (Mrs. R. O.), 168; H. D., 223; Harry, 170; Robert O., 169-170.
Aron, J., (illus.), 21.
Ashworth, Drew W., Mrs., 244.
Atlanta Constitution, The, 39, 166.
Austin, Helen, 44; Mabel P. (Mrs. P. T.), 225.
Ayres, Clara H. (Mrs. James), 196; James, 196.

Baldwin County, The History of, 95n.
Bank of Covington, 127, 180, 227; of Newton County, 14, 22, 23-24, 26, 85, 127, 198.

303

Baptist Church, First, 4, 6-7, 49, 107, 142, 223, 224, 234.

Barnes, Thomas G., 105.

Bates, Ella D. (Mrs. G. J.), 137; Gustavus J., 137, 140; Horace J., Dr., 57, 136-140, 157, 167, 174, 178, 178; Jacqueline, 137, 174; Mary H. (Mrs. H. J.), 137; Mary Lucy, 55, 57, 137; -Terrell House, 136-144; Virginia C., 138.

Battey, Frances S. (Mrs. H. I.), 179; Hugh Inman, Dr., 179.

Batts, McAllen, 34, 37; Sarah Ann, 33; Sidney (Mrs. AcAllen. Nee Graves?), 34.

Bass, John H., 209.

Beatie, John J., 89.

Beebe, Eliza (Mrs. W. L.), 12; William L., Rev., 12.

Belcher, Ethel, 207; Leonora, 14.

Belfield, Mary Frances L., Mrs., 194.

Bellamy, Mary Washington, Mrs., 242.

Benton, Julia, 27.

Berry, George, 103; William P., 151n.

Bethany Assembly, 48.

Bethlehem Baptist Church, 6.

Bibb Company, 221, 235.

Biggers, James F., 142; Mary S. (Mrs. J. F.), 142-143.

Bigham, Kate, 167.

Billups, Mary R., 16, 18.

Bleckley, Logan, Chief Justice, 39.

Blue, Martha K., 156.

Bolton, Cora, 212; Dolly, 87; Dorothy G. (Mrs. L. D.), 87n, 93, 129-130, 133; Elsie (Mrs. J. G.), 93; John G., 93; John G., Jr., 130; Louis D., 87n, 129-130; Louis D., 2nd, 130; Mollie Reeves (Mrs. J. G.), 130-131, 133.

Bomar, A. R., Capt. and Mrs., 194, 208-209, 211; Ava, 194; Maud, 208.

Bonaparte, Jerome, 271(n41); Napoleon, Emperor, 271(n41).

Bonner, Allan, 53; Lucy A., (Mrs. Allan), 53; Jerustha, 53.

Borella, Jean, 144; John, 144; Julie, 144; Sally, 144; Suzann, 144; Terry, 144; Virginia G. (Mrs. W. G.), 144; William G., Lt. Col., 143-144.

Bower, Augustus R., Mr. and Mrs., 133; Lyda Sue, 133; Mary Patricia, 134.

Boyd, Jane Elizabeth, 174.

Bradshaw, Annie (Mrs. J. N.), 107, 117; James N., Rev., 116-117; Oliver, 117; Sarah Margaret, 117.

Branch, Lucy Hyde, 55.

Braswell, Hortense, 189.

Bray, Jerry, Mrs., 156.

Brazil, Samuel, 4.

Brewer, Oby T., Mr. and Mrs., 51.

Brick Store, 2.

Briscoe, Ferdinand A., 74; Kate E., 74; Mary Alice M. (Mrs. F. A.), 74; Otto T., 74.

Brittain, Henry, 222; Ida C. (Mrs. J. M.), 223; George, 222; J. M., Rev. Dr., 107, 222-225; Lillian, 223; Luther, 223; M. L., Dr., 223.

Brown-Anderson House, 11-15; Coleman G., 11, 43; Fannie R. (Mrs. C. G.), 11, 43; Ike W., 212; Joseph E., Gov., 57; William, 101; Winfred W., 68.

Bryan, Amanda, 72; Jasper, Dr., 72; Samuel, Dr., 72.

Buchanan, Martha V. (Mrs. B. H.), 107.

Burge-Bolton House. See Burge Plantation; Diary of Dolly Lunt, The, 92n; Dolly L. (Mrs. Thomas), 87n, 92, 93, 96, 129; Eliza, 93; Hamilton, 79; Louisiana, 93; Mary C. (Mrs. Thomas), 93; Plantation, 79, 87n, 92, 96, 129, 130; Rebecca, 93; Sarah Cornelia ("Sadai"), 93, 129; Thomas, 79, 92, 93; Thomas, Jr., 93; Wiley C., 93.

Burney, Albert S., 128; Florence H. (Mrs. A. S.), 128; Martha, 170.

Bush, Anna M. (Mrs. T. B.), 212; Eugenia G. (Mrs. Tandy), 120, 213; Tandy E., 120, 213; Thomas B., 212.

Butler, Cleo P., Mrs., 226; David, 197; Eleanor, 197; George D., 195, 196; George D., Jr., 197; Joseph B., Rev., 194; Katharine, 197, 207; Laura, 194; Laura G. (Mrs. David), 197; Mary Lucy, 197; Mary Lucy H. (Mrs. G. D.), 196, 197.

Callaway, Ackie W. (Mrs. T. G.), 44; E. E., 84; Edgar A., Rev., 134; Helen A. (Mrs. Thomas, Jr.), 44; Ida, 223; John, 207; Lamar, 197; Martha C. (Mrs. Thomas, Jr.), 44; Mary Lucy B. (Mrs. Lamar), 32, 197; Sarah White, 44; Thomas G., 44; Thomas G., Jr., 44, 87.

Calloway, Mattie, 189.

Camp, Archibald L., Dr., 84, 217, 218-221, 222n, 223, 229; Archie, 217, 221-222; Avah, 217; Benjamin F., 148; Carrie C. (Mrs. Archie), 222; Charles, 217, 218-220, 221, 240; Charles Josephine, 220; Eulah, 217; Gerard, 34, 148, 188, 217; Germaine, 217; Hannah, 217; Harry, 103, 148; J. Randolph, 34-35, 217; "Jennie." See Virginia B.; Julia McC. (Mrs. Charles), 220; Lucinda Jane M. (Mrs. J. R.), 35; Marietta S. (Mrs. A. L.), 217; Martha, 217; Martha L. (Mrs. Gerard), 188, 217; Samuel, 218; Sarah A. (Mrs. Harry), 148; Sarah Frances, 217; Septimus C., 35, 217, 218; Virginia B. (Mrs. S. G.), 35, 154; William J., 217.

Campbell, Charles E. T. W., 111, 173; E. W. (Mrs. C. E. T. W.), 111; William C., 173.

Candler, Asa G., 44, 226; Caroline, 226; Charles, 226; Frances, 226; Frances G. (Mrs. Charles), 226; John S., Judge, 151; Martha, 44; Warren A., Bishop, 166, 226.

Carithers, Mary, 240; Sudie, Mrs., 240.

Carr & Cureton, 178; Alethia W. (Mrs. G. T.), 152, 153; Amanda M., 69, 102; Angeline McC. (Mrs. N. C.), 102; Anna Belle, 102; Annie, 105; Benjamin, 102; Benjamin Franklin, 102; Carlton, 152; Cebelle M. (Mrs. Benj.), 102; Clara, 105, 152, 207; Clara C. (Mrs. E. P.) 105; Clarence H., 102; -Cody-Corley House, 72, 101, 108; Corrie, 152, 153; E. P., 105; Flora, 207; Florella, 102; Frances, 69, 102, 104; George T., 102, 152, 153, 178; John P., 4, 69, 101-104, 152; John W., 102; Lizzie, 102; Martha T. (Mrs. J. P.), 102, 152; Mary Elizabeth H. (Mrs. B. F.), 102; Mary T. (Mrs. J. P.), 102; Nathan C., Capt., 21, 102, 105; Wilson, 152.

"Carr's Corner," 153.
Carroll, Carrie, 222.
Carter, Ann Briggs, 179; Jane A., Mrs., 186.
Cedars, The, 17, 165-167, 171.
Central of Georgia Railroad, 6, 195, 198, 236; Central Railroad & Banking Co., 113.
Champion, Eloise S. (Mrs. James P.), 179.
Chancellor, John L., 147; Sarah (Mrs. J. L.), 147.
Cherry, Kate B. (Mrs. S. D.), 74-75; Samuel D., Rev., 74.
Chestnut, Adelaide W. (Mrs. J. C. B.), 167; Constantine, 166; J. C. Benjamin, 167.
Chiang Kai-shek, Generalisimo, 38.
Childs, Florence, 167; Hugh, 65; Maggie C. (Mrs. Walter), 64-65, 212; Mattie G. (Mrs. Walter), 272(n46); Walter, 65, 272(n46);Walter, Jr., 65, 212.
Childers, Eleanor S. (Mrs. Reid), 100.
Christian Science Church, 7, 227.
Cienfuegos, Marquis, 38.
Circuit Rider's Wife, The, 71.
Civil War era in Covington, 6, 19, 56, 57-58, 60-61, 70, 81-82, 94-96, 114, 124-125, 138-139, 147-149, 152-153, 160-163, 174, 175-176, 192, 203, 204-206, 217-221.
Clark Banking Co., 14, 85, 127, 150, 196, 207, 212; John, 112; John, Gov., 4; May Belle, 83; Mary Elizabeth, 83; Sallie E. (Mrs. W. C.), 83-86; Sarah Isabella, 83; Sarah W. (Mrs. John), 112; Tempe White, 83; Temperance C. (Mrs. W. W.), 79, 83; Walter, Sgt. (CSA), 82; Walton C., 86, 207; William C., 23, 83-87, 168; William W., 2nd., 83, 112, 117, 118; William W., 47, 78-79, 81, 83, 86, 103, 118, 207.
Clarke, Florence (Mrs. L. A.), 212; John P., 212; Julia L. (Mrs. R. W.), 212; Lillian, 207, 212; Love A., 211, 212; Maggie, 65, 212; Mary, 212; Robert W., 212; William L., 212.
Clark's Grove, 76-78, 81-84, 87-88;
Clarkston, 79.
Clayton, Augustin L., Judge, 2.
Cleveland, Adele F. (Mrs. King), 51; King, 51.
Cobb, Howell, Gen. (CSA), 90, 113, 146.
"Cobb's Legion," 59(n1, n4), 94.
Cody, Amanda C. (Mrs. J. M.), 69, 104; Benjamin, 69; Derrell. *See* Madison D.; Elizabeth, 68; Frances, 69; Frances C. (Mrs. M. D.), 69, 104; James, 68; Jeptha M., Dr., 68-69, 71, 72, 73, 104; Julia L. (Mrs. J. M.), 69; L. L., 69; Louisa Amanda, 68; Madison D., 68, 69, 72, 102-104; Madison D. (Jr.), 104n; Mary McC. (Mrs. James), 68; Mary Rebecca, 69; Michael, 68; Missouri C. (Mrs. J. M.), 69; Rebecca R. (Mrs. Michael), 68.
Cohen, Abe, 47, 269(n37); Callie H. (Mrs. Leon), 46; Leon, 46-47; Wolfe, 46-47.
Colbert, Frances, 123; Mary, 89.
Colley, Huldah B., 82; Joel, Elder, 6-7; 82, 151n.

Comer, Sarah Lee S. (Mrs. T. J.), 55, 56, 57; Thomas J., 55, 56.

Confederate Monument, 140.

Confederate States of America, 78, 174-177.

Conyers, Amanda C. (Mrs. W. D.), 8, 14, 80; Betsey D. (Mrs. Ross), 79; Chloe P., 61, 80, 137; Elizabeth D., 80; Elizabeth P. (Mrs. W. D.), 80; Rebecca, 138; Ross, 79; Temperance B., 79, 81; (town of) 80; Virginia B. (Mrs. W. D., Jr.), 138, 140-141; William D., Dr., 3, 11, 14, 49, 52, 79-80, 86, 111, 113, 137, 167; William D., Jr., Major (CSA), 59, 80, 86, 137-139, 167, 205; Willie Rebecca, 138, 139.

Cook-Adams-Williams House, 202, 215; Anna Maria G. (Mrs. S. A.), 95n; C. J., Mrs., 215; Carter, 14; Sallie Mae P. (Mrs. W. S.), 14; Samuel Austin, 95n; Sarah, 14; Virginia, 167; William S., 14; William S., Jr. (Dr.), 14; Willie (Mrs. C. W.), 139.

Corley, Annie B. (Mrs. J. J.), 107, 117; Emma, 107; James T., 6, 71-72, 73, 106, 234, 240; James T., Mrs. (née Skinner), 107; John J., 107, 117; Kate S. (Mrs. W. T.), 107; Leonora A. (Mrs. Tom), 107; Martha Vashti, 107; Mary, 107; Tom, 107; Walter T., 107; Will, 107.

"Corley's Hill," 72, 103.

Cottage, The, 201-203, 204, 208, 216.

Covington & Oxford Street Railway Company, 9, 22, 127; Book Club, 30; first commissioners of, 3; Garden Club, 30, 32, 142; incorporation of, 3; Leonard, Gen., 3; Mills, 23, 24, 26, 85, 87, 88, 127, 168, 170, 232, 236; Municipal Building, 119; naming of, 3; News, The, 127, 152, 169, 231, 238; Public Schools, 31; Public Square, 3, 8, 18, 123, 156, 185, 195, 227; School System 118-119; Service Guild, 156; Star, The, 5-8, 12, 107, 111, 126, 150, 192; Tennis Club, 64.

Cox, Emily E. (Mrs. Sidney), 181.

Crawford, Ransom, 167.

Crawley, Frank, 190; Mary Virginia A. (Mrs. Frank), 190.

Creek Indians, 1, 3.

Crimmins, J. A., 244.

Crowe, House, 105; Thankful B. (Mrs. Wendell), 105; Wendell, 105, 133.

Cunningham, Agnes P. (Mrs. George), 184; George, 184; Lucy H., 184; Susie, 47.

Cureton, Alfred M., 105, 178; Amanda P. (Mrs. A. M.), 105.

Cuyler, Robert R., 113.

Daniel, George B., 188, 224; George H., Capt. (CSA), 81-82; Huldah B. (Mrs. George), 82; Mary W. (Mrs. George), 82.

Daughters of the Confederacy. See United Daughters of the Confederacy; Daughters of the American Revolution, 133, 142.

Davis, Carrie W. (Mrs. Fletcher), 141; Corinne R. (Mrs. J. B.), 147, 149, 150; Fletcher, 141; J. C., Maj. Gen. (USA), 160; Jefferson, President (CSA), 174; John B., 21, 149, 150; Nannie F., 141; Thomas, 157.

Dearing, A. E., 231; Eugenia, 189; Hortense B. (Mrs. Perino), 189; Indie (Mrs. J. J.), 88, 189; John J., Dr., 117, 189, 231; John M., 88, 189, 231; Mattie C. (Mrs. J. M.), 189; Perino, 189; Plantation, 189.

Dietz, Iola P. (Mrs. Harry), 225.
Delaney Hotel (illus.), 8, 79.
Delaney, James, 12.
Dennis, Belmont, 152; Mabel S. (Mrs. Belmont), 152.
Denson, Betsey, 79.
DeVane, Eleanor B. (Mrs. Fulton B.), 197.
DeWald, Solomon, 173; Solomon, Mrs., 173.
Dickson, David, 157.
Dietz, Iola (Mrs. Harry), 225.
Dillard, Ella, 137.
Dixie Manor, 145-156.
Dorsett, Martha C., Mrs., 217.
Douglass, Peyton W., Dr., 20; Susie, Mrs., 20.
Dried Indian Creek, 4, 6, 33, 76, 101, 103, 104; Common, 4.
Dupre, Celeste (Mrs. J. H.), 51; James H., 51.
Dutton, Mary Elizabeth, 91; Sarah Ward, 51, 91.
Dyer, Elizabeth C. (Mrs. J. R.), 16, 80; John R., Col. (CSA), 16, 80; Mary H.,
    80n.

Echols, Addie, 84; Charles, 84; John, 84; John H., 84; Leila, 84; Place, The,
    16, 84; Sallie, 83; Sarah Jane (Mrs. J. H.), 84.
Edwards, Amanda B. (Mrs. E. F.), 72, 75; Annie N. (Mrs. W. A.), 73; Ellijay
    F., Col., 72-74, 75; House, 68-75; Ida, 73; Mamie, 73; Mary E. (Mrs. E.
    F.), 72; Minnie, 73; Samuel, 72; William A., 73.
Ellington, V. C., 46.
Elliott, Charles, 181; Emily, 181; Elizabeth, 181; George, 29, 181; Georgie S.
    (Mrs. J. L.), 181; Jackson L., 181; Maria C. (Mrs. George), 29; Ruth, 181.
Emmel, Walter C., Mr. and Mrs., 51.
Emory College, 17, 39, 40, 49, 51, 52, 70, 71, 77-78, 81, 82, 94, 114, 123,
    166, 184, 196, 210, 223, 226, 235, 236.
Emory, John, Bishop, 77.
Episocpal Church of The Good Shepherd, 31, 65, 105, 131-133, 157, 158.
Estes, C. C., Mrs., 105.

Faulkner, Lucinda, 135; Priscilla B., 135; Priscilla G. (Mrs. R. L.), 134-135;
    Robert L., Dr., 134-135.
Fears, Emma Jones, Mrs., 46.
Felton, Rebecca Latimer (Mrs. W. H.), 94; William H., Dr., 94.
Few, Ignatius, Dr., 77.
First National Bank, 141, 180, 231.
Fiske, Minnie, Mrs., 73.
Flanegan, Joel, 145; 157; Sarah (Mrs. Joel), 33, 145, 157, 230.
Flint Judicial Circuit, 3;
Floyd, Ann S. (Mrs. John B.), 89; Florida, 94-95; Frances Ann, 92; *House* 18,
    89-100; John B., Major (USA), 89; John C., Lt. (CSA), 59, 92, 94; John
    J., Judge, 18, 19, 61, 72, 89-91, 92, 95-97, 114, 118, 122, 201, 202-203,
    207, 215; Mary C. (Mrs. John J.), 89, 95, 97, 123, 207; Mary Louisa, 92;
    Sarah Elizabeth, 92; Stewart, 92; William B., 92.

"Floyd's Newton Cavalry," 95.
Foreman, Mary L. (Mrs. W. B.), 209; William B., 209.
Fortson, Adele, 51; William D., Jr., 198, 199-200.
Fowler, Florence, 88; Louly, 88; Louly T. (Mrs. R. R., Jr.), 87, 88, 168; Robert R., Jr. 87, 88; Robert R., 3rd., 88.
Franklin, Felix, Mrs., 179; Wright Park, 157, 166, 173.
Freeland, Nix, 103.
Fulton, Creed, Rev., 113, 114.
Furlow, Timothy M., Col., 113.

Gaither, Cecelia W. (Mrs. W. H.), 18; William H., 18.
Gardner, J. D., 225.
Garrard, Kenner, Brig. Gen. (USA), 6, 60, 82, 125, 148.
Gay, S. H., 111.
Georgia Conference of the Methodist Church, 76, 78.
Georgia Enterprise, The, 12, 23-24, 64, 97.
Georgia: Historical and Industrial, 167.
Georgia Rail Road & Banking Company, 7, 18, 78-79, 80, 103, 120, 183, 184, 187, 207.
Gheesling, Louise, 238.
Gibson, Count, 152; Julia T. (Mrs. Count), 152.
Ginn Apts., 49, 66, 67; Elizabeth, 199; Frances, 199; Frances D. (Mrs. T. R.), 66; Lois S. (Mrs. S. A.), 66, 198, 199-200; Mary Ellen, 66, 199; Rucker, 65-66, 198; Rucker, Jr., 66, 198, 199; S. A., 36, 66, 198, 199; Sally D. (Mrs. Rucker), 66; Stephanie, 199-200.
Glass, J. (illus.), 21; Manson, Judge, 111.
Glenn, Julia, 119-120.
Godfrey & Candler, 227; Frances, 226; P. W., Mr. and Mrs., 7, 226, 227.
Goneke, John D., 52-53; Margaret G. (Mrs. J. D.), 52-53.
Gone With The Wind, 100, 199, 208.
Gordon, John B., Gen. (CSA), 39.
Graham, Fannie, 53; Frances G. (Mrs. W. P.), 49, 50, 52-53; John, 53; Margaret, 52, 53; William P., Dr., 18, 49, 55.
Grand [Masonic] Lodge of Georgia, 97, 113-118; 159.
Graves, Barzillia, 50; Cornelia, 51; Dutton, 51; Fannie, 50; Frances, 49, 50; Frances L. (Mrs. Solomon), 50; Henrietta M. (Mrs. Henry), 51; Henry, 51; Henry, 2nd., 51; Irma T. (Mrs. Henry), 51; Iverson L., 49, 50-51, 53, 91; John L., Dr., 50; Sarah D. (Mrs. Iverson), 51, 91; Sidney, 50; Solomon, 2, 4, 49, 50; William, 50.
Gray, Davis, 129; Dorothy, 93, 129; Esther C., Mrs., 74, Fannie, 129; Ida, 129; Ida E. (Mrs. W. H.), 73; Joe, 129; John D., Rev., 129; Sarah Cornelia ("Sadai." Mrs. J. D.), 93, 129; Wade H., 73.
Green, Anna Maria, 94-95; Louise R. (Mrs. Paul), 147.
Greer, W. Thomas, Mr. and Mrs., 227.
Groves, Elizabeth A., 160.
Guinn, Dudley, 207; Eugenia, 120; Julia E. (Mrs. R. C.), 119, 120; R. Chessley, 120; Robert, 120.

Hagins, Suzann (Mrs. Wydell), 144.

Hall, John H., 134; Lyda Sue B., Mrs., 133, 134.

Hamilton, Emma, 233; Jane, 233; Julia R. (Mrs. R. W., Jr.), 93, 232; Robert W., Jr., 51, 93, 232.

Hammond, Florida (Mrs. George H.), 92.

Hamrick, David, Rev., 144; Terry B. (Mrs. David), 144.

Haralson, Hugh, Gen., 39; Leonora, 39.

Hardman, Martha (Mrs. Lanier), 191; S. Lanier, 191.

Hargrove, James. S., Capt. (CSA), 102; Lizzie C.(Mrs. J. S.), 102.

Harper, Robert G., Col. (CSA), 36; Sarah N. (Mrs. R. G.), 36.

Harris, Aerie, 159; -Cody House, 68-75; Corra W. (Mrs. Lundy), 71; -Corley House, 42; Dora, 159; Elizabeth G. (Mrs. J. P., Jr.), 160; Isaac, 159; Jack N., 159, 163; Joel Chandler, 167; John, Rev. Sol., 158; John, Judge, 18, 68, 69, 73, 113, 115, 142, 157, 158-163, 164, 171; John P., Jr., 72, 159-160, 186; Joseph, 159; Julian, 166; Louise F. (Mrs. J. P., Jr.), 160; Lucy Catherine A. (Mrs. J. P., Jr.), 106; Lula N. (Mrs. R. H.), 36; Lundy, Rev., 71; -Metcalf-Wright House, 167, 170; Richard H., 36; Susan S. (Mrs. J. P., Jr.), 159, 160; Susan H. (Mrs. John), 158; Susan P. (Mrs. I. P. H.), 159; Walker, Mayor, 156; William, 159.

Harris' Quarters, 142, 160, 163.

Harwell, James, 111.

Hawkins, Sion W., 12.

Haygood, Atticus G., Bishop, 147; Mary R. (Mrs. W. F.), 147; William Fletcher, 147.

Hay, Frances D. (Mrs. S. B.), 88; Louly F. (Mrs. S. B., Jr.), 88; Samuel B., Rev., 88; Samuel B., Jr., 88. Hays, A. N., 150.

Heard, B. Simms, 98, 207; Edward, 55, 97-98, 231; Edward, Jr., 98; Elizabeth E. (Mrs. Joseph), 181; Emily D. (Mrs. Fitz), 98; Fitz, 98; Grant D., Capt., 140; Herbert, 98; "Hyda." See Lucy Hyde; Joseph, 98; Lucy Hyde, 98, 207; Lucy Jane S. (Mrs. Edward), 55, 62, 98; Mattie, 140; Stephen, Gov., 98; White & Thompson, 231.

Hemphill, Emma S. (Mrs. W. A.), 39-40, 207; William A., 39-40.

Henderson, Cary W., 20; Charles, 20; Clara (Mrs. C. Y.), 152; Claudia, 20; Clifford (son of J. F.), 207; Clifford (son of R. J.), 20; Fannie, 207; Florence, 128, 167; Frances, 127; Hattie H. (Mrs. Clifford), 128; Isaac P., 19, 62, 80n, 106, 158; Isaac P., 2nd. (son of R. J.), 20, 80n; Isaac P., 3rd., 80n; John F., 20, 23, 125, 127-128, 151, 168; John T., Col. (CSA), 18, 56, 158; Julia U. (Mrs. J. F.), 125, 127-128; Laura W. (Mrs. R. J.), 18, 19-20, 80n, 97, 127; Martha W., 104; Mary Elizabeth, 102; Mary D. (Mrs. I. P., 2nd), 80n; Mary Ruth, 20; Paulina W. (Mrs. J. T.), 18; Robert, 20, 128; Robert J., Brig. Gen. (CSA), 18, 19-20, 80n, 97, 127, 158; Ruth S. (Mrs. I. P.), 106, 158; Sarah; Sarah B. (Mrs. I. P.), 158; Susan; Susan Ann, 158; William, 20.

Hendrick, Gen., 136; John B., Dr., 4, 110; 113, 136; Mary Ann, 137; Zalema W. (Mrs. J. B.), 110.

Hendry, Harold M., 15; Nina A. (Mrs. H. M.), 15.

Hennessey, Mr., 191.
Henry, Aerie (Mrs. J. A.), 159; Clara, 196; Eleanor, 196; Elizabeth A. (Mrs. H. T.), 186, 196; Elsie L. (Mrs. Hugh), 196; George, Rt. Rev., 132; Gertrude, 196; Henry T., Dr., 56, 118, 142, 196, 293(n33); Hugh, 196; Mary Lucy, 196; Patrick, 196; William R., 196.
Herring, Chloe C. (Mrs. W. F.), 61, 80, 139; William, Mr. and Mrs., 80n; William F., 61, 80, 139.
Hicks, Ophelia Jane S. (Mrs. John H.), 37.
Hightower Trail, 3.
Hill, Benjamin H., 104.
Hines, Edward R., Judge, 179; Nelle W. (Mrs. E. R.), 179-180.
Hitchcock, Henry, Major (USA), 163, 187-188.
Hood, John B., Gen. (CSA), 80n.
Hopkins, A. S., Dr., 213; Isaac S., Rev. Dr., 166, 223.
Hopper, Jack, Rev., 132.
Horton, Elizabeth, 190.
Hospital Aid Society, 205, 206.
Hotel, Cox, 8; Delaney, 8, 79; Flowers, 8; Pitts, 8, 227.
Hunt, Caroline C. (Mrs. Lowry), 226.
Hunter, Hattie, 128; Nathan, Mrs., 40; Nicholas P., 184-185, 192.
Hurst, Katharine B., Mrs., 197.
Hurt, Eva, 62; Joel, 62; William, 137.
Hutchins, James B., Mr. and Mrs., 154n; James E., 215; Margaret W. (Mrs. J. E.), 215; Sarah Clyde.

Ivy, Martha, 236.

Jackson, Sarah, S. T., 61.
Jarrard, Florence, Mrs., 212.
Jenkins, Clara C. (Mrs. Crawford), 105.
Johnson, Andrew, President, 186; James, Prov. Gov., 97; Ruth S., Mrs., 158.
Johnston, Joseph E., Gen. (CSA), 174.
Jones, Elizabeth S. (Mrs. Thomas F.), 146; Francis M., 71; Harrison, 4; James L., Prof., 115; Louise F., Mrs., 160; P. B., Major, 146; Presley, 82, 153; Rebecca P. (Mrs. Thomas), 146; Sam, Rev., 166; Thomas, 4, 145-146; Thomas F., 113, 145, 146, 156.
Jordan, Arthur D., Mr. and Mrs., 117; Charles M., 2.
Journal of A Milledgeville Girl, 95n.

Kaplan, N., 47.
Kelly, H. Baron, 231; Gladys (Mrs. H. B.), 231.
Kilpatrick, Gertrude A., Mrs., 65; Mr., 65.
King, Charles C., 240; H. W., 225; Harmon, Mr. and Mrs., 225.
Kiwanis Club, 156, 198.
Knox, Belle W., Mrs., 237; James, 237.
Kolb, Martin W., Capt., 4, 80n; Mary P. (Mrs. M. W.), 80.
Ku Klux Klan, 87, 88, 213.

Lacy, Martha, 217.

"Lady Haw Haw," 38.

Ladies Memorial Association, 139.

"Lamar Infantry," 59 (n1, n3), 94, 205.

Lamar, Jennie L. (Mrs. L. Q. C.), 52-53; Jefferson M., Lt. Col. (CSA), 59,
    112, 138, 205; L. Q. C., 4, 36, 52-53, 59 (n4), 77, 205.

Langtry, Lily, 167.

Latimer, Julia A., 69; Rebecca, 92-94.

Lawrence, Samuel, 115.

Lee, Augustus H., 104, 106; Augustus J., 194; Ava B. (Mrs. E. E.), 194;
    Berto, 231; Carlton, Dr., 231; Caroline, 240; Dorothy, 231, 233; Ernest
    E., 194, 211; Eugene O., 194, 212, 230-231, 240; Eugene O., Jr., 231;
    Eugene O., 3rd., 240; Gladys, 231; Jack, Dr., 231; James, 194, 240; John
    W., Dr., 194, 212; Julia, 194; Laura B. (Mrs. W. B.), 194; Lester, 207, 231,
    240; Lester, Jr., 240-241; Lillian, 231; Margaret A., 194; Martha H. (Mrs.
    A. H.), 104; Mary C. (Mrs. Lester), 240-241; Mary Frances, 194; Mary W.
    (Mrs. W. S.), 194, 212, 230; Richard, Hon., 53; Robert E., Gen. (CSA), 61,
    176, 186; -Rogers-Hamilton House, 230; Sarah Louisa, 194; Tommie A.
    (Mrs. E. O.), 230, 240; Walter E., 194; William B., 192, 193-194, 195, 196,
    197; William Bell, 194, 212; William S., Judge, 194, 212, 230.

Levy, J. M., 118.

Lewis, Dolly L. (Mrs. S. H. B.), 92, 93; Frances, 50; Samuel H. B., Dr., 92;
    Sue P. (Mrs. Charles), 182.

Leyden, Austin, Major (CSA) and Mrs., 80n.

Lincoln, Abraham, President, 60, 163.

Livingston, Allie M., 209; Eliza McG. (Mrs. R. B.), 209; Elizabeth B. (Mrs.
    Joseph), 209; Joseph, 209; Leonidas F., Cong., 209; Mary, 209; Robert B.,
    70, 85, 209.

Loganville Railroad Company, 96.

Longstreet, Augustus Baldwin, Judge, 51, 52, 77, 184; Jennie, 52, 77n.

Longwood, 109-111.

Loyal, A. B., Mrs., 226.

Loyall, John, 234.

Luckie, Alexander F., 38; Eliza B. (Mrs. W. D.), 37; Emma S. (Mrs. L. F.), 37,
    39-40, 42, 71; Hezekiah, 37, 38; Jane (Mrs. Hezekiah), 37, 38; Lorena,
    110; Lorenzo F., Capt. (CSA), 37, 39; Mary Ann, 38; Masonic Lodge, W.
    D.; William D., Judge, 37-38, 39, 110; William D., Jr., 39.

Lumpkin, Joseph Henry, Chief Justice, 79; Wilson, Gov., 79.

Lunt, Cornelia, 129; Orrington, Mr. and Mrs., 129.

Lurkin, Elsie, 196.

McCord, Mary Ellen G., Mrs., 66.

McCracken, Julia, 220; William D., 17.

McDaniel, Henry D., Gov., 236.

McDonald, Lettie, 223.

McGarity, A. S., 225.

McKay, Coleman, 196; Gertrude H. (Mrs. Coleman), 196.

Maddox, Mary Sue (Mrs. J. B.), 48; Nannie R. (Mrs. R. F.), 43.
Mahoney, Mamie E. (Mrs. P. D.), 73; P. D., Dr., 73.
Male Academy, 4, 52, 118, 223.
Man Called Peter, A, 70.
Manne, M. L., 170.
Manual Labor School, 17, 49, 76-78, 81, 8, 101, 112, 114.
March To The Sea, 162, 176, 187.
Marsh, Adelaide B. (Mrs. E. W.), 34; E. W., 34; McAllen B., 34; Spencer, 267(n5).
Marshall, Peter, Rev., 71.
Martin, Edgar G., 190; Lucinda J., 35; Mary Virginia A. (Mrs. E. G.), 190.
Matthews, Cebelle, 102.
Maybank, Nellie N. (Mrs. Theodore), 206, 207; Theodore, 206.
Meacham, Elsie R. (Mrs. J. F.), 191; John F., 191.
Meadors, Clarence, 226, 228; Lily Mae W. (Mrs. T. C.), 228.
Means, Alexander, Rev. Dr., 52, 76, 114, 184, 218, 280(n18).
Melson, Davis, Mrs., 107.
Memorial Association, The, 206.
Merck, Ernest G., 212; Mary C. (Mrs. E. G.), 212.
Meritt, Fannie R. (Mrs. G. A.), 11, 43; Gustavus A., Dr., 11, 43.
Metcalf, Frances U. (Mrs. W. J.), 125, 126, 164; William J., 125, 126, 163-164.
Methodist Church[, First United], 4, 22, 69, 70-71, 74, 95, 97, 127, 136, 149, 154, 158, 179, 181.
Middle Branch Rail Road Company, 136.
Middle Georgia & Atlantic Railway Company, 194-195.
Middlebrooks, Emma C. (Mrs. L. L.), 107; Lucius L., Col., 107.
Milledgeville and Baldwin County, A Treasury Album of, 179.
Miller, Edward F., 30; Frank M., 29-30; Julia B. (Mrs. Frank M.), 29-30
Milner, Anna M. (Mrs. R. W.), 212, 214; Cora B. (Mrs. R. W.), 212; Robert W., 47, 212-213.
Mitchell, Anna, 212.
Mixon, S. B., Mrs., 230.
Mize, James, 3.
Mobley, Carrie S. (Mrs. R. M.), 191, 196; Robert M., 196; Sarah, 196.
Montgomery, W. S., 218.
Moore, Fannie, 147; Leslie J., Mr. and Mrs., 132.
Morehouse, Dutton, 130; Ida G. (Mrs. M. J.), 129, 130; Louise (Mrs. Dutton), 130; Merritt J., 129, 130.
Morgan, James, 191; Olga R. (Mrs. James), 47, 191.
Morris, James, 160; Lisor, 160; William, 160.
Morrow, William H., 4.
Moses, Raphael J., Major (CSA), 175.
Mt. Pleasant, 49, 50-51, 51, 53, 129.
Murray, Ethel P. (Mrs. Hugh), 225.
Murrell, J. W., 4.

Napier, Annie Foster, 73.
Natural Grove, 79.
Neal, Clara P. (Mrs. McCormick, Jr.), 206, 208; Corrine, 36; Elizabeth C. (Mrs. Thomas), 68; Frances F. (Mrs. McCormick), 92, 201-207; George, 36, 37; Jack, 208; John, 37, 104; Louisa, 36; Lula, 36; Mary, 206; McAllen, 36; McCormick, 33-34, 36-37, 41, 42, 44-45, 68, 71, 106, 147, 157, 203, 208; McCormick the younger, 36, 59, 71, 92, 106, 118, 201-208, 211, 215; McCormick, Jr. (third of name) 206, 208; Nellie, 36, 206; -Patterson House. *See* The Cottage; -Sanders House, 33-34, 41, 48, 64, 130; Sarah, 36; Sarah Ann B. (Mrs. McCormick), 33, 34, 36-37, 41, 147, 208; Thomas, 68.
Newell, Alfred, 167.
Newsome, H. T., Mr. and Mrs., 93.
"Newton Anderson Guards," 152.
Newton, John, Sergeant, 1. Superior Court, first session of, 2-3.
Newton County Academy, 4, 84, 145; courthouses, 3, 9, 183; creation of, 1; Historical Society, 2, 31, 32; Library, 33; settlers of, 1-2.
Newtonsboro, 3-4, 9, 183, 234.
Nichols, George, Major (USA), 161-162.
Nixon, Nell (Mrs. Otis), 151.
North Georgia Conference of the Methodist Church, 118.

Oglesby, James, Mr. and Mrs., 110.
Orr, Gustavus J., 116.
Overby, Basil H., 39.
Owsley, Leonora, 207.
Oxford, 17, 54, 77-78, 114, 185.
Oxford College, 31, 131.

Pace, C. D. & Co., 178; Carr & Cody, 178; Carr & Cureton, 178; Columbus D., Judge, 38-39, 91, 113, 118, 178; James M., Capt. (CSA), 39, 47, 112, 118, 140, 192; Leonora H. (Mrs. J. M.), 39; Martha E. (Mrs. C. D.), 39; Mary Ann L. (Mrs. C. D.), 38; Mary Elizabeth D. (Mrs. C. D.), 39, 91; Richard, 6; William, 102.
Page, Sarah W. (Mrs. Earl N.), 55.
Parker, Alma, 225; Earnest, 225; Ethel, 225; Fannie, 225; Grady, 225; Iola, 225; Julius, 225; Lizzie P. (Mrs. M. E.), 225; Mabel, 225; Maurice A., Mrs., 15; Millard E., 225; Rena, 225; Robert, 225; Ruby, 225; Ruth, 225; William A., 2.
Parkinson, Mollie R. (Mrs. William), 133; William, Rev., 133.
Parks, Dolly L. (Mrs. W. J.), 92; William J., Rev., 71, 92.
Patrick, Agnes, 184.
Patterson, George W. D., Mrs., 38; Mamie E., Mrs., 74; R. H., 214-215; R. H., Jr., 214; Sarah Clyde H. (Mrs. R. H.), 214-215, 216; Sarah Margaret, 214.
Peacock, Florence (Mrs. James L.), 88.
Peddy, Lizzie, 225.

Perkins, W. R., 195.

Perry, A. C., Dr., 80, 110; Clara, 206; Elizabeth, 80; J[osiah;], 21; Jeremiah, Col., 80; Mary, 80; Temperance, 80, 110; Wiley, Dr., 80, 110.

Pharr, Clara, 154; Frank, Dr., 98; Lucy B. (Mrs. Frank), 98.

Philips, James E., Mr. and Mrs., 208.

Pickett, Clara Belle S., Mrs., 207; S. P., 140, 141; Sallie H. (Mrs. W. H.), 14; Sallie Mae, 14; William H., 14, 79, 107-108; William H., Jr., 14.

Pierce, George, 58, 59; Thomas F., Rev., 95.

Piper, Cleo, 226; Howard, 225-226; Ida (Mrs. Howard), 226; Virgil, 226.

Pope, O. C., 196.

Porter, Elizabeth T. (Mrs. O. W.), 241-243; Harriett, 242-244; James H., 24, 234-236, 237; Julia, 242-244; Julia, Memorial Methodist Church, 236; Julia McC. (Mrs. O. S.), 149, 220, 221, 241; O. W. ("Wick"), 181, 241, 243; O. W., Jr., 242-243; Olive S. (Mrs. J. H.), 24-27, 198, 235-236, 237, 242; Oliver, 149, 242; Oliver S., 23, 42, 168, 220, 223, 235, 241.

Poverty Hill, 183, 18, 190, 192, 193, 196, 197-198.

Pratt, Daniel, 17; Everett H., 181-182; Everett H., Jr., Capt. (USAF), 182; Lily Mae W. (Mrs. P. W.), 156, 229; Michael, 182; P. W., 181, 229; Ruth E. (Mrs. E. H.), 181-182; Sue, 182.

Presbyterian Church [,First], 70-71, 116, 117, 237, 241, 243.

President's House, The, 109-121.

Pritchett, E., 55; Sarah Lee S. (Mrs. E.), 55.

Purington, Cynthia C. (Mrs. J. L.), 151n; Joseph L., Elder, 151n.

"Queen of Floyd Street." See *Swanscombe*.

Rainey, Annie C. (Mrs. William N.), 65, 105; Mary S. (Mrs. W. T., Jr.), 100; William T., Jr., 100.

Ramey, Elizabeth B., 187.

Ramsey, C. D., 47-48; C. D., Jr., 48; George, 48; Martha, 48; Mary Sue, 48; Spence, 48; Susie C. (Mrs. C. D.), 47-48.

Ray, Emma C., 237.

Raybun, Marcelle R., Mrs. 190.

Reconstruction era, 96.

Reid, Neel, 27.

Reynolds, Ada, 43; Emily, 43; Fannie E., 11; Fletcher, 43; Frances, 43; John, 43; Katherine, 43; Martha, 43; Mary Ann, 43; Nancy K. (Mrs. P.), 11, 43; Nannie, 43; Purmedus, 11, 43, 218.

Rheburgh, Carl W., 190; Christine, 190; E. S., 190; Elsie, 190; Fannie A. (Mrs. S. C.), 190, 193; Francis A., 190; John L., 190; Marcelle R. (Mrs. E. S.), 190; Mildred, 190; Olga, 190; Olga B. (Mrs. S. C.), 190; Otto R., 190; Richard, 190; Rose, 190; S. C., 142, 190; Stephen C., Col. (USAF, Ret.), 190.

Richardson, J. Milton, Rt. Rev., 132.

Roberts, Daisy S. (Mrs. W. F.), 179; James, 103; Mae W. (Mrs. Raymond), 180; Raymond, 180; Walter F., 179.

Robertson, Luke, 6.
Robinson, Caroline Julia, 178; Guy, 153; Luke, Dr. and Mrs., 16; Marcelle, 190.
Rogers, Belle W. (Mrs. J. F.), 237; Cary W., 147; Corinne, 147, 148-149; E. B. ("G. W."), 170, 231-232; Emery R., 237; Emma R. (Mrs. J. F.), 237; Fannie M. (Mrs. O. T., Jr.), 147; James F., 236; Julia, 232; Louisa N. (Mrs. O. T.), 36, 146; Louise, 147; Martha I. (Mrs. J. F.), 236; Mary, 147; Mary Jane W. (Mrs. O. T.), 18, 84, 147, 149, 150, 151; Mary S. (Mrs. Osborn), 146; Natalie T. (Mrs. E. B.), 168, 170, 231, 232; Osborn, Rev., 146; Osborn T., 18, 36, 118, 146-147, 149, 150, 176-178, 230; Osborn T., Jr., 147; Perry S., 236; Rebecca, 68; Sarah, 147.
Roosevelt, Theodore, President, 167.
Rosser, E. B., 47; John E., 118; Laura S. (Mrs. J. F.), 45.
Russell, Martha R. (Mrs. J. M.), 43.
Ryan, Catherine G., 186.

Sams, Clara N., 156; Clara P. (Mrs. J. R.), 154; J. Roscoe, Dr., 153-156; Margaret L., Mrs., 194; Marion, 154.
Sanders, Bretton, 37; Charles H. Rev., 4, 37, 40-41, 69, 71, 184, 188, 203, 208, 217, 240; Charles H., Jr., 40, 59, 205; Emma B., 37; Eugenia Adelaide, 37; Georgianna C. (Mrs. C. H.), 37; Georgianna Cook, 37; Julia Eliza, 37; Ophelia Jane, 37; Osgood, 40, 42, 71; Sarah Ann B. (Mrs. C. H.), 37, 40-42, 43, 71-72, 188, 203, 208.
Sanford, Charles V., 42; Lizzie (Mrs. C. V.), 42; Steadman Vincent, Dr., 42.
Sayers, Marietta, 217.
Schermerhorn, Mary B. (Mrs. R. W.), 134; Richard W., 134.
Schley, William, 113.
Scott, Elizabeth, 146; Julia E., 120; Winfield, Gen. and Mrs., 120.
Scurry, John, Dr. and Mrs., 242, 244; Ralph, Dr. and Mrs., 242, 244.
Searcy, Helen N., Mrs., 207.
Secession Convention, 218.
Selden, Estelle (Mrs. George K.), 179.
Sergeant Newton Chapter, D. A. R., 31;
Seward, William, Secty. of State, 218.
Schackleford, Richard S., 3.
Shelby, Mary Louisa F. (Mrs. W. A.), 92; William A., Dr., 92.
Shepherd, Birdie, 45; Charles, 45-46; Caroline ("Callie") S. (Mrs. W. B.), 45, 46; Ethel, 45; Ralph, 45; T. J., Mr. and Mrs., 85, 230; Thomas, 185; William B., 45, 185, 230; Willie Beck, 45.
Sherman, William T., Gen. (USA), 19, 60-61, 106, 125, 148, 153, 160, 162, 163, 174, 187.
Shields, Inez A. (Mrs. T. J.), 190; Thomas J., 190.
Sibley, Amory W., 192; Josiah, 192.
Simkins, Leroy H., Jr., Lieut., 171; Sarah T. (Mrs. L. H., Jr.), 171.
Simms, Arthur Benjamin, 47, 55, 57, 59, 60, 61-63, 118, 234; Arthur Benjamin, Jr., 62, 64; Arthur L., 54; Bonner, 62, 64; Elinor L. (Mrs.

James), 53; Eva H. (Mrs. A. B., Jr.), 62; James, 53; James P., Brig. Gen. (CSA), 55, 56-57, 58-60, 61, 62-63, 137, 205; Jerustha B. (Mrs. R. L.), 53-61, 98; Lucy B. (Mrs. R. L., Jr.), 55, 57, 58, 98; Lucy Jane, 55, 57, 58, 98; Mary Lucy B. (Mrs. J. P.), 55, 57, 137; Richard L., Judge, 3, 53-55, 85, 98, 122; Richard L., Jr., Lieut. (CSA), 55, 57, 58-59, 138, 205; Richard L., 3rd., 98; Sarah, 62, 64; Sarah J. (Mrs. A. B.), 61-62, 63-64; Sarah Lee, 55, 57.

Sinclair, Rena P., Mrs., 225.

Slack, Susan E., 160.

Slaughter, Amanda C. (Mrs. M. G.), 80; Martin G., Dr., 80.

Smith, Boykin, 166; Margaret B. (Mrs. JD), 32.

Snapping Shoals R. E. A., 69.

Sockwell, Charles A., 141-142, 191; Fannie H. (Mrs. J. W.), 142; J. W., 142, 164, 191; Jessie U. (Mrs. C. A.), 142; Lucy C. (Mrs. J. W.), 142; Mary, 142; Sallie Mae, 191.

Soong, Mei Ling, 38.

Southern Female Academy, 113; Female College, 22, 78, 91, 92, 94, 112, 188, 227; Masonic Female College, 42, 62, 97, 112-118, 146, 149, 188.

Spears, Lois, 198.

Speer, Eustace W., Rev., 71.

Spence, Adeline, 45; Anderson H., 45; Caroline F., 45; Charles C. Rev., 45; David W., 44-45; Laura, 45; Sophia (Mrs. D. W.), 45.

Spencer, Clara Belle, 207; Cleo S. (Mrs. N. W.), 207; Elizabeth (Mrs. W. A.), 207; Helen, 207; Mary N. (Mrs. W. A.), 206, 207; Neal W., 207; "Rosebud." See Clara Belle; William A., 206, 207.

St. Augustine's R. C. Church, 48.

Stage coach, 5; route, 2, 5.

Stansell, Matthew R., 71.

Stanton, Edwin M., Secty. of War, 218; Lee P. (Mrs. C. Ben), 56; Frank L., 167.

Stark, Frances G. (Mrs. John), 199.

Starr, Kate, 107; Silas H., Jr., Capt. (CSA), 107; Tyra A., 23.

Steadman, E. Stoney, 42, 65, 212; Enoch, 42-43, 64; Lizzie, 42; Maggie C. (Mrs. E. S.), 65, 212; Mary (Mrs. Enoch), 42; Sanford C., 64, 65.

Stephenson, Ed, 207; J. R., 207; Lelia, 44.

Stewart, Adger, 179; Annie C. (Mrs. Adger), 179; Anita, 179; Caroline R. (Mrs. J. A.), 178; Daisy, 179; Eloise, 179; Estelle, 179; Frances, 179; J. A. B., 20, 178; John L., 178; Joseph A., 21, 178; Julia H. (Mrs. J. L.), 178.

Stillwell, Eulah C., Mrs., 222.

Stokes, Chas. Wm. Young, 18, 147; Irma T., Mrs., 51; Mary Jane W. (Mrs. C. W. A.), 18, 147.

Stone Mountain Judicial Circuit, 3.

"Stoneman's Cavalry," 148.

Stowers, Sarah Elizabeth, 24.

Strickland, Charles D., 120-121; David, 121; Louise N. (Mrs. Charles), 121.

Strong, Charles, 4, 84.

Swann, Coy, 213; -Davis Co., 22, 24, 178, 232; Dorothy, 100; Eleanor, 100; Elizabeth S. (Mrs. T. C.), 24, 25, 26, 32; James, 213; John T., 213; Julia B. (Mrs. Thomas C. [Jr.]), 27-29, 132, 169; Mary A., 100; Olive, 23, 24, 25-26, 207, 235; Paul, 100; Stella, 24; Stella U. (Mrs. W. K.), 99-100, 142; Stewart & Co., 21, 178; Stewart & Thompson, 21, 178; T. C., 20-24; 85, 97, 99, 127, 168; T. C. Co., 22, 178; Thomas C. (Jr.), 24, 26-28, 170, 178, 198, 207, 213; Thomas C., 3rd., 28, 29, 131, 133, 242-243; W. Kirk, Jr., Dr., 100, 213; William K., Dr., 98-100
Swanscombe, 16-32.

Tara of Covington, 199.
Tate, Janie M., 167.
Taylor, Deems, 38; W. H., 167.
Terrell, Clarence D., 141; Henry D., 141; Joseph B., 141; Nannie D. (Mrs. H. D.), 141.
Thomas, Edward L. 183; George H., Gen. (USA), 80n.
Thomason, Florence, 125; Julia U. (Mrs. Oscar), 125; Oscar, 125; Usher, 125.
Thompson, Charles S., 62, 64, 191; David A., 20, 117, 178, 231; Clara S. (Mrs. Lewis E.), 156; Elizabeth, 62; Jessie B. (Mrs. W. H.), 100; John Riley, 100; Mary Ann L. (Mrs. J. R.), 100; Sam, 117, 152; Sarah Margaret B. (Mrs. D. A.), 117; Sarah S. (Mrs. C. S.), 53n, 62, 64.
Todd, Elizabeth, 241.
Toombs, Robert, 174, 218.
Tours of homes, 32, 158-159, 242.
Townsend, Farr H., 4.
Trammell, Sarah (Mrs. Godfrey), 36.
Travis, A. C. W., Dr., 209; Allie L. (Mrs. A. C. W.), 209; Allie Louise, 211; John L., 210; Julia, 211; Maud B. (Mrs. W. D.), 209; Parepa M. (Mrs. W. B.), 194, 211; Paula S. (Mrs. W. D., 3rd.), 211; Robert F., Brig. Gen. (USAF), 210n; Robert J., Maj. Gen. (USA), 210; William B., 211; William D., Dr., 140, 208, 209, 210-211; William D., 3rd., 211.
Tribble, R. A., Mrs., 131; Samuel J., Cong., 237.
Trotti, Mary Louise, 128.
"Troup Artillery," 72;
Tuck, Goodwin G., Dr., 131, 238; Louise G. (Mrs. Reuben), 237, 238; Reuben M., 237-238; Reuben M., Jr., 238.
Turner, Addie E., Mrs., 84; Allen, 78, 111; Bonner S. (Mrs. Ralph L.), 62; Florence, 168, 169-120; Frank B., 170; Green B., 78; Julia T. (Mrs. N. S.), 168; Louly, 168; Louly T. (Mrs. N. S.), 168, 224; Martha, 102; Martha B. (Mrs. N. S., Jr.), 156, 170; Mary, 102; N. S., 23, 167-168, 185, 208, 224, 231; Natalie, 168; Nathaniel S., Jr., 168; Nathaniel S., 3rd., 170; Ralph L., 62, 98; Sarah, 170, 171.

United Daughters of the Confederacy, 31, 139, 142, 206, 227, 237.
Upshaw, Berrien K., 100; Claude, 142; J. C., 119; Jessie, 142; Margaret M. (Mrs. B. K.), 100; Ora, 169; Stella, 99-100.

Usher & Anderson, 184.
Usher, Fannie, 125; Florence, 95, 125; Frances C. (Mrs. R. O.), 61, 123, 164;
    House, 122-135; Julia, 125; Robert O., 18, 49, 61, 80n, 122-124, 184;
    Robert O. (Jr.), 125, 164.

Van-Horne, Adeline (Mrs. J. T.), 45; James T., Dr., 45.
Vonderau (Vondereaux), Francis J., 190; Miriam A. (Mrs. F. J.), 190, 192.

Walthour, John B., Rt. Rev., 132.
Ward, J. C., Mr. and Mrs., 7, 237, 238.
Washington, George, President, 242.
Weaver, Robert I., Mr. and Mrs., 69.
Webb, John, Rev., 194; Lily Mae, 228; Mary, 82, 194.
Welborn, Amos, 234.
Welburn, Sanford, 157.
Weldon, Frank, 166-167; Jeannie W. (Mrs. Frank), 165, 166-167.
Wellborn, James M., 68; Louisa C. (Mrs. J. M.), 68, 69; Marshall H., 68.
Wells, George T., 14; Nellie A. (Mrs. G. T.), 14.
Wesley, Charles, 78; John, Rev., 78.
Western Judicial Circuit, 2.
Wharton, Dorothy S. (Mrs. Robert), 100.
Wheeler, Joseph, Gen. (CSA), 148.
White, Ackie, 44; Charles H., 44, 231; Leila S. (Mrs. C. H.), 44.
Whitehall, 157-172.
Whitehead, J[ames L.?], 21.
Williams, Margaret, 215; Sarah C. (Mrs. W. F.), 215; William F., 214, 215.
Williamson, John N., Gen., 109-111, 112; John P., 110; Lorena L. (Mrs. J.
    N.), 110; Louisa (Mrs. J. N.), 109; Temperance P. (Mrs. J. N.), 80, 110;
    Wiley B., 110; Zalema, 109-110.
Williford, Julia B. (Mrs. W. B.), 30-32, Lawrence, 30, William Bailey, 30-32.
Willingham, Emma W. (Mrs. Wilkins), 234; Wilkins, 234.
Wilson, Alethia A., 152; Elias, 152; Temperance S. (Mrs. Elias), 152.
Winton, 2.
Wofford, William T., Brig. Gen. (CSA), 139.
Womack, Eleanor W. (Mrs. Emmett), 179; Emmett, 179-180; Nelle, 167,
    179-180.
Woman's War-Time Journal, A, 92n.
Women's Sewing Society, 57-58, 95, 205.
Wood, Bessie, 166; Cary, 3, 16-18, 21, 32, 33, 77, 80n, 84, 85, 97, 127, 147,
    173, 197, 234; Cary, 2nd., 174, 178; Cecelia, 18; Edgar, 85, 105; Irene,
    174; Jacqueline B. (Mrs. R. R.), 137, 174, 178, 179; Jane B. (Mrs. R. R.
    Jr.), 174; John, 18; John H., 85, 105; Laura, 18; Mary B. (Mrs. Cary), 16,
    18, 19, 147, 178, 234; Mary Jane, 18; Paulina, 18; Robert R., Major
    (CSA), 18, 137, 173-178; Robert R., Jr., 174, 178; Stevens, 18; William,
    18.
Wright, Boykin R., 165; Christopher C. (Mr. and Mrs.), 179; Corrie C. (Mrs. J.

A.), 152, 153-154; Emma, 234; Emmett, 207; Frances H. (Mrs. Hugh), 128; Frank, 166, 179; Franklin, 21, 164-167, 171, 179, 230; Hugh, 128; Hugh, Jr., 129; J. W., 225; James C., 167; Janiet (Mrs. R. F., Jr.), 167; Jeannie, 166-167; Joseph A., Dr., 132, 153; Madge, 166; Mae, 180; Margaret Adelaide, 167; R. E., Capt. and Mrs., 151; Robert F., 165, 167; Salina P. (Mrs. Franklin), 164-167, 178; Tate, 167; Virginia C. (Mrs. Tate), 167; William B., 151n; Wilson Carr, 154.
Wynne, Samuel, 17.

"Young Guards," 106.
York, Martha C., Mrs., 44.